52 Bible Lessons

for YoungReaders™

Carol A. Jackson, units 1, 2
Nancy Karpenske and Dianna Golata, unit 3
Becky Reilly and Lisa A. Horrell, unit 4

Christine Spence, units 5-7
Sarah J. Lyons, units 8-10
Tracy L. Harrast, review lessons
and key verse activity ideas

STANDARD
PUBLISHING
Cincinnati, Ohio

Reproducible
Permission is granted to photocopy patterns and pages
from this book (except for lessons 1-52)—for classroom use only.
The Standard Publishing Company, Cincinnati, Ohio.

Cover design by Roberta K. Loman
Inside illustrations by Andra Chase and Roberta K. Loman
Design and typography by Sherry F. Willbrand
Syllabus development by Carol A. Jackson
Curriculum consultant, Barbara Bolton
Reading specialist, Diana Crawford
Project editor, Linda Ford

03 02 01 00 99 98 97 96   5 4 3 2 1

ISBN 0-7847-0459-7

Table of Contents

Unit 1

Unit 2

Unit 3

Unit 4

Unit 5

Bible Lessons for Young Readers

Primaries read Bible stories and find Bible verses

Many courses have been written that teach through the Bible in 52 lessons. *Bible Lessons for Young Readers* is unique because it teaches fundamental Bible skills, as well as fifty basic Bible stories. Bible stories are grouped in chronological units focused on action aims appropriate for primary learners: worship, obey, tell. Unit key verses emphasize these themes.

Build enthusiasm for reading Bible stories

Children are encouraged to read Bible stories from *The Young Reader's Bible* at their own levels. Some will look at pictures and retell the story. Others will be able to read a few sentences. Still others will have the confidence to read aloud to others.

Prepare a special reading area for your room. Make the area cozy with carpet squares, an area rug, or pillows. Provide copies of *The Young Reader's Bible,* a cassette player, and cassette-taped stories. (*The Young Reader's Bible Audio Cassette* provides all seventy stories from *The Young Reader's Bible* including the fifty stories used in this curriculum.) Children can follow along, listening to the cassette and reading words they know.

Photocopy the twenty complete reproducible stories from pages 259-318. Stack the stories into booklets and arrange the booklets on a bookshelf or in a decorated book-box. Children can read and color these pages.

Provide skill-building practice

Children learn to separate the Old and New Testaments. They learn to find Genesis, Psalms, Matthew, and Acts. They learn to name the Gospels: Matthew, Mark, Luke, and John.

Children learn how to decode a Bible reference: book, chapter, verse.

Easy to teach!

❶ **Get Ready to Read** offers an activity to introduce the content of the Bible story.

❷ **Read the Bible Story** includes several experiences with the written story. A *purpose* for listening is given. Children *listen* as the teacher reads the story. (Good news: You need not be a great storyteller. You simply practice so you can read with enthusiasm and expression.)

Children are given ways to *participate* as the story is read a second time. Then, children are given time to *read* the story at their own levels—from reading and coloring pictures to reading aloud for others.

❸ **Practice Using a Bible** allows even nonreaders to begin developing Bible skill. Equipping young readers with this useful skill is exciting and satisfying. Confidence blossoms as children learn to read Bible stories *and* find Bible verses.

❹ **Share What We've Learned** completes the learning cycle as children show their new skills and talk about their newly acquired knowledge.

The Singing Bible, ©1993 Word Publishing, 1501 LBJ, Suite 650, Dallas, TX 75234

Kids on the Rock! More Songs, ©1994 Gospel Light, Ventura CA 93006

Follow the Leader, I'm a Helper, Good News, ©1991 Integrity Music, Inc., P.O. Box 16813 Mobile, AL 36616

Options and **Materials** are listed in the narrow column. Scan other lessons for **option** ideas to adapt to the lesson you are teaching. Scan the lesson for **materials** to gather before class.

Including music is easy. Suggestions from the following seven tapes are given with each unit: *The Singing Bible* (3 tapes); *Kids on the Rock! More Songs;* The Donut Man (3 tapes) *Follow the Leader, I'm a Helper, Good News.* Songs emphasize unit themes or lesson content—at least one new song for each unit.

Teaching at Home offers help for families to adapt group activities or expand learning activities. **Reading tips** are especially helpful for those who are using *The Young Reader's Bible* as a supplemental reading text.

Reproducible pages

- Three pages of supplemental activities with each unit
- Three story excerpts from *The Young Reader's Bible* with each unit
- Two complete Bible stories are included for every unit—twenty Bible stories in all! Reproduce these stories (pages 259-318) to make a mini-*Young Reader's Bible* for each child.

Teach so they can learn

Each unit provides a balance of fun activities to help every child learn. Some learn more easily by seeing information. So *Bible Lessons for Young Readers* includes ideas for easy-to-make visual teaching ideas. Many children learn more readily as they handle items, and participate in games, dramas, crafts, and cooking. Select learning activities to involve all five senses. Guided conversations and recorded stories will help auditory learners. Simply cue the cassette to a story on *The Young Reader's Bible on Cassette,* and let readers and nonreaders follow along in a *Young Reader's Bible.* Two young readers narrate the stories. Background music and sound effects capture a young child's attention.

Using music will help children hear and remember the lesson content and build unit themes. For ideas, see the music charts on the unit pages.

Teaching is a breeze with these helps from Standard Publishing

The Young Reader's Bible (seventy easy-reader Bible stories)
50 Bible Paper Pop-Ups (one hands-on paper craft for every lesson in this book)
The Young Reader's Bible Audio Cassette (every story from *The Young Reader's Bible*)
Devotions for Young Readers
The Young Reader's Bible Double Fun Pads
God Made Me Special (reproducible journal for primaries)
Big Picture Books: *What Is the Best Thing About God?*   *Who Brought the Bread?*
                     What Is the Best Thing About Jesus?   *Who Wrecked the Roof?*
                     Just Like Everybody Else
Choose from fourteen titles of Really Reading! Books (reading levels 1.7—2.1)

Other supplemental helps

Christian bookstores offer a variety of video Bible stories. The videos vary in technical quality as well as biblical accuracy. Series include: *Superbooks Video Bible,* Tyndale Family Video; *The Greatest Adventure, Stories From the Bible,* Turner Home Entertainment; *Family Classics From the Stars; Rabbit Ears: The Greatest Stories Ever Told.* Focus on the Family Films with Zondervan (in association with Shepherd Ltd. Production) is expanding a line of basic Bible stories.

Computer resources are increasingly available. Look for Bookie Bookworm Interactive Talking Books (CD-ROM for DOS and Windows) from Zondervan Publishing House (Division of Harper Collins).

Encouraging Young Readers

Parents and teachers influence young readers by simple example.

Read newspapers and magazines. Read the Bible. Read a novel. Read to yourself and read to the child.

Give the child time to read. Listen to him read stories over and over. Do echo reading (let the child repeat each phrase). Make puppet shows.

Reading and writing go hand in hand. Balance reading, writing, speaking and listening. Provide rich multisensory experiences with vocabulary words.

Build on what children already know. Prior knowledge is the base on which new knowledge builds most securely. Explore the library. Visit bookstores and Christian bookstores.

Parents and teachers help young readers use reading strategies.

Successful reading experiences encourage independent reading!
- Look at pictures for clues.
- Read carefully one word at a time. Make sure what you *say* is what you *see*.
- Use beginning letter cues and familiar endings to sound out a word that fits.
- Reread a passage to get the context and gather clues.
- Ask yourself questions. Make a guess. Try it out.
- Skip the word. Maybe you will understand it when you reread the story.

Young readers have fun learning vocabulary with hands-on practice.
- Write letters and words in all kinds of substances: finger-paint, dry cornmeal, pudding.
- Handle letters to spell words: magnetic letters, pasta or cereal letters, letters cut from sandpaper, clay, or sponges.
- Write words or letters and then trace them in other colors to make rainbow letters or words.

Parents, teachers and young readers should read and write every day.
- Write letters, cards, and postcards.
- Read and write daily schedules and chores lists.
- Keep journals.
- Create a family or class diary or family history.
- Write captions for photo albums.
- Read and write songs, jokes, and riddles.
- Write copy to go with cartoon balloons or drawings.
- Make booklets of family celebrations.

Although *Bible Lessons for Young Readers* is not a complete reading curriculum, it offers a helpful supplement to other reading materials.

I Can Use My Bible

It is filled with good lessons and it is true.

It is the B ___ ___ ___ ___ ,

God's Book for you.

If we divided the Bible in two,

Its parts would be the

O ___ ___ T ___ ___ ___ ___ ___ ___ ___ ___ ___

and N ___ ___ .

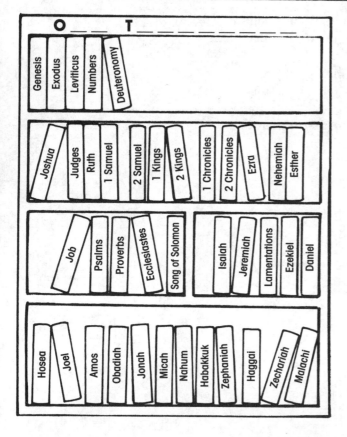

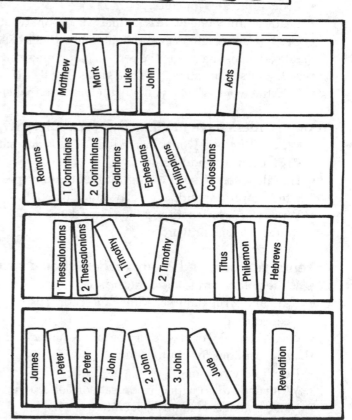

Table of Contents

Genesis ___

Matthew ___

Psalms ___

Revelation ___

I Can Use My Bible

Genesis, Psalms, and Matthew,
Revelation—take a look.
The testaments are divided into parts,
Each called a B ___ ___ ___ .

Most Bible books have several parts,
And so we often say,
"We will read a C ___ ___ ___ ___ ___ ___
From our Bibles every day."

Each chapter is divided into parts of smaller size.
Each part is called a V ___ ___ ___ ___ ,
That's what we memorize.

Psalm 1

1 Blessed is the man
   who does not walk in the counsel of the wicked
  or stand in the way of sinners
   or sit in the seat of mockers.
2 But his delight is in the law of the LORD,
   and on his law he meditates day and night.
3 He is like a tree planted by streams of water,
   which yields its fruit in season
  and whose leaf does not wither.
   Whatever he does prospers.

4 Not so the wicked!
   They are like chaff
   that the wind blows away.
5 Therefore the wicked will not stand in the judgement,
   nor sinners in the assembly of the righteous.
6 For the LORD watches over the way of the righteous,
   but the way of the wicked will perish.

New International Version

Unit 1

We Worship God Because He Is Powerful

Key Verse

"O Lord my God, you are very great."   Psalm 104:1, NIV

Unit Vocabulary

angels
animal
ark
beginning
count
cupbearer
dove
dream
earth
evening
flood
grain
heavens
human beings
ladder
laugh(ed)
message
morning
obey(ed)
pillar
pillow
prison
promise
rainbow
remember
visitor

Unit Aims

By the end of the unit, learners will be able to
• tell five Bible stories about God's power.
• feel interested in finding books in a Bible and reading *The Young Reader's Bible*.
• locate books, chapters and verses in their own Bibles.
• read (at their level) at least one story from *The Young Reader's Bible*.
• worship God because He is powerful.

Unit Projects

Questions in Rhyme

Recruit someone to help you write question and answer rhythms to a "military march cadence."

Who told Noah "Build a boat"?	God told Noah, "Build a boat."
Who sent water to make it float?	God sent water to make it float.
Who made it rain for forty days?	God made it rain for forty days.
Who said obeying always pays?	God said obeying always pays.

Then chant: God sent the water
God sent the flood
And when He sent a rainbow
Noah worshiped God.

Worship Songs

The theme for units 1, 2, 5, and 6 is worship. Teach children several of the worship songs during unit 1. You will be able to use them regularly during Share What We've Learned.

	The Singing Bible (3 tapes)	Kids on the Rock (More Songs)	Follow the Leader (The Donut Man)	I'm a Helper (The Donut Man)	Good News (The Donut Man)
Lesson 1	God Made the Universe				This Is the Day
Lesson 2	Noah Build a Boat				
Lesson 3	God Began a Nation				
Lesson 4	The Blessing That Will Be				
Lesson 5	Seven Fat Cows				
Key Verse		Lord, I Trust in You			
Unit Theme		Singing Together; Time to Worship	Make a Joyful Noise	What a Mighty God	
All Lessons	The Books We Love the Best	God's Word Is for Me			
	The Bible Book Is True				

The Singing Bible (3 tapes), ©1993 by Lightwave Publishing, Inc. Manufactured and distributed by Word Publishing, Dallas, TX 75234
Kids on the Rock! More Songs, ©1994 Gospel Light, Ventura CA 93006
The Donut Man (3 tapes): *Follow the Leader,* ©1990; *I'm a Helper,* ©1991; *Good News,* ©1991; Integrity Music, Inc., P.O. Box 16813 Mobile, AL 36616

Key Verse Activities

Materials

- transparent acetate report covers or page protectors
- scissors
- permanent marker
- paper reinforcements
- paper punch
- paper towels
- fluorescent paint pens (glow-in-the dark are especially fun)
- transparent tape
- stapler
- 12-inch and 36-inch pieces of twine
- at least two colors of inexpensive, fluorescent surveyor's tape (from a hardware store) or gift wrapping curling ribbon

Flying Colors Windsocks

Before class, open the report covers and cut them apart along the fold. If the pages have holes punched in them, cut off a strip to remove the holes. Write the memory verse with permanent marker near the center of each acetate page. Evenly space four paper reinforcements about ½-inch from the bottom edge. Place two reinforcements ½-inch from the top edge and about 2½ inches from each side. Stick reinforcements on the back of the acetate facing all six reinforcements. Punch holes in the middle of them.

When someone does something well, people say the person did it with "flying colors." God does _everything_ well. When you memorize Psalm 104:1, you can make a windsock with flying colors.

When you memorize the verse today, you earn the tube of the windsock to decorate however you like. If you can still recite the verse "with flying colors" at the beginning of the next four lessons, you can earn a streamer each time to tie onto the windsock.

Let the children decorate the acetate pages with paint pens. When the paint has dried, roll the acetate into a tube shape and tape the edges together inside and outside the tube. Staple the taped edges together also. Tie the ends of the 12-inch twine to the top holes. Tie one end of the 36-inch twine to the middle of the 12-inch piece. In each upcoming week, put a streamer through a reinforced hole and let the children knot it. They take their windsocks home after the last lesson of the unit.

Materials

- seeds
- photocopies of the pattern from page 11
- scissors
- glue stick
- markers

Seed Packets

Before class, cut out the packets and fold along the dotted lines.

What does our memory verse say? (We can praise God for His power.) **He made plants on the third day and we can still see His power making plants grow. We're going to decorate seed packets and then we'll put seeds in them to take home. First, color in the letters and draw different kinds of flowers. Then we'll glue the side flaps down, put seeds in the packet, and glue down the top flap.**

Sound and Show

Let's stand in a circle for a game. We'll recite the memory verse as a group and then one person will say, "God made _____ ," and make a sound and motion of that thing (for example, a dog barking and begging or the wind whistling and making you sway). Everyone copies that sound and motion. Then the group repeats the memory verse and the next person makes a sound and motion to be repeated. Continue until everyone has had a turn.

God Makes Everything

Tell why God's creation is so amazing.
Worship God because He made everything.
Show the Old Testament and New Testament.

"O Lord my God, you are very great."   Psalm 104:1, NIV

① Get Ready to Read

Before class, make a sample cube. Prepare colored paper and art from page 31 for the days of creation. 1—light/dark, yellow/black; 2—sky/water, light and dark blue; 3—land, sea, plants: tree growing by pond; 4—sun, moon, star; 5—fish, bird; 6—animal, person. Tape the lid of a box closed securely. Cover all six sides of a box with plain wrapping paper. Put the art and paper on the sides of the creation cube.

God did an amazing thing when He made everything in the world. All He said was, "Let there be . . . each thing" and there it was!

Show the sample cube. Let the children make creation cubes or a creation tower. Glue the colored paper or art for each day of creation to each side of the boxes. To make a tower, use wrapping paper to cover six boxes of graduating sizes and glue one day of creation on each box.

Sing songs on the topic of creation. As you sing, the children can stack the tower boxes in order. (Day 1/light on bottom, etc.) or find the corresponding day on the creation cube.

Use the cube to talk about God's power. Explain how amazing the creation was. How God is so powerful He can make something out of nothing.

What did God make on day 1? What's the biggest light you've ever seen? How much bigger was the light God made? (It's like a blanket around the whole earth.)

Day 2—What are some things that come from the sky? (Rain, snow, wind, and light come from the sky.)

Day 3—What is one amazing thing about plants? (They die in winter and come back alive in spring. One seed grows a plant with many seeds.)

Day 4—What would happen if the sun were not in the right place? (People might burn up if it were too close or freeze if it were too far away. God did it just right!)

Day 5—What is so amazing about fish and birds? (Birds fly south in winter and back to the same places in spring—without a map!)

Day 6—What is so amazing about animals? (Cats have special eyes to see in the dark. Each animal has just what it needs.)

What is so amazing about people? (We are made in the image of God. We can think, plan, choose, and someday go to live with God in Heaven!)

Materials
- photocopies of page 31 (option: enlarge the art for use on larger-sized boxes)
- a small box for each child or a set of 6 boxes in graduating sizes
- plain wrapping paper
- construction or colored paper (yellow, blue, green, black)
- tape
- scissors
- music for songs about the creation

Options
- For younger children or if time is limited, prepare the cube or tower before class. This way you can use class time to learn about God's power. Remember the aim of the activity is learning about God's power in creation—decorating boxes is part of the method and not the aim.
- Small groups can work together to make one cube or tower. Large groups and children who learn by moving around will enjoy making the cube or tower out of the biggest boxes you can find. Stack them up to the ceiling!
- Singing will help children who learn best by hearing. The children who learn best by seeing will do well if they can have their own cubes or towers.

Materials
- *The Young Reader's Bible*, pages 14-19
- photocopies of the Bible story (pages 259-261)
- *The Young Reader's Bible Audio Cassette* or a cassette on which you have recorded unit stories
- cassette player(s), earphones optional
- creation cube or tower made earlier
- small index card with "God" printed on it
- pencils
- crayons or markers

❷ Read the Bible Story

"The Beginning"
Have children use their creation cube(s) or tower to report what God made on each day. **As I read the story, listen for the number of each day of creation.**

Listen
Gather the children around as you read dramatically the story from the *Young Reader's Bible*.

Focus the follow-up conversation on what God did in the story. Add some of your own questions and review the story.

What did God do in the very beginning of the world? (He made heavens and earth. But it was dark.)

What did God do first? (He made light.) **What did He do next?** (He made sky.)

What is your favorite thing that He made? What is so amazing about God and His power? (He does things no one else can do!)

Prayer Example
"God, You are special because only You can make such a wonderful world with everything just right for every plant and animal. God, only You could make people. You are greater than us, God. We honor You in Jesus' name. Amen.

Participate
Let the children participate as you read the story again. They can hold up the correct number of fingers and count aloud each day of creation as it is named in the story. They can stand up and smile when you name their favorite creation. (Help them understand that if their favorite creation is a cat, then they will want to stand up when you say "living things for the land.") Or they can choose a sound effect to make for each day. If you do sound effects, tell them you will signal when to begin and end each sound effect.

Finally, in response to God's great power in creation, ask the children to pray a worship prayer with you. Let them echo your example, phrase by phrase.

Give each child a copy of the Bible story (pages 259-261). As they look at the pictures, ask them what they think God made first, second, etc. They can match the pictures to the ones they used on the story cubes.

Explain that the story has some words they know and some new words for them to learn. Begin to communicate joy and excitement about the possibility of reading God's words for themselves. Show the index card on which you printed the word *God*. Help them circle the word *God* on the first page of their story. Emphasize this story shows God made everything in the world.

Note
The word *God* is used sixteen times in this story booklet.

Read
Allow time for the children to get comfortable and to enjoy reading the story. Children who are not yet readers can look at the pictures while listening to the recorded story or "read" the story by finding a picture to go with each day of creation. Beginning readers can look for the number words for each day. Readers may enjoy reading aloud to other children.

Snacks
Serve basic foods God created, such as, sliced apples and cold water. Before eating you can worship God for the many foods He created.

❸ Practice Using a Bible

Materials
- Bible for each child
- paper or ribbon bookmark for each child

Using My Bible
The Bible has two parts: Old Testament and New Testament. The Old Testament is this big. (Show them and let them feel it.) **And the New Testament is this big.** (Show them and let them feel it.) **Right at the beginning of the New Testament is a book called Matthew.**

Give each child a bookmark to put where the New Testament begins. Demonstrate how to find Matthew, the first book of the New Testament, by turning to the table of contents and finding the page number for Matthew. Help each child mark the New Testament/Matthew with a bookmark. Close the Bible and again see how much is Old Testament and how much is New Testament.

Right in the middle of the Bible is a book called Psalms. Psalms is in the Old Testament. (Show them. Let them experience how to find Psalms by using their thumbs to open to the middle of their Bibles.) **Right at the front of the Bible is a book called Genesis. Genesis is also in the Old Testament.** (Show them. Let them turn to the front of their Bibles to find Genesis.)

Let's remember what we found today. (Review with the following questions.)

What are the two big parts of the Bible? (Old Testament, New Testament) **Which is first?** (Old Testament) **Which is last?** (New Testament)

What book is at the beginning of the New Testament? (Matthew) **Old Testament?** (Genesis) **middle of the Bible?** (Psalms)

Which book tells how God made everything? (Genesis)

Allow practice time for building skill in locating different parts of the Bible. If your children can all show how to find each testament, they can begin to work on finding three books: Psalms, Genesis and Matthew. Work on one book at a time. Stop when interest declines. Work on it again in the next session.

Finding Bible Verses

The Bible story about God making everything is in the book of Genesis. Let's find the very first words of that story. Show how to turn pages until you come to Genesis. Show where the story begins in verse 1. If you have readers in your group, let volunteers take turns reading the first sentence aloud (Genesis 1:1).

Ask children to practice finding Genesis 1:1. Be sure they include all three steps: find the book, find the chapter (big number), and find the verse (small number). Then allow enough time for each child to read or listen while you read the first verse in the Bible, Genesis 1:1. **You found the first verse in the Bible.**

4 Share What We've Learned

Let the children tell what they have learned! Be patient while they are learning what you expect. Even if the conversation seems unproductive today, try it at the end of each lesson. In future lessons add creative ways to report what was learned. But for now, keep the reporting simple and direct.

Gather everyone in a circle to talk about what they have been learning. Use the lesson aims as an outline for the questions you ask.

What did God do in today's story? (created everything in the world)

Why was that so amazing? (He made it out of nothing just by speaking and everything was perfect.)

What can we do to let God know we think He is a great God? (Worship Him and tell Him He is great in a prayer or even in a song.)

What two parts of the Bible can you show me? (Old Testament, New Testament) **What three books of the Bible can you find and show me?** (Matthew, Psalms, Genesis) **Which book did our story come from?** (Genesis)

Play a game called "I'm Thinking Of." The first person in the circle says "I'm thinking of something God made that is ____ and ____." Fill in the blanks with two words that describe something God made, like *tall* and *green*. One word should be a color. Whoever guesses correctly gets a turn to say, "I'm thinking of . . ."

Option
Paper can be laminated or covered with clear adhesive to make it sturdy.

Options
• Children who learn best by listening can begin to learn a chant/rap to help them find Bible verses. Use the reference rhyme on page 32.
• The visual learners can look at the pictures to help them understand the process of how to find parts of the Bible.

Options
• Teacher says "I'm thinking of . . ." Children search room to find item.
• Teacher puts each item in a bag. Child looks into bag and says, "God made something ____ and ____."

Teaching at Home

Make creation riddles to share with the family:
I am (color, size, shape).
I eat . . .
I have . . .
God created me. What am I?

Reading tips
• Make snakes with play clay. Form the letters for simple words like *God* or *good*.
• Sound out *human beings.* Help child find the little words *be* and *man.*

God Sends a Flood and a Rainbow

Tell why God's flood and the rainbow were so amazing.
Worship God because He saved Noah from the flood.
Say and copy a Bible reference and locate a Bible verse.

"O Lord my God, you are very great."   Psalm 104:1, NIV

1 Get Ready to Read

Materials
- play dough
- large plastic pan
- small buckets of water
- towels

God did an amazing thing when He covered the world with a great flood. He sent water from under the earth, water from above the earth (rain) and water from the oceans to flood the world all at the same time. Show the children the picture on page 33 of the *Young Reader's Bible*. Read the words, "Water will cover the whole earth. Every living thing will die."

God did another amazing thing when He kept Noah and his family safe from this flood of water. Review the flood story. **How did God keep Noah and his family safe?** Talk briefly about the ark that housed Noah, his family, and animals.

Options
- In a large class, group the children in pairs or trios so each child can help make the play-dough model. In a class with few children, let each one make a model.
- Children will enjoy adding small plastic figures (trees, houses, etc. borrowed from play sets of toys) to the "model" of the flood. Add a small plastic boat and watch it float to the top as you pour in water.

Let the children simulate a flood with play dough and water. Work together to make play dough mountains, valleys, rivers and lakes in a large tub or pan. Let them pour water over the "land" to make a flood in the tub. Use your finger to make "cracks" in the model to simulate where water would come up from under the earth. Move the water with your hands to simulate the great tidal waves that would have resulted from the earth's movement. Emphasize the destructive power of the flood so that the children can sense how powerful God is.

Focus the conversation on what God did and why it was so amazing. **Why did God send the flood?** (People were wicked and didn't listen to God.) **Where did the water come from that God used to flood the earth?** (under/above earth, ocean) **Why is that so amazing?** (Floods have never covered the earth all at once. Only God has that power.) **What else did God do that was amazing?** (He saved Noah, his family, and animals in an ark.)

2 Read the Bible Story

Materials
- *The Young Reader's Bible,* pages 32-37
- photocopies of the Bible story (pages 262-264)
- *The Young Reader's Bible Audio Cassette* or a cassette on which you have recorded unit stories
- cassette player(s), earphones optional
- cassette of favorite song(s) about Noah and the flood (See page 11.)
- model of flood made earlier
- pencils and crayons or markers
- large sheet of paper

"Water, Water Everywhere"

Do pantomimes of things to do with water (drink, wash, walk in rain with umbrella, fish, swim). Let volunteers think up something to do or do what you whisper in their ears. The rest can guess what they are doing with water.

Creation is the first story in the Bible. Today's story about God is also in the book of Genesis. God made all the water in the world. Long ago He used all the water in a very powerful way. Listen to find out what God did.

Listen

Gather the children around as you dramatically read the story from the *Young Reader's Bible* about what God did with all the water in the world.

Talk about the model of the flood. Ask them to tell about the power God showed and what that water power did to the world.

Participate

Before class, print the following word list in a column on a large sheet of paper: *ark, two, forty, flood, dove, rainbow.* On another paper, print *Noah.*

Give each child a copy of the story (pages 262-264). Ask children to find the picture that is similar to the flood they made with play dough and water (page 263). As they look at the picture, ask, **What do we learn about God from this story?** (He has power to destroy life and power to save the life of Noah and his family.)

Ask them to find the picture that shows God's promise, "I will never send another flood like this one." **God said the rainbow helps us remember that He will not use His power to flood the whole earth again.** See page 264.

What are the people in the picture doing? (Hands are raised to God in worship.) **What might they be saying?** (God, only Your power could send the flood to cover the earth. Your power is great. We praise and worship You alone.) **If you had been one of the people on the boat what might you have said to worship God for being so powerful?**

Show the children how to draw a simple boat outline around the name *Noah.* Tell them Noah is the father in this story. Help them pronounce the sounds in his name. Then tell them to circle or draw a boat shape around the name *Noah* in the story. (It is used nine times.) Choose and play songs about Noah as they work.

Let the children choose a word from those you listed before class (ark, two, forty, flood, dove, rainbow). Have them find the words in the story. Then guide them in using the words in sentences. Older children can print sentences on strips of paper and put the strips in order to retell the story.

Have the child do hand motions as you reread the story. Choose a motion for the six words used earlier.

After the story, ask the children to pray a worship prayer with you to acknowledge God's great power. Let them echo your example.

Read

Use photocopies of the Bible stories for lessons 1 and 2. Display them in a special reading area where the children can use the cassette and the *Young Reader's Bible* to enjoy Bible stories.

Encourage nonreaders to look at the pictures to see what happened first, second, next. Rejoice with the efforts of each child to "read."

❸ Practice Using a Bible

Using My Bible

Before class, fill in the blank on a photocopy of Task Card #5 with "Psalm 104:1." Prepare bookmarks for the children to use when they copy the Bible reference, Psalm 104:1. For young children, make dots for them to trace to spell out Psalm 104:1.

Soon we will be able to find many Bible stories and verses in our Bibles. We know the story of creation and the story of the flood are in Genesis. Our key verse is in Psalms. Remind the children how to find the Old Testament and how

---

Hand motion ideas

ark—make roof with hands over head; **two**—two fingers; **forty**—count by tens to forty by holding up ten fingers at a time; **flood**—wave hands over your head like flood waters splashing; **dove**—hook thumbs together and flap hands like wings of bird flying away; **rainbow**—use hand to make the shape of a rainbow in the sky

Prayer Example

"God You are special
because only You have the power
to make a flood cover the whole
   world.
God, only You could make a
   rainbow
to help us remember Your power.
You are so great!
We worship You in Jesus' name.
   Amen."

Snacks

Serve animal crackers and cold water. Ask children what it might have been like to ride with the animals in the ark.

Materials

• Bible for each child
• paper or ribbon bookmarks
• photocopies of Task Card #5
   (page 111)
• drawing paper
• large sheet of paper
• markers, pencils

---

they marked the New Testament with a bookmark. Ask them to find both the Old Testament and New Testament.

1. Open to the "middle" of the Bible. (This should be Psalms.)

2. Look for the BIG numbers on the pages of Psalms. Keep turning pages until you find number 104. It might be helpful to find 100 and then count to 104. This is chapter 104.

3. Look for the small numbers in chapter 104. (There are 35 small numbers or verses.) Locate the number "1" at the beginning of the chapter. This is verse 1.

Show the children the three parts of writing the Bible reference (book, chapter, verse) they just found in Psalms. Print the reference on a large sheet of paper. Ask them to read the reference with you as you point to each part: Psalm, chapter 104, verse 1.

Then give them a bookmark and Task Card #5 to complete on their own. Older children can copy the reference onto their bookmarks. Younger children can trace the reference on a bookmark.

Focus the conversation on the privilege of having a Bible for everyone to read and find verses. Enable them to talk about what they have just learned about finding verses.

What are the two big parts of the Bible? (New Testament, Old Testament) **Which is first?** (Old Testament) **last?** (New Testament)

What book is at the beginning of the New Testament? (Matthew)

What book is at the beginning of the Old Testament? (Genesis)

What book is in the middle of the Bible? (Psalms)

How do we read this Bible reference? (Show Psalm 104:1.)

How can we find Psalm 104:1? (Find the book in middle, then the chapter, then the verse.)

Spend some time practicing. Let children help one another use their Bibles.

Finding Bible Verses

Repeat the three steps to show how to find a Bible reference in Psalms. Close all Bibles. Then have everyone follow the steps to find Psalm 104:1 in their own Bibles. Read aloud the key verse for this unit, Psalm 104:1.

4 Share What We've Learned

This is a time to let the children tell you what they have learned! Use the aims for this lesson as a conversation guide.

What did God do in the story? (He sent a flood of water to cover all the earth.)

Why was that so amazing? (No one else can do that.)

What can we say to let God know we think He is a great God? (God, only You have the power to cover the whole earth with water!)

What does this Bible reference say? (Show card with "Psalm, chapter 104, verse 1.")

What can you find in your own Bible? (Old Testament, New Testament, Matthew, Genesis, Psalm 104:1)

What Bible stories have you read so far? (Creation, Noah)

Your careful listening will give you clues for what needs to be re-emphasized in the next lesson. So let them talk freely with you.

God Promises Abraham and Sarah a Son

Tell why God's gift of a son to Abraham and Sarah was so amazing.
Worship God because He gave Abraham and Sarah a son.
Say and copy a Bible reference and read a Bible verse.

"O Lord my God, you are very great."   Psalm 104:1, NIV

1 Get Ready to Read

Before class, print "Can you count the stars? So shall your family be." on strips of paper, one per child.

God made a powerful promise in the book of Genesis. He promised Abraham there would be so many people in his family that Abraham wouldn't be able to count them. That seemed impossible because Abraham had no children. His wife Sarah laughed because she thought she was too old to have children. She didn't believe God's promise!

Use paint brushes to smear thin glue on black paper. Then sprinkle glitter over the glue. Shake excess glitter into a shallow box to recycle onto the next child's picture. Glue the promise printed on the strip of paper to the black, starry sky paper. Read the promise aloud. The glittery star pictures help children grasp the vast number of people that would come from Abraham and Sarah's promised family.

Focus the conversation on what God promised and why that was so amazing.

What amazing promise did God make to Abraham? (Can you count the stars? So shall your family be.)

Try to count the grains of glitter drying on your paper. (Wait a little bit before commenting. Explain that counting glitter is what it would be like for Abraham to try to count the stars in the sky—impossible.)

What does God's promise mean? (Abraham's family would be so big he could not count them all.) **Why was that so amazing?** (When God made the promise, they had no children. Sarah thought they were too old to have children.)

How would you feel if God promised your Grandma was going to have a baby? (perhaps not believe it or think it was not really true) **What did Sarah do that showed it was hard for her to believe God would keep His promise?** (She laughed.) **What do you think Sarah would say if it really did come true?** (Only God could do this!)

2 Read the Bible Story

"A Surprise for Sarah"
Look at one of the "glittery stars at night" pictures. Ask how many stars they

Materials
- black art or construction paper
- thin glue (2 parts glue, 1 part water)
- ½- to 1-inch wide paint brushes
- glitter
- 1-by-8-inch strips of paper
- pencils or markers
- shallow box

Options
- For large groups, make the starry sky more awesome to count by displaying all their black papers with glittery stars together.
- Auditory learners benefit from chanting or singing the promise to a familiar tune—such as "Farmer in the Dell."

  Can you count the sand
  *   that goes beside the sea?*
  Can you count the stars?
  *   So shall your family be.*

- For active learners or younger nonreaders, play a counting game to show how hard it would be to count all the stars. While seated in a circle, each child pretends to be a star. Starting with number 1, each child stands and says the next number in order around the circle until they tire of it. Comment on how far they have counted, but how many more Abraham could count in a whole night of looking at the stars!

Materials
- *The Young Reader's Bible*, pages 38-43
- photocopies of the Bible story excerpt (page 28)
- *The Young Reader's Bible Audio Cassette* or a cassette on which you have recorded unit stories
- cassette player(s), earphones optional
- glittery star pictures made earlier
- yellow construction paper
- star pattern
- marker
- scissors

Option

Plan actions for the entire group to do together to mime the story action as you reread it.

Prayer Example

"God, You are so great because Your power helped Abraham and Sarah
have a son when they were very old.
You are the only one
who could make Abraham have a family
as big as the number of stars in the sky!
So we worship only You.
Through Jesus we pray. Amen."

Option

Kinesthetic learners will enjoy playing a circle game with the vocabulary words. Let them pass the star-shaped word cards around while counting to ten. Whoever has a star when the counting stops says the word and tells what it means.

Snacks

Serve a star-shaped snack such as Jell-O Jigglers or cookies.

Materials
- Bible for each child
- three bookmarks per team or per child (optional)
- photocopies of Task Card #6 (page 111)
- crayons or markers, pencils

---

think might be in the picture (accept all guesses). Then ask how Abraham and Sarah might have felt when God promised them a family with as many people as there are stars in the sky.

Let's read to find out who brought the surprise to Abraham and Sarah.

Listen

Gather the children around you to listen as you dramatically read the story from the *Young Reader's Bible*.

Talk about how Abraham and Sarah might have felt.

How did Abraham feel when God said his family would be like the stars? (happy, curious) **when visitors told him Sarah would have a son?** (happy, amazed)

How did Abraham feel when Isaac was born? How did Sarah feel? (very happy)

Participate

Let volunteers mime the action of the story as you reread it. You will need at least two characters: Abraham and Sarah. If you have a large group, you can add some or all of the following characters: servants, flocks, three visitors, baby Isaac.

Invite the children to pray a worship prayer with you to acknowledge God's great power. They can echo your prayer as they did in the last two lessons.

They may be ready to offer their own prayers after hearing your example. Encourage volunteers to offer their worship by starting out "God, You are so great because . . ." Either way, help them to understand that their worship prayers can tell God about the great thing He did.

Before class, cut out three star-shaped word cards from yellow construction paper and print the following words on them with a marker: *Abraham, servants, flocks.*

Remind the children that all the stories so far are found in Genesis, the first book in the Bible. Give each child a copy of the two-page excerpt (page 28) from "A Surprise for Sarah."

Show the children the vocabulary words printed on star shapes (*Abraham, servants, flocks*). Ask them to listen for those words as you read the two pages aloud. After you read, show the three vocabulary word cards and ask the children to sound out each word with you. Hearing the words in context will provide clues for their meaning when you ask these questions.

Who do you think Abraham is? (the father in the story)
What do you think a servant is? (person who helps do your work)
What do you think a flock is? (group of animals like sheep or goats)

Read

Give the children a few minutes to look at or read today's story. They can find and circle the four vocabulary words on a copy of the story pages. Children who can read may choose to read any or all of the first three stories. Children who are not yet readers can look at the pictures while listening to the story on cassette.

❸ Practice Using a Bible

Using My Bible

Before class, prepare bookmarks for non-writers to trace the reference Psalm 104:1. Print *Psalm 104:1* and the word *great* in the blanks on Task Card #6.

For an extra challenge, make a second Task Card #6 with the reference Genesis 15:5 and the word *stars* printed in the blanks.

Tell the children you are glad they are learning to find verses in their Bibles. Let them copy "Psalm 104:1" or "Genesis 15:5" onto a bookmark. Younger writers can trace the reference on a bookmark.

Guide the group in the following review.

1. Find the Old Testament. (Open to front; look for Genesis.)
2. Find Psalms. (Open to the middle.)
3. Find the New Testament and place a bookmark there.

Use Task Card #6 to review how to find Bible verses (book, chapter, verse). Let them copy the reference, find the verse as directed on the Task Card, and mark it with their bookmarks.

Focus the conversation on the joy of being able to find verses and read them. Enable the children to talk about what they have done to find Bible verses.

Finding Bible Verses

Ask the children to tell you what to do to find a Bible verse. When they can describe the process correctly (find book, find big number for chapter, find small number for verse), encourage them to find the key verse for this unit, Psalm 104:1, and a verse from today's story, Genesis 15:5.

To practice this skill, provide Bibles with three bookmarks inside the front cover. Play in teams or let each child work alone. At a given signal, they race to put the bookmarks at the start of the New Testament, at the start of the Old Testament, and in Psalms.

4 Share What We've Learned

Before class, use the lesson aims to write questions. Print them on star-shaped cards, one question per card. Punch a hole in each card and use fishing line or yarn to hang them in one area of your classroom.

This is the time for the children to shine like stars as they show and tell what they have learned. Let them talk freely, note what they have learned and what they need to work on in the next lesson. Read the questions from the stars to guide the conversation time.

What did God do in the story? (He promised Abraham that trying to count the people in his family would be like trying to count the stars.)

Why was that so amazing? (At that time, they were old and had no children.)

What can we say to let God know we think He is a great God? (God, only You could give them a baby when they were very old.)

What does this Bible reference say? (Show Task Card #6: Psalm 104:1 or Genesis 15:5.)

What can you find in your own Bible? (Old and New Testament, Matthew, Psalms, Genesis)

What Bible stories have we read? (creation, Noah and flood, son for Abraham and Sarah)

Learn a star song.　　Twinkle twinkle little stars.
No one knows how many there are.
God promised Abraham a son.
Isaac was the promised one.
Now Abraham's family is like the stars.
We can't count how many there are.

Fill in Task Card #6
Copy this Bible reference:
Psalm 104:1.
Find Psalm 104:1 in your Bible.
Read the verse. Find the word great.
Copy this Bible reference
Genesis 15:5.
Find Genesis 15:5 in your Bible.
Read the verse. Find the word stars.

Materials
• photocopies of Task Card #6 (page 111)
• six star-shaped cards
• felt marker
• fishing line or yarn
• paper punch

 Teaching at Home

Choose a cloudless night for a field trip to the country to count the stars.

Reading tips
• Add lots of vocabulary words to star cutouts. Just as the angel challenged Abraham to count the stars, the children can count the stars they can read.
• Make tent-shaped and star-shaped cards. Work on words that rhyme with tent and star.

God Repeats His Promise to Jacob

Tell why God's promise to Jacob was so amazing.
Worship God because He kept His promise to Jacob.
Read and copy a Bible reference and find a Bible verse.

"O Lord my God, you are very great."   Psalm 104:1, NIV

Materials
- paper grocery bags, one for every two children
- scissors
- painting supplies
- marker, pencils
- Option: tempera paint and painting supplies for decorating stone pillows

Options
- For younger children, outline the words of the promise in dots to trace.
- For small groups, find enough real stones for each child to have one. If you find large stones, let children paint the stones and print the promise on one side.
- Provide a blank cassette and recorder. Let good readers read God's promise to Jacob in their "awesome" voice from a Bible (Genesis 28:13-15), or from the *Young Reader's Bible* (page 52).

Materials
- *The Young Reader's Bible*, pages 50-55
- photocopies of the Bible story excerpt (page 29)
- *The Young Reader's Bible Audio Cassette* or a cassette on which you have recorded unit stories
- cassette player(s), earphones optional
- large stone or rock for a pillow
- sleeping bag or blanket
- paper stones made earlier
- small index cards
- markers or crayons, pencils

① Get Ready to Read

Before class, cut two 11-by-18-inch sections from each paper grocery bag. Throw away the rest of the bag.

Abraham and Sarah had a grandson named Jacob. God made a powerful promise to Jacob in the book of Genesis. God made this promise while Jacob was sleeping—with a stone for a pillow.

Let each child draw a large stone shape on the plain side of an 11- by-18-inch paper you cut from the bag. Inside the outline of the stone, he or she can print the promise or part of the promise: "I am with you always."

Cut out the stone shape, wad it up to texturize it and then flatten it out to look like a stone. Talk about using a stone for a pillow; try using it on the floor as a pillow. Then read the promise that God made to Jacob when he had a stone pillow.

② Read the Bible story

"A Pillow and a Promise"

Ask the children to name one important thing to have when you go to sleep at night. Then show them the stone. Let several children try to use the stone for a pillow. Ask them to tell how it feels.

Explain that Jacob went on a journey. Emphasize how Jacob's travel was different from what we expect (no motel or home to stay in, sleep on ground, hard stone instead of soft pillow).

Listen to find out how Jacob used his stone in two ways in the story.

Listen

Gather the children on a sleeping bag or blanket with you (and your helpers) as you read the story from the *Young Reader's Bible*. If you have a small group of children who have good self-control, you might let them lay in a circle around you (like spokes of a wheel with you at the center) with their heads propped up on their hands. They can use their paper "stones" as pillows.

Participate

Compare the story with the children's experiences:

If you were visiting your uncle, how would you travel? How did Jacob travel?

If you were sleeping away from home, where would you stay? Where did Jacob stay?

When you have good dreams, what do you see? What did Jacob see in his dream?

When you wake up in the morning, what do you do with your pillow? What did Jacob do?

How do you feel when you see your family again? How did Jacob feel?

Let the children participate as you reread the story. Whenever you come to an action word, act it out together instead of speaking it.

Focus the conversation on what God promised and why it was so amazing. Review the promise to Jacob. **God promised 1) to give Jacob the land where he was sleeping; 2) to make the number of people in his family like the number of dust grains in the earth; 3) to always be with Jacob; 4) to always care for Jacob; 5) to bring Jacob back to the land he was leaving. This was amazing because Jacob had no wife or children, and he was running away to a new home.**

How many people do you think Jacob would have in his family? (more than we can count)

Why do the promises to Abraham and Jacob sound alike? (Abraham is Jacob's grandfather. God is telling Jacob He will keep his promise to Abraham. Now Jacob is part of the promise too.)

What does God's promise mean? (Abraham and Jacob's family will be too big to count.)

Why was that so amazing? (When God made the promise to Jacob, he had no wife or children. He was running away from the only family he had. Extra note: It seemed impossible for Jacob to come back because his brother hated him and would kill him.)

Invite the children to pray a worship prayer with you to honor the power of God to care for Jacob in this story. The children may want to echo your prayer as they have in past lessons.

They may be ready to offer their own prayers after hearing your example. Encourage volunteers to offer their worship by starting out "God, You are the only one who . . . " Either way, help them to understand that their worship prayers can talk to God about the promise He made and kept in today's story.

Remind the children that all four stories are from Genesis, the first book in the Bible. Give each child a copy of the two-page Bible story excerpt (page 29). Ask them to name things they see in the pictures (Jacob, stone, pillow, angels, ladder). Then ask them to find and underline those items in the printed words (picture of Jacob and the word *Jacob*.) Remind the group that pictures in a book give us clues for what words say.

Next, read the story again. Pause to let them fill in the five words that go with the pictures. Signal the next word by pointing to the picture. Use these questions to help the children recall what happened next.

What did God do? What did God say?

What did Jacob do? What did Jacob say?

Did Jacob ever see his family again? What promise did God keep?

Read

Display copies of the *Young Reader's Bible* stories in your reading area. Children who can read may choose to read any or all of the first four stories.

Option

Use the paper stones to play act the story. If you have a calm, safety-conscious group, use real stepladders for the angels to climb. Include giving worship to God when Jacob uses his stone for a pillar.

Prayer Example

"God, You are so great
because Your power kept Jacob
 safe
when Jacob was not with his family.
You are the only one
who could help Jacob not be afraid.
We worship You, God.
Through Jesus we pray. Amen."

Snacks

Serve angel food cake and fruit juice as you pretend to be Jacob enjoying breakfast.

Children who are not yet readers can look at the pictures while listening to the story on a cassette player. They can also color the story pictures (page 29).

Materials
- Bible for each child
- paper bookmarks
- photocopies of Task Card #7 (page 111)
- photocopies of page 32
- pencils

③ Practice Using a Bible

Using My Bible

As you review the skills the children have been working on, be ready to rejoice with the children who can show you how to do the following:

Find the New Testament and mark it with a bookmark. (Find page for Matthew in the Table of Contents.)

Find Psalms. (Open to middle of Bible.)

Find the Old Testament. (Open to front; look for Genesis.)

Finding Bible Verses

Review, or ask children to show you, how to find specific verses in the Bible (book, chapter, page). The reference rhyme on page 32 can help. Give each child a copy of the reference rhyme. Talk about the directions and the pictures. Use the rhyme to locate Genesis 28:12.

Before class, print *31* and *angels* in the blanks on Task Card #7. Let the children follow the directions on the card. Let them copy (or trace) the reference, Genesis 28:12, on a bookmark.

How do we read this Bible reference: Genesis 28:12? (book of Genesis, chapter 28, verse 12)

What do we do to find Genesis 28:12? (Find Genesis, find big 28, find small 12.)

What did you learn about angels and a dream in Genesis 28:12? (In the dream, the angels went up and down a ladder.)

Show me where we learned that same thing in a *Young Reader's Bible.* Encourage the children to practice finding the key verse for this unit: Psalm 104:1 and a verse from today's story, Genesis 28:12.

Materials
- stone-shaped papers
- marker
- strips of paper

Option

Print your conversation questions on stone-shaped papers. Turn them upside down on the floor. To ask questions in order, number the back of each "stone." Children could hop to collect question stones.

Teaching at Home

Put the action word cards near the television. As children watch a program, they can identify the actions listed.

Reading tip

Print verbs on rock-shaped flash cards: spoke, woke, bowed, ran, hugged, cried, gave. Tell children these are verbs. Verbs are words that tell what we do. Read each word and let the children act out the motion. Pantomime each word as it is read.

④ Share What We've Learned

Before class, make a game with five stone shapes cut from art paper. Print one word of the promise on each paper stone: "I am with you always." Also, print Bible references Psalm 104:1 and Genesis 28:12 on a strip of paper.

Gather in an informal circle, and use the goals for this lesson to plan your conversation.

What did God do in the story? Why was it so amazing? (Jacob had no wife or children, he was running away from the land God said He would give him.)

What can we say to let God know we think He is a great God?

Read this Bible reference. (Show Psalm 104:1, Genesis 28:12.)

What can you find in your own Bible?

What Bible stories have you read so far?

Play a game with the stones you prepared before class. Arrange the paper stones on the floor. Let the children take turns saying the promise as they step on the correct words. For an extra challenge, add several extra stones with words that are not in the promise.

God Helps Joseph Explain Dreams

5

Tell why Joseph's explaining dreams shows that God is amazing.
Worship God because He knows everything.
Read and copy Bible references and find Bible verses.

"O Lord my God, you are very great."   Psalm 104:1, NIV

❶ Get Ready to Read

Give each child a copy of the Bible story excerpt (page 30). Ask a volunteer to read aloud the first side (*The Young Reader's Bible*, page 65) to find out what Pharaoh dreamed. Or read it aloud to them.

Help the children work together to make puppets to illustrate the first half of the dream. Let some children make seven fat cows out of paper lunch bags stuffed with newspaper. Use the bottom of the sack for the cow's face; glue on paper ears, draw on a mouth and nose with a marker. Keep the neck of the sack shut with a rubber band. Leave the band loose enough for a child to be able to stick one hand into the puppet.

Let the rest of the children make the seven skinny cows. Draw or trace a cow's head onto seven 8-by-11-inch sheets of poster board. Color and cut out the heads. Tape a tongue depressor or dowel rod to the backs for a handle.

Turn a table on its side for a simple puppet stage. Put the seven fat cows on one side of the stage and the seven skinny cows on the other side. Let the children take turns acting out the dream as you reread it from the booklet. Let the skinny cows walk up to the fat ones. The fat cows can disappear behind the skinny cows and then down behind the puppet stage.

What did Pharaoh dream? (Seven skinny cows ate seven fat cows; seven skinny grain heads ate seven fat ones.)

God did an amazing thing for Joseph. He helped Joseph tell the meaning of the Pharaoh's dreams.

Materials
• photocopies of two-page Bible story (page 30)
• 7 paper lunch bags
• newspaper
• art paper
• glue
• 7 rubber bands
• 7, 8-by-11-inch pieces of poster board
• crayons or markers
• 7 tongue depressors or 8-inch long dowel rods
• tape
• long table turned on side for puppet stage

Option
For children who work more slowly, stuff the fat-cow puppets and cut out the skinny-cow puppets ahead of time.

❷ Read the Bible story

"Double Dreams"
Let children show and describe the pictures or puppets of Pharaoh's dreams.
Listen to find out how Pharaoh learned that Joseph could tell him the meaning of his dreams.

Listen
Gather the children around you and read the story. Focus the conversation on

Materials
• *The Young Reader's Bible*, pages 62-67
• photocopies of the Bible story excerpt (page 30)
• photocopies of page 33
• *The Young Reader's Bible Audio Cassette* or a cassette on which you have recorded unit stories
• cassette player(s), earphones optional
• picture or puppets made earlier
• pencils or markers

what God did and why it was so amazing.

What amazing thing did God do? (God helped Joseph tell Pharaoh what the dreams meant.)

What did the dreams mean? (There would be seven years with plenty of food and seven years with no food.)

Why was that so amazing? (No one else could tell what the dreams meant. Everything happened just as God said it would.)

What would you do if you knew there were going to be seven years with plenty of food and then seven years with no food? (Perhaps someone will suggest "save food for bad years.")

Participate

Today's story has the numbers two and seven. Pharaoh had two dreams. He had seven of something in each dream. Let's look at the story together.

Give each child a copy of the rebus (page 33). Show the rebus and tell what word goes with each symbol. Together, read aloud the rebus. Reinforce the number seven in Pharaoh's dream.

Give each child a copy of the Bible story excerpt (page 30). Ask the children to find and circle each number seven (fat cows, skinny cows, fat grain, thin grain, good years, bad years). Have children confirm that the number of cows, grain and years in the rebus are the same as in the story.

Use the following riddles to talk about who was in the story,

I was put in prison for something I did not do.

My dream came true three days after Joseph told me what would happen.

I had two dreams I did not understand.

I told the Pharaoh Joseph could explain his dreams.

I told the Pharaoh what his dream meant.

I put Joseph in charge of the land to save grain for the bad years.

Invite the children to pray a worship prayer to acknowledge the power of God helping Joseph in this story. They can echo as you lead them.

Or they may be ready to offer their own prayers after hearing your example. Encourage volunteers to offer their worship by starting out "God, You are great because . . ." Help them to understand that in worship prayers we can talk to God about what He has done.

Use these questions to help the children remember the ways God's power is shown.

What did God help Joseph do? (tell meaning of dreams—no one else could)

What did God promise Jacob? (always be with you, bring you back here, give you this land)

What did God do when Abraham and Sarah were very old? (promised a son, gave them Isaac)

What did God do when the people of the earth only did wrong? (sent flood, saved Noah and his family)

What did God do in the very beginning of the world? (Made everything!)

What is so amazing about God and his power? (He does things no one else can do!)

Read

Remind the children that the five stories we are learning to read are all in Genesis, the first book in the Bible. Allow time for the children to go to a special area of the room to enjoy reading any of the first five stories. Children who are not yet readers can color story pictures while listening to a cassette story. Some children will enjoy looking at the rebus as they listen.

Option

Kinesthetic learners will enjoy "doing" the pictures on the rebus. Let them stand in a group and listen to the story again and again. They can demonstrate the rebus pictures.

Prayer Example

"God, You are greater than us because You alone helped Joseph explain dreams. We worship You, God. Through Jesus we pray. Amen."

Snacks

Serve whole grain bread or crackers and cheese.

❸ Practice Using a Bible

Using My Bible

Before class, print *65* on the blank on Task Card #8. Print Psalm 104:1 in large letters on a sheet of paper.

Begin by reviewing the skills the children have been learning in this unit. **Find the Old Testament**. **Find Psalms**. **Find the New Testament.** (Find Matthew's page number in the table of contents.)

Continue by asking the following questions.

What book is at the beginning of the Old Testament? (Genesis) **in the middle of the Bible?** (Psalms) **at the beginning of the New Testament?** (Matthew)

Give each child a small index card on which to copy (or trace) a reference from today's story: Genesis 15:5. Ask for a volunteer to tell how to read the reference.

Focus the conversation on the joy of finding and reading verses. Use Task Card #8 as a review.

Before class, print Bible references on index cards. Place the cards around the room in plain sight.

State a reference the children are to find first. Upon your signal, they race to find a card with a reference. If they find the wrong one(s), they must put them back. The person with the correct reference can read it aloud. Give everyone a turn to read a reference.

Finding Bible Verses

Use the reference rhyme (page 32) to guide the children to find Genesis 15:5. This will help them see that the stories they read come from the Bible. When they can describe the process correctly (find book, find big number for chapter, find small number for verse), help them find the key verse for this unit, Psalm 104:1, and a verse from today's story, Genesis 41:15, 16.

❹ Share What We've Learned

Instead of asking questions, let the children tell you what they have learned. By now, the children should have reached the unit know, feel and do aims. Use the unit aims and lesson aims to guide your conversation. For example:

What did God do in the stories we have been reading and why was that so amazing? How did God show His power?

What can we say to let God know we think He is a great God?

What does this Bible reference say? (Show references.)

What can you find in your own Bible? (Old and New Testaments, Genesis, Matthew, Psalms)

Before class sketch (or photocopy from the Bible story pages of this unit) these picture pairs. Adam and Eve/world (creation), Noah/ark (flood), Abraham and Sarah /baby (promise), Jacob/stone (promise), Joseph/7s (dreams). Make a banner that says "Bible Hall of Fame Game." Post it on the wall.

Play a "Bible Hall of Fame Game" with people in this unit's stories. Post pictures for each story in two rows under the "Bible Hall of Fame Game" banner. Put people on the top row; put items underneath, but not in matching order. Each child takes a turn to exchange two pictures to match one person to an item. When the matches are correct, take turns making a worship statement about each match. For example, "God, You are great because . . ." (Fill in with something from each story.)

Materials
• Bible for each child
• *The Young Reader's Bible*
• small index cards
• pencils
• photocopies of Task Card #8 (page 111)

Materials
• banner paper
• art paper
• markers
• Plasti-Tak or tape

Teaching at Home

Talk about saving for the future. Choose a family goal. Plan ways that every family member can help save (e. g. collect and sort recycle items to turn in for cash). Younger children will need goals set in the very near future!

Reading tip

Emphasize opposites such as fat/skinny, thin/full, and happy/sad. Draw or cut out shapes to represent opposites. Let child demonstrate action ideas such as fast/slow and loud/quiet.

A Surprise for Sarah

God told Abraham
to leave his country.

"I will bless you in a new land,"
God said. Abraham obeyed.

He took his wife, his servants,
and his flocks.

"Can you count the stars?"
God asked Abraham.

There were too many to count!

"So shall your family be,"
said God.

"But I have no children,"
said Abraham.

"Don't worry," said God.
"I will give you a son."

28

A Pillow and a Promise

On his way to see his uncle,

Jacob stopped to sleep.

He used a stone for a pillow.

While Jacob slept,

God sent him a special dream.

In his dream, Jacob saw angels

going up and down

a tall ladder.

The ladder led to heaven.

At the top stood God.

29

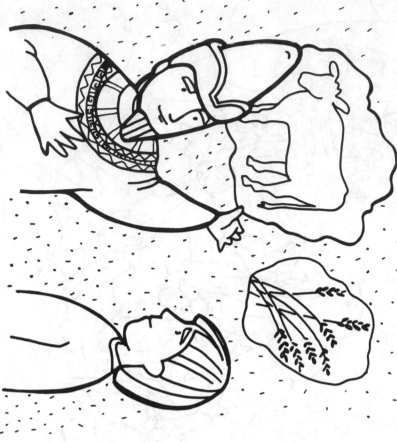

Pharaoh told Joseph his dreams.

"I saw seven fat cows," he said.

"Seven skinny cows ate them up.

Then seven thin heads of grain

ate up seven full heads."

"God gave you two dreams

that mean the same thing,"

said Joseph.

"There will be seven good years

with plenty of food.

Then there will be

seven bad years with nothing."

"God has made you wise,"

said Pharaoh. "I will put you

in charge of the land."

30

Creation Days

Color, cut out and tape each picture onto boxes (or sides of one box).

Use a sheet of black and a sheet of yellow construction paper for dark and light.

Use two shades of blue construction paper for water and sky.

Reference Rhyme

First I find the book

  or the page number of the book.

Then I find the chapter;

  the big number's where I look.

 Last, I find the verse;

    the small number is the one.

I've got it now!

  Finding verses is such fun.

God Helps Joseph Explain Dreams

 was put into prison for something he did not do.

Two years later, the king had strange dreams.

The cupbearer remembered .

 called for and told Joseph his dreams.

"I saw fat 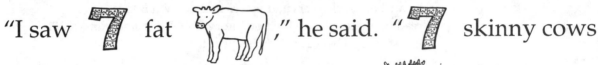 ," he said. " skinny cows ate them up. Then thin heads of ate up full heads."

Joseph said, "God gave you dreams that mean the same thing. There will be good years with plenty of . Then there will be bad years with nothing to eat."

"God has made you wise," said . "I will put you in charge of the land."

Unit 2

We Worship God Because He Helps People

Key Verse

"The Lord is my helper; I will not be afraid."   Hebrews 13:6, NIV

Unit Vocabulary

basket
boils
camped
commandment
crossed
darkness
desert
doorframes
firstborn
gnats
ground
Hebrew
hungry
livestock
locusts
magicians
manna
mountain
pharaoh
princess
quail
shepherd
slaves
soldiers
staff
swallowed
thirsty
troubles
wilderness
worship

Unit Aims

By the end of the unit, learners will be able to

• tell five Bible stories about how God helps people.
• feel interested in finding verses in a Bible and reading *The Young Reader's Bible*.
• locate books, chapters and verses in their own Bibles.
• read (at their level) at least one story from *The Young Reader's Bible*.
• worship God because He helps people.

Unit Project

Our Worship Book About Moses

God is bigger than any predicament. The Israelites saw and heard with their eyes and ears just what God's power could do to rescue them from crisis after crisis. The awesome power that brought the Israelites out of Egypt is the same power we can depend on to help us today. This unit can help us refocus on feeling grateful for what God has done.

Make a big worship book about Moses. Use five sheets of newsprint or chart paper to fit inside a cover made from large sheets of poster board. Make one page for each Bible story. (You can use a photocopy machine to enlarge the Bible art from pages 52, 53, 54, 266, and 269 of this book.)

On the five story pages, children can draw pictures or color the enlargements you provide. Decide together what worship statements to print on each page. The lessons focus on God's power in Moses' life.

    6. God protects baby Moses.
    7. God tells Moses what to do.
    8. God's power challenges Pharaoh.
    9. God rescues His people from the Red Sea.
    10. God gives rules to guide people.

When we feel truly grateful, the most natural thing to do is worship. Children can be helped to grow in their worship of God. Together we can lift up our God who has all power and who uses that power to help people—us!

	The Singing Bible (3 tapes)	Kids on the Rock (More Songs)	Follow the Leader (The Donut Man)	I'm a Helper (The Donut Man)	Good News (The Donut Man)
Lesson 6	Baby Moses				
Lesson 7					
Lesson 8	Pharaoh Told Them No				
Lesson 9	The Red Sea	My Heavenly Father Cares			
Lesson 10	Ten Commandments		With All My Heart		
Key Verse					
Unit Theme		The Lord Is a Mighty God	Sing Unto the Lord	Sing, Shout, Clap	
All Lessons	The Books We Love the Best The Bible Book Is True	God's Word Is for Me			

The Singing Bible (3 tapes), ©1993 by Lightwave Publishing, Inc. Manufactured and distributed by Word Publishing, Dallas, TX 75234
Kids on the Rock! More Songs, ©1994 Gospel Light, Ventura CA 93006
The Donut Man (3 tapes): *Follow the Leader*, ©1990; *I'm a Helper*, ©1991; *Good News*, ©1991; Integrity Music, Inc., P.O. Box 16813 Mobile, AL 36616

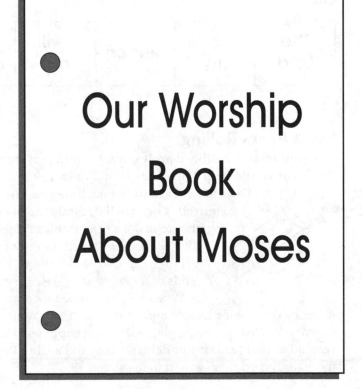

Our Worship Book About Moses

Key Verse Activities

Bravery Bandages

Materials
- clear or plain adhesive bandages
- several colors of ball-point pens

Before class, print "Hebrews 13:6" on the bandages.

Are you afraid when you get hurt? (Response.) **Jesus is always with us to help us so we don't need to be afraid. As soon as you memorize Hebrews 13:6, you can each have three bandages to decorate. Later when you need to use the bandages, you can remember the verse and know that Jesus is helping you so you won't be afraid.** Help the children practice the verse until each of them can recite it.

Fears Pop Like Bubbles

Materials
- five-foot strip of butcher paper or plain shelf liner
- scissors
- brightly colored permanent markers
- index cards
- pen
- masking tape
- one bottle of bubble solution with a wand

Before class, print the memory verse on an index card for each child. Print the memory verse on the strip of paper (draw lines between groups of words as shown). Tape the banner to the classroom floor and make a tape line to show the children where to stand.

If fears were like bubbles, what would happen to them when you remembered that Jesus was helping you? (They would pop.) **We're going to play a bubble game that will help us learn Hebrews 13:6.** Give the children their index cards.

Let's read the verse aloud together and then you'll take turns blowing one bubble onto a section of the memory verse banner. We'll say those words aloud and I'll put check marks above those words on the bubble blower's card. We'll play until everyone has check marks above all of the words on their cards.

The Lord	is my	helper;	I will not	be afraid.	Hebrews 13:6

Send Fears Rolling

Materials
- several marbles per child
- paper tubes (from gift wrap, toilet paper, and paper towels)
- masking tape or brightly colored electrical tape
- optional decorations (sequins, stickers, gift wrap scraps, ribbon scraps, markers)

If your fears were like marbles, what would they do when you remembered that Jesus would help you? (They would roll away.)

You can earn a marble each time you can say our memory verse by yourself. Then we'll decorate the paper tubes and tape them together to make a fun marble slide.

Cut "peek-a-boo" sections out of some of the tubes so the children can see the marbles roll through them. Cut the ends of the tubes at angles. Tape together the angles.

When you have taped together the slide, write the memory verse along its side and let the children take turns rolling their marbles down it. While they are playing, ask, **What happens to our fears when we remember that Jesus is our helper?** (They roll away.) Let the children bring more cardboard tubes to add to the slide.

God Protects Baby Moses

Tell what God did to help His people.
Worship God because He helped Moses and his family.
Find and read in the Bible that it is from God.

"The Lord is my helper; I will not be afraid."   Hebrews 13:6, NIV

① Get Ready to Read

Materials
- *The Young Reader's Bible*
- large cake pan or flat waterproof container (e.g., old baby bathtub)
- clean sand
- water
- small basket-boat (bottom 1-inch section cut from a plastic margarine or milk container)

Show the picture of Moses and his family on page 75 of *The Young Reader's Bible*. Read aloud to the children that page of the story.

If you needed a basket to keep a little baby safe, what would you use?

How would you feel about sending a baby out in a basket on a big, wide river? How do you think Moses' family felt? What would you have to do to your basket before you could put the baby in it in a river?

Help the children pretend to be Moses' family preparing a basket for him. Put sand on one side of the cake pan for the shore of the river. Add enough water to float your "basket-boat." Let several children use your basket-boat to take turns showing what Moses' mother, might have done and said when she brought the basket to the river.

Help the children put what they have heard into their own words: **What would Moses' family have to do before they put him in the basket? If you were Moses mother what would you have said to Moses when you closed the basket? What would you have done after you left him?** (prayed, worried)

② Read the Bible Story

Materials
- *The Young Reader's Bible*, pages 74-79
- photocopies of the two-page Bible story (page 52)
- photocopy of baby Moses (page 52)
- *The Young Reader's Bible Audio Cassette* or a cassette on which you have recorded unit stories
- cassette player(s), earphones optional
- a large sheet of paper
- basket-boat from last activity
- review questions printed on boat-shapes
- strip of blue paper or cloth
- purple, red, and blue crayons
- crayons or markers

"Baby Moses' Riverboat"

Have you ridden in a boat? How does it feel to ride in a big boat? In a little boat? What size boat did baby Moses ride in? (Show the basket-boat from previous activity.) **Listen for how God used a little basket-boat to keep baby Moses safe.**

If you plan to make a big book, *Our Worship Book About Moses*, plan time to make the cover and page 1. See the unit project on page 34.

Listen

Gather the children around you and read the story to them from *The Young Reader's Bible*. Give special attention to making your voice help the children feel as if they were really watching by the riverbank. After the story, help the children tell you what they heard.

Before class, print the story questions on boat-shaped pieces of paper. Tape a copy of a picture of baby Moses on boat #10. Turn all the story questions face down on the blue paper river. Let the children take turns answering each question and trying to find the basket with baby Moses in it.

1. *Who was afraid of the Hebrew people?*
2. *Who made the Hebrews to be his slaves?*
3. *Who made a law about the Hebrew baby boys?*
4. *Who hid a baby in a basket?*
5. *Who found the baby in the basket?*
6. *Who was watching when the princess opened the basket?*
7. *Who did Miriam bring to care for the baby?*
8. *Who took care of the baby when he grew older?*
9. *Who named the baby?*
10. *"Surprise! You found the basket with baby Moses in it."*

Participate

Seat the children in three different groups. Give each child a copy of the Bible story excerpt (page 52). Let them help read from *The Young Reader's Bible*.

The groups can read the parts about 1) the princess, 2) Miriam and 3) the mother. Before reading the Bible story, let the children mark the sentences for each person.

Use a purple crayon to circle the first two sentences (about the princess).
Use a red crayon to circle the next three sentences (about the sister).
Use a purple crayon to circle the next sentence (the princess' answer).
Use a blue crayon to circle the last two sentences (about the mother).

Each group can use the color code to help them remember when to read. Help each group practice reading their part. Then let the three groups participate by reading their part at the right time in the story.

Read

Give the children time and a quiet area to read their copy of the Bible story by themselves. Very early readers may want to color the pictures and describe in their own words what happened on these two pages. Fluent readers may want to sit in groups of three and "read" the story with each child doing a different character. Let them enjoy what they can do!

❸ Practice Using a Bible

Using My Bible

Before class, make bookmarks with three colored ribbons. Punch a hole an inch from one end of the index card, push the ends of the ribbons through the hole and staple them securely.

Place the index card in the top end of the spine of the *Young Reader's Bible*, so that the three colors of ribbons hang out.

If some children can find the Old Testament and New Testament by themselves, let those children demonstrate to the rest of the group how to open a Bible to the beginning of the Old Testament. Give a volunteer a ribbon bookmark. Have the volunteer mark the Old Testament with a red ribbon. Choose another volunteer to open to Psalms (in the middle of the Bible) and mark it with a blue ribbon. Then have a third child open to the beginning of the New Testament and mark it with a green ribbon. Then give each child a ribbon bookmark. Let pairs of children work to find the Old Testament, Psalms, and New Testament and mark each with a three-ribbon bookmark.

Option
Limit the number of readers in each group to two or three children. As they read, others can act out what is being read to allow more children to participate.

Snacks
Make small basket shapes using chow mein noodles mixed with melted butterscotch chips. Mold the baskets while the butterscotch is still warm. Pretend to eat your snack by the Nile, in the river weeds, just waiting for the crocodiles or the princess to come by.

Materials
• *The Young Reader's Bible*
• Bible for each child
• 1-by-5-inch strips of index cards or poster board
• 12-inch lengths of 1/4 inch wide ribbon in 3 colors (red, blue, green)
• paper punch
• stapler
• photocopies of page 55 (for use in unit 2)

Option
Invite several children to help you make the bookmarks before class.

Finding Bible Verses

Give each child a copy of page 55. Talk about the picture clues for finding verses, as you chant aloud the Reference Rhyme (page 32).

First I find the book or the page number of the book.
Then I find the chapter; the big number's where I look.
Last I find the verse; the small number is the one.
I've got it now! Finding verses is such fun.

Then let the children match each phrase of the chant with one of the pictures. This will help them see what they are chanting. Cut apart the cards from page 55. Children can put them in order as they chant the rhyme.

Work together to find a verse that says the Bible is the Word of God. As a group, find the table of contents. Then find the page number for the book of 2 Timothy. Look on the page for the big number 3 and the small number 16.

This verse tells us that the Bible is from God. Because it is from God, we want to know it and listen to it and do it. We're learning the Bible when we learn to read Bible stories by ourselves.

Ask the children to close their Bibles and try to find 2 Timothy 3:16 again, either by themselves or in groups of two or three.

For more practice, use the chant to help the children locate Exodus 2:10. Let them read the verse. **Find the name of a baby she got out of the water.** (Moses)

④ Share What We've Learned

Before class, draw a tic-tac-toe outline on blank paper and make a copy for every two children.

Let's play a game of tic-tac-toe. The X's will be Pharaoh and his men. The O's are Moses' family.

At the end of a round of play, more X's than O's means Pharaoh won that round.

More O's than X's means Moses' family kept the baby safe in that round.

Every time Moses' family wins a game, let the winners suggest a worship statement to honor God for how He really kept Moses safe over 2,000 years ago. Say, "God, only You could keep Moses safe in a basket-boat" or "God, You are so special because your power was stronger than Pharaoh."

Gather the children around you by your imaginary Nile river. Use this time to help the children connect the first three steps of this lesson and be able to worship God for how He helps people. As you talk together, include the following questions and listen to see if the children have reached the lesson goals.

What did God do to help Moses and his family in the story? (He protected them from Pharaoh's law.)

How do you think Moses' family felt when they put him in the basket-boat?

How do you think Moses' mother felt when she was bringing Moses back home?

What do you think Moses' mother said to God when she got back home with her baby?

What could we say to tell God what we think about His great power to help people?

What verse can you find in the Bible today?

What does that verse tell us about God and His Word?

Option

Help very early readers or no readers find the chapter and verse numbers. Read it aloud to them before you talk about what it means.

Materials
• blank paper
• marker

Teaching at Home

A trip to the library can expand children's understanding of the land of Egypt.

Reading tip

Notice how verbs change form: grow, grew; make, made; hid, hide; find, found; run, ran; come, came; think, thought; take, took.

7

God Tells Moses What to Do

Tell what God did to help Moses.
Worship God because He helped Moses do his work.
Say and copy a Bible reference.

"The Lord is my helper; I will not be afraid."   Hebrews 13:6, NIV

Materials
- *The Young Reader's Bible*
- small box
- several kinds of gift wrap and ribbon
- stick
- mirror

① Get Ready to Read

Before class, wrap the stick and mirror in a box so it looks like a birthday gift. For extra fun, wrap the box in several layers of gift wrap so more children can have a turn unwrapping it.

Show the picture of the burning bush on page 81 of a *Young Reader's Bible*. **God spoke to Moses from a burning bush and told him to lead the Israelites out of Egypt. Moses didn't want to go. Let's unwrap this gift box to help us learn what help God gave Moses. This is not a Christmas gift, not a birthday gift, but an "I-will-help-you" gift.**

Let children take turns unwrapping the box. When they open the box, explain the meaning of the stick and mirror inside. **The little stick reminds us of a big stick called a staff. God gave Moses a special staff that could do miracles. In the mirror we can see friends standing by us. God gave Moses a friend (Aaron) to go stand by him and help him speak to the Pharaoh.**

Help the children put this information in their own words by having them answer these questions. **What message did God speak to Moses? What did Moses tell God? What did God give Moses to help him do his work?**

Materials
- *The Young Reader's Bible*, pages 80-85
- photocopies of the two-page Bible story (page 53)
- *The Young Reader's Bible Audio Cassette* or a cassette on which you have recorded unit stories
- cassette player(s), earphones optional
- a branch decorated as a burning bush
- photocopies of story pages from units 1 and 2
- highlighting markers or crayons

② Read the Bible Story

"I Am Sending You"

When you need help, who do you go to? Who does your mom or dad or brother or sister ask to help?

When God told Moses what He wanted Moses to do, God also gave Moses some help. What two things did God give him? (staff, Aaron to go along) **Listen for how the special staff and special friend helped Moses do his work.**

Listen

Before class, decorate a branch with green leaves and red flames. Place it in your story area. Gather the children around the imaginary "burning bush" and read the story to them from *The Young Reader's Bible*.

Help them feel the power of God's voice speaking to Moses. Let them sense the whining tendency in Moses' part of the conversation.

After the story use some no-noise talking to help the children recall the facts of the story. For each word in the list below, make your mouth form the word, but do not say it aloud. When the children guess your word, they should use it to make a sentence about the story. If after several tries they cannot guess your word, give them another clue by speaking the first sound in the word. Try these words: *Moses, bush, fire, slaves, staff, Aaron.*

Participate

Read the story again, using two groups of children: one represents God, and one represents Moses.

Let the groups stand on opposite sides of the room. As you read the story, they can pretend to be speaking to each other. Each group can stand up when you read their part. If you prefer, after you speak each sentence, the appropriate group can echo what you say. This will help the children experience the two-way conversation that takes place in the story.

If you have several confident readers, let two groups mark their own copies of the Bible story excerpt (page 53). One group can highlight sentences about God and what God said. The other group can highlight sentences about Moses and what Moses said. Then they can use their copies to read aloud together their parts of the story.

If you are making a big book, *Our Worship Book About Moses,* continue with page 2. (See unit 2 page 34.)

Read

Give the children time to read or listen and follow along in their own copies of the Bible story excerpts from this unit. Very early readers will be more interested in the pictures (perhaps coloring them with crayons or markers). Fluent readers may want to read alone or in small groups, taking turns for each character in the story. Keep the Bible story copies in a decorated box or file so they are readily available for this part of each lesson.

Snacks
Serve pretzels and cold water. Pretend to eat your snack by a burning bush in a desert area.

❸ Practice Using a Bible

Materials
• Bible for each child
• three-ribbon bookmarks from lesson 6
• photocopy of page 55 for every four children
• copies of Task Card #5 (page 111)

Using My Bible

Let children work in pairs or alone to find and mark the key parts of the Bible.
Find the beginning of the Old Testament. (Genesis)
Find the book of Psalms. (in the middle of the Bible)
Find the beginning of the New Testament. (Matthew)
They can mark each place with their three-ribbon bookmarks.

Finding Bible Verses

Ask for volunteers to help you chant aloud the guidelines for finding Bible verses (page 32).
First I find the book, or the page number of the book.
Then I find the chapter; the big number's where I look.
Last, I find the verse; the small number is the one.
I've got it now! Finding verses is such fun.
Before class, cut apart photocopies of the four pictures on page 55 (or use the ones prepared for the last lesson).
Make enough sets so every child in your class can have at least one picture. Let

each child stand or hold up the picture as you chant the guideline that goes with that picture. This will be particularly helpful for children who need to see what they are learning.

Before class, print *Exodus 3:2* in the blank of Task Card #5. Make photocopies of the filled in Task Card. Help the children follow the instructions on Task Card #5 to find a Bible verse (Exodus 3:2).

4 Share What We've Learned

Materials

- photocopies of page 57
- cassette tape
- cassette player
- a sack containing objects related to the Bible story (plastic or rubber snake, sheep, branch with orange/red tissue, stick for staff, sand)

Before class, ask someone to help you record the words for "God Cares" on a cassette tape. (Sing to the tune of "Do Your Ears Hang Low?")

Play the song for the children. Listen to the song several times, encouraging the children to join in when they can. The words are printed on reproducible page 57.

Play a game to help the children recall the story content. Let children take turns removing an object from the sack. They can tell the part of the story that includes the object.

If you have time, let children hold the objects and assemble themselves in story order (sheep, bush on fire, staff, snake, sand).

Gather the children around you (perhaps by your "burning bush") to help them put together what they have learned. As you lead the conversation, listen for evidence that they reached the goals for this lesson. Some questions to include are:

What did God do to help Moses in today's story?

How do you think Moses felt when God was speaking to him?

How do you think Moses felt when God gave him a staff and a helper?

What do you think Moses might have thought about as he walked back to Egypt with his staff in his hand?

What kind of worship might Moses have spoken?

What could we say to worship God for His great power to help people?

What verse(s) can you find in the Bible today?

What does that verse tell us about God and His Word?

Teaching at Home

Activities designed for two groups can be done at home with the parent and child each taking a part—just as Miriam helped her mother.

Reading tip

Develop a word family for the verb *to cry*: cry, cries, cried, crying. Think of other rhyming words that work the same way such as spy, fry, and dry.

God's Power Challenges Pharaoh

8

Tell how God changed Pharaoh's mind.
Worship God because He helped the Israelites leave Egypt.
Find Bible references.

"The Lord is my helper; I will not be afraid."   Hebrews 13:6, NIV

❶ Get Ready to Read

Show Moses and Aaron in front of Pharaoh on page 86 of a *Young Reader's Bible*. Explain that every time Moses and Aaron asked Pharaoh to let the Israelites go, Pharaoh said, "No." God sent ten terrible troubles so Pharaoh would change his mind.

Give each child a copy of page 56. For each picture of a terrible trouble, let the children choose a sound to help them remember that terrible trouble. For example, for water turned to blood, make a gurgling or rushing water sound. When needed, explain the terrible trouble shown in each picture. Help the children work together to think of sounds for all the plagues.

What did Moses and Aaron ask Pharaoh? (Let the people go!) **What did Pharaoh say?** (No, No, No!) **So what did God do to make Pharaoh change his mind?** (Use sounds to name each trouble.)

The following dramatic interchange between what God said and what Pharaoh said is a creative way for the children to report the sounds of the plagues. For each plague, repeat the first two lines together, and then make a sound of the plague. Speak the words rhythmically:

God said "Let my people go." And Pharaoh said, "I will not. No, No, NO!" (Respond with the sound of a plague.)

❷ Read the Bible Story

"Ten Terrible Troubles"

Today's story is about ten terrible troubles. Let the children make the sound of all the troubles. **Listen to find out how such terrible troubles could actually help God's people!**

Listen

Gather the children around you. **Let's imagine we are in Pharaoh's court watching Moses and Aaron talk to the Pharaoh.** As you read the story from a *Young Reader's Bible*, use your voice to make the ten troubles sound simply terrible.

Before class, print the words in the list that follows on a large sheet of paper.

Materials
• *The Young Reader's Bible*
• photocopies of page 56
• construction paper, optional

Option
Photocopy a set of plague cards (from page 56) for each child to color. Let pairs of children play a matching game. Mount the pictures on heavy paper so you can't see through from the back of the picture. Lay out two sets of cards face down in a four by five arrangement. Let children take turns turning over two cards. If they match, have the child make a sound to go with that plague. Continue until all cards are matched and all plagues are sounded.

Materials
• *The Young Reader's Bible*, pages 86-91
• photocopies of the Bible story (pages 265-267)
• a large sheet of paper
• *The Young Reader's Bible Audio Cassette* or a cassette on which you have recorded unit stories
• cassette player(s), earphones optional
• photocopies of Bible story pages from units 1 and 2

After the story, play "Which doesn't fit?" **I will name three words. You must decide which two go together** *best.* **Then use those two words to make a sentence to help us retell the story.**

1. *Moses, Aaron,* Pharaoh (*Moses* and *Aaron* traveled to Egypt.)
2. *Desert, worship,* magicians
3. Lamb, *frogs, flies*
4. *Hail,* worship, *gnats*
5. *Door frames, blood,* flocks
6. *Firstborn male,* obey, *die*

Participate

Read the story again. The children can participate by making a sound for each plague as you mention it in the story. Agree on a signal you will give them for when they must stop making each sound, such as raising your hand. Clearly set the boundary before you begin reading, so you are in control and the story does not become chaos.

Give each child a copy of the Bible story (pages 265-267); then let each child underline each terrible trouble. Readers can help nonreaders find the words. Then have the children draw a circle around how God kept the people safe. Circle the words *lamb* and *blood* to show what God told them to do to be safe from the final plague.

Read

Give the children some time to read today's story by themselves. A special area of the room ready for reading shows the children this is an important part of the lesson. Children who are in the "working very hard to read" stage may prefer listening to the stories from units 1 and 2 on cassette as they follow along in a *Young Reader's Bible* or photocopied portion of a Bible story. Children who are beginning to enjoy the process of figuring out new words will be eager for this opportunity to read the story all by themselves. In either case, stay close by to give encouragement to any who lose their concentration or feel like giving up.

If you are making a big book, *Our Worship Book About Moses,* continue with page 2. (See unit 2 page 34.)

❸ Practice Using a Bible

Using My Bible

Children who have been present for the past few lessons should be able to find three main parts dividing their Bibles. Have them use a three-ribbon bookmark to find the beginning of the Old Testament (Genesis), the middle of the Bible (Psalms) and the beginning of the New Testament (Matthew). If you have newcomers, pair them with someone who can show them how to find these three guideposts in their Bible.

Today, show how to use a Table of Contents to find the page number for the book of Exodus. Guide the children to find the page on which Exodus begins in their own Bible.

Finding Bible Verses

Gather the copies of the cards cut from page 55 you have been using in this unit. Make more if you will need them.

Ask for volunteers to help you chant the reference rhyme (page 32) to remind

---

Snacks

Eat a royal snack in your imaginary royal palace for Pharaoh. Try finger Jell-O Jigglers gelatin snacks cut in the shape of Pharaoh's crown.

Materials
- Bibles
- *The Young Reader's Bible*
- three-ribbon bookmarks from lesson 6
- photocopies of page 55 for each four children
- photocopies of Task Card #6 (page 111)
- blank paper
- crayons or markers

everyone how to find Bible verses.

First I find the book, or the page number of the book.
Then I find the chapter; the big number's where I look.
Last, I find the verse; the small number is the one.
I've got it now! Finding verses is such fun.

For an added challenge, give a set of four pictures (page 55) to each group of four children. They can work together to remember which comes first, second, etc. Then they can arrange themselves to hold the picture up in the correct order to show how to find Bible verse references.

Before class, fill in the blanks on Task Card #6 with the reference *Exodus 10:21* and the word *darkness*. Help the children follow the instructions on Task Card #6 to give them an opportunity to find a Bible verse (Exodus 10:21) and do something with it. You can provide blank paper and crayons or markers if the children choose to draw what the verse says.

Option
For children who are eager to find more verses, provide more copies of Task Card #6 with the reference Hebrews 13:6 or Psalm 118:7a and the word helper printed in the blanks.

④ Share What We've Learned

Gather the children around you, perhaps in an imaginary palace in Egypt. Help them think through what they have learned in this lesson. As you lead the conversation, notice which children have reached the lesson goals.

Questions to include are:

What did God do to help Moses in today's story?

How do you think Moses felt when he spoke to Pharaoh?

How do you think Moses felt when each plague came to the Egyptians?

What kind of things might Moses have said as he worshiped God?

What could we say to worship God for His great power to help people?

What verse(s) can you find in the Bible today?

What does that verse tell us about God or His Word?

Before class, make ten small index cards with the pictures of plagues (page 56) and ten small index cards with numbers from 1-10.

Play a Ten Terrible Troubles Concentration game. Turn all twenty cards face down. Players take turns choosing two cards. They must find the picture of the first plague and the number "1" card for the first match. Continue taking turns to find each plague in order and its number. Continue until all ten plagues are matched to their numbers.

For extra help, provide a copy of page 56 to show the order of the plagues.

Materials
- photocopies of plague pictures (page 56)
- twenty small index cards (colored cards are great)
- felt markers
- scissors

 Teaching at Home

Count ten of *everything*: cups, spoons, crackers, cracks in the sidewalk. Older children can "count by tens."

Reading tip
Find compound words (two little words that make one new word): *everywhere, livestock, firstborn.*

God Rescues His People From the Red Sea

Tell how God protected the Israelites from the Egyptians.
Worship God because He helped the Israelites be safe.
Find and read Bible references.

"The Lord is my helper; I will not be afraid."   Hebrews 13:6, NIV

Materials
- *The Young Reader's Bible*
- white poster board
- yellow poster board
- cotton balls or batting
- yardstick
- tape or stapler
- red marker

Option
Let groups of two or three children work together to make sections of a tall pillar of cloud and fire. Use yellow and white construction paper. Some can work on clouds. Some can work on fire. Staple a cloud/fire pair together and slide each cloud/fire onto a long broom handle so each group's work is part of one tall pillar. Tape securely. Use in the "Follow the Pillar" game.

Materials
- *The Young Reader's Bible*, pages 92-97
- photocopies of the Bible story (pages 268-270)
- a large sheet of paper
- *The Young Reader's Bible Audio Cassette* or a cassette on which you have recorded unit stories
- cassette player(s), earphones optional
- photocopies of Bible stories from units 1 and 2
- ten cards, each with one word (or picture): Pharaoh, Moses, cloud, fire, staff, wind, God, chariot, Red Sea, Miriam
- chairs or blue fabric or sheets

① Get Ready To Read

Before class, make a cardboard model of a pillar of cloud and pillar of fire. Cut a large, tall cloud shape from the white poster board. Cut the same size and shape piece from the yellow poster board. Tape or staple the pieces together, leaving a space at one end to insert a yardstick for a handle. Glue cotton balls or batting to the white side. Draw red flames on the yellow side.

Show the picture of the Israelites traveling (page 92 of a *Young Reader's Bible*) as you read that page of the story. Then show the pillar of cloud and fire to help explain what a pillar of cloud or fire might have been like.

Instead of "Follow the Leader" play "Follow the Pillar." Whoever is first in line carries the pillar; when the cloud faces the people, everyone marches briskly in line. When the leader turns the fire side toward the people, everyone must "freeze" in position until the leader turns the pillar around again. Have fun marching around the room as if you were traveling from Egypt to the Red Sea.

Help the children describe in their words what God did to help His people travel.

How did God's people know where to go? (follow pillar)
What kind of pillar could they see in the day? (cloud)
What kind of pillar could they see in the night? (fire)

② Read the Bible Story

"Pharaoh's Biggest Mistake"

What is a pillar? Where do we see pillars? How are our pillars different from a pillar of cloud or a pillar of fire? (One helps hold up buildings; the other helped people know where to go, like a tall flag at the front of a parade; one you can touch, the other you can't touch.)

How are building pillars the same as a pillar of cloud or a pillar of fire? (Both are tall, stretch up above your head, you can see them from way back.)
Listen to find out how God used His kind of pillar to help the people.

Listen

Gather the children around you as you read the story from a *Young Reader's Bible*. If your children have good imaginations, suggest that they pretend to be sitting on the far side of the Red Sea watching the Israelites coming toward the sea—and being chased by Pharaoh!

Participate

After you read the story, pass out the ten cards for the children to hold up in answer to your questions.

1. I was sorry I let God's people go.
2. I told the people, "Don't be afraid."
3. I was in a pillar in the daytime.
4. I was in a pillar in the nighttime.
5. I was raised up and pointed to the sea to make it part and go back.
6. I blew to part the water.
7. I held back the water of the Red Sea all night long.
8. I carried Pharaoh when he chased the Israelites right into the sea.
9. I flowed back onto Pharaoh and all of his army.
10. I led the women in a celebration dance.

Read the story again and let the children act out this breathtaking example of how God used His power to help people. Involve as many characters as you can: Moses, Pharaoh, Israelites, Egyptian soldiers, Miriam, etc.

One child can carry the pillar of cloud/fire you used at the beginning of the lesson. Two rows of chairs or blue fabric held by teachers, children or teens can represent the water of the sea. Move fabric up and down to show the water, standing up to make a path for God's people. Be sure to read slowly enough to allow for all the action that the children want to include.

Before acting out the story, talk together about the conversation in quotation marks in this story.

Help the children underline Pharaoh's question and exclamation on the second page of the story. On the next page have them circle Moses' statement that begins "Don't be . . ." On the next to last page, they can draw a box around God's statement, "Lift your staff again."

Help the children look to see how these quotations are illustrated in the pictures. Ask how Pharaoh and Moses might have felt when they spoke their words. These insights can help the children put more meaning into what they do and say as they act out the story.

Option

If you have more than ten children, make multiple sets of cards. If you have only a few children, share the cards among them.

Read

Before class, check to see if you need to recopy any of the stories for today's reading time.

There is nothing quite like reading a story for yourself. Having a special part of the room set up for reading makes it even more enjoyable. You can provide the story for today as well as other favorites from units 1 and 2.

Very early readers can focus more on the pictures and look for a few words in the story they can recognize or sound out. They can listen to the cassette stories as they color their copy of the Bible story and look at the pictures.

Children who have acquired more reading skills will appreciate the opportunity to sit down and enjoy reading the story by themselves.

If you are making a big book, *Our Worship Book About Moses*, continue with page 4. (See unit 2 page 34.)

Snacks
Eat a celebration snack of rice cakes and peanut butter as you sit resting on the banks of the Red Sea.

Materials
- Bibles
- small cube or dice
- masking tape
- marker
- photocopies of the Reference Rhyme pictures (page 55)
- photocopies of Task Card #7 (page 111)

❸ Practice Using a Bible

Using My Bible

If you have newcomers, pair them up with someone who can show them how to find three key parts in the Bible: Genesis, Psalms and Matthew.

Before class, cover a small cube or dice with masking tape. Print an abbreviation on each side: OT, NT, Gen, Ps, Matt and Ex. Then play a game to help the children develop more skill in using their Bibles. Review what each side of the cube stands for. Take turns rolling the cube you made so everyone can find the part of the Bible named on the top of the cube.

Finding Bible Verses

Together, chant aloud the Reference Rhyme guidelines (page 32) for finding Bible verses. Refer to the set of four pictures (from page 55) as you do the chant.

First I find the book, or the page number of the book.
Then I find the chapter; the big number's where I look.
Last, I find the verse; the small number is the one.
I've got it now! Finding verses is such fun.

Use the rhyme to help the children find Exodus 14:21 in a Bible and listen as you read what God did to help the people.

Before class, fill in the two blanks of Task Card #7: 1) *pages 94-95,* 2) *Moses.*

Help children follow the instructions on Task Card #7 to give them an opportunity to see how the Bible and a *Young Reader's Bible* include the same story!

Option
For children who are eager to find another verse, fill in a second copy of Task Card #7. Use *Exodus 13:21* and look for the description of the *pillars* God gave the people.

❹ Share What We've Learned

Materials
- 6-inch poster board circle for spinner game
- pencil and paper clip to make the spinner
- marker
- large sheet of paper

Option
If you think they will need clues, list an assortment of possible answers on a large sheet of paper. The children can pick one and cross it out when they use it.

Before class, make a "spinner" with two sections: one section says "Moses"; the other section says "Me." Use the spinner to play a "Moses and Me" game. Hold the paper clip in place with the pencil tip. After the players take a turn spinning the paper clip, they have 15 seconds to tell either how God helped Moses or how God helped them—depending on which side the paper clip lands. They can fill in the blanks: God helped Moses when . . . or God, You are great because you help me . . .

As you gather the children around you to close the lesson, imagine you are near the Red Sea watching Miriam lead a celebration dance. As you talk together about what you have learned, be aware of which children are reaching the goals for this unit.

Questions to include are:

What did God do to help Moses in today's story?

How do you think Moses felt when he lifted his staff up over the sea? when the sea crashed down on the Egyptians?

What kind of things might Moses have said as he worshiped God?

What could we say to worship God for His great power to help people?

What verse(s) can you find in the Bible today?

What does that verse tell us about God or His Word?

Teaching at Home
Keep a pillar of cloud and fire in your home to signal both night and day.

Reading tip
Read and write question marks and exclamation marks. Let the children practice writing questions and exclamations.

God Gives Rules to Guide People

Tell how God helped His people.
Worship God because He helped the people by giving them rules.
Find Bible references and read Bible verses.

"The Lord is my helper; I will not be afraid."   Hebrews 13:6, NIV

1 Get Ready to Read

Before class, tape someone singing the lyrics to "God Cares" (page 57). Sing to the tune of "Do Your Ears Hang Low?"

Give each child a copy of page 57 and ask the children to use the pictures for clues to help them name ways God helped Bible people (e.g., basket—kept Moses safe). Then listen to the song and point to the pictures as you name them in the song. Let the children help choose an action to go with each **bold** word. Have fun with the actions as you sing it several more times.

Help the children describe what God did to help His people.

What help did Moses' family need?

What help did Moses need when God sent him to Egypt?

What help did the people of Israel need to get out of Egypt?

What help did the people of Israel need when they were traveling?

What help did the people of Israel need so they would know what is right and what is wrong?

Provide crayons or markers for everyone to color a set of the pictures on page 57.

Cut them apart and glue them on 3-by-4-inch pieces of art paper. Place two sets of cards face down randomly scattered on the table. Take turns choosing two cards. If they match, name the way God helped people and lay the match aside. When the game is done, sing the song again.

Give everyone a picture to hold up as you sing the song. Instead of singing the name of what is in the picture have children hold up a card.

Materials
- *The Young Reader's Bible*
- photocopies of page 57
- cassette player
- cassette cued to "God Cares"
- scissors
- crayons or watercolor markers
- art paper
- glue stick

2 Read the Bible Story

"A Special Treasure"

Ask for volunteers to sing the song and do the actions to "God Cares." When they finish, ask the whole group to **listen for one way God helped in the story today.**

Listen

Gather the children around you as you read this final story about how God

Materials
- *The Young Reader's Bible,* pages 98-103
- photocopies of the two-page Bible story (page 54)
- a large sheet of paper
- *The Young Reader's Bible Audio Cassette* or a cassette on which you have recorded unit stories
- cassette player(s), earphones optional
- photocopies of Bible stories from units 1 and 2
- 2-by-20-inch strips of poster board
- marker

helps Moses and the people of Israel. Imagine you are at the foot of the smoking, fearsome Mt. Sinai, waiting for God to come talk to you.

Participate

After the story, read the following statements and ask what is wrong with each statement. If you print the statements on strips of poster board before class, the children can also work to put the corrected statements in the correct order to retell the story.

Statements (italicized words are wrong)

1. God covered the *sky* with manna bread.

2. Water *dripped* from the rock.

3. The people *parked* by a mountain.

4. Moses went *into* the mountain.

5. Thick *clouds* covered the mountain because God was there.

6. One commandment said, "*Always* take what is not yours."

7. God gave Moses the Ten Commandments on two stone *idols*.

Read the story again, making a mistake in about every other sentence. Before you begin to read, tell the children to raise their hand when they hear a mistake. Let them correct what you said. Choose five or six mistakes to help them focus their attention on what you are doing.

Read

Provide a few extra minutes, if you can, to let the children enjoy reading several stories from units 1 and 2. This will help them build confidence. When they begin to see themselves as capable of reading Bible stories, you will have given them a very precious gift. Rejoice with each child at his or her level of accomplishment—from managing to sit still and look at pictures to reading fluently every story you provide.

As always, provide the cassette-taped stories so children can listen as they follow along in a *Young Reader's Bible*.

If you made a big book, *Our Worship Book About Moses*, finish page 5 today, (See unit 2 page 34.)

❸ Practice Using a Bible

Using My Bible

Before class, on a large sheet of paper, list the following parts of a Bible: *Genesis, Psalms, Matthew, Old Testament, Exodus, New Testament.*

Play a game to help the children improve their Bible skills. Arrange the children in groups of four to six. In each group, let the children take turns being the "leader."

The leader's job is to name a place from the list to find in the Bible. The leader says, "Let's find . . . (Genesis). Ready, Set, Go!" You may want to use a stopwatch to challenge the children to improve their speed. Children can mark the places they find with the three-ribbon bookmark made in lesson 6.

Finding Bible Verses

Print the following Bible references on small index cards. Arrange them in one column on a wall. Place pictures (pages 56 and 57) of the items in these verses or real items in a basket or box.

Snacks

Pretend you are sitting at the foot of Mount Sinai, waiting for Moses as you eat a snack of "bread and meat."

Materials
• Bibles
• a large sheet of paper
• marker
• three-ribbon bookmarks
• stopwatch
• photocopies of Reference Rhyme cards (page 55)
• small index cards
• photocopies of Task Card #8 on page 111.

baby/basket	*Exodus 2:3*
bush	*Exodus 3:3*
staff	*Exodus 4:2*
darkness (plague)	*Exodus 10:21*
fire and cloud	*Exodus 13:21*
sea	*Exodus 14:21*
quail	*Exodus 16:13*
manna	*Exodus 16:31*
water	*Exodus 17:6*
rules	*Exodus 20:12, 13*

Together, chant aloud the Reference Rhyme (page 32) for finding Bible verses.
First I find the book, or the page number of the book.
Then I find the chapter; the big number's where I look.
Last, I find the verse; the small number is the one.
I've got it now! Finding verses is such fun.

Point to the illustrations for the chant in the set of four pictures (from page 55) as you do the chant. Help the children work together to read and find verse references for ways God helped people. Then they can match each reference card with a picture (or object) that shows the way God helped.

Option

On Task Card #8, print in the blank *pages 98, 99*. Help the children follow the instructions on Task Card #8 to give them an opportunity to see how the Bible and the *Young Reader's Bible* have the same story.

❹ Share What We've Learned

This is the final opportunity in this unit to talk about how God helped Moses and the Israelites. As you gather the children around you to close the lesson, ask which place from this unit the children would like to visit. Imagine you are there as you talk together about what you have learned. Sincerely affirm the ways the children are reaching the goals for this lesson and this unit. Questions to include are:

What has God been doing to help Moses and the Israelites?

What did God do to help Moses in today's story?

How do you think Moses felt when he went up on the mountain? when he carried the rules back down?

What kind of things might Moses have said as he worshiped God?

What could we say to worship God for His great power to help people?

What verse(s) can you find in the Bible today?

What does that verse tell us about God or His Word?

Before class, place an item in each of the bags to go with one of the stories from this unit (e.g., basket, stick, flashlight or cotton, water and bread or meat, and two stones).

Play a Feel and Shake game. Let the children feel, pinch, smell and shake the bags as they try to guess what is in each one. When they have guessed it or are done guessing, they may pull out the item. Encourage them to use it to speak in a worshipful manner to God for the way He helps people.

Here are some examples to get you started:

basket	God protected baby Moses.
stick	God gave Moses a special staff (and brother) to help him talk to Pharaoh.
flashlight/cotton	God showed people where to go.
water/bread/meat	God gave the people water and food. (Let the children taste.)
two stones	God gave rules to guide people.

Materials
• basket
• stick
• flashlight
• cotton
• water/bread/meat
• two stones
• five paper bags

Teaching at Home

Let your children be the leaders, challenging you to find places in the Bible.

Reading tip

For older readers, point out abbreviations, *Mt.* for *mount* or *mountain*. Children can name other abbreviations they have seen, e.g., *Dr.* for *doctor*.

The princess of Egypt
found the little baby.

"This is a Hebrew baby,"
she said softly.

The baby's sister was watching.

She ran to the princess.

"Shall I find a Hebrew woman

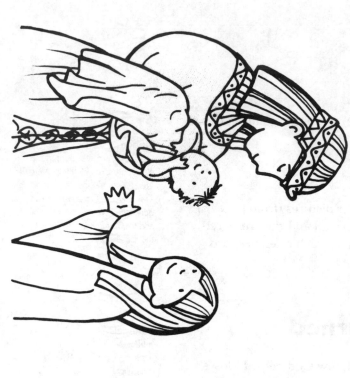

to nurse the baby for you?"

"Yes, please do,"
said the princess.

The girl came back
with the baby's own mother!

Surely God is watching over
this baby, the mother thought.

Then God called to Moses

from the bush.

Moses covered his face

because he was afraid

to look at God.

"I have heard the cries

of my people," said God.

"And I am sending you

to bring them out of Egypt."

"But God, why me?" said Moses.

"I will be with you," said God.

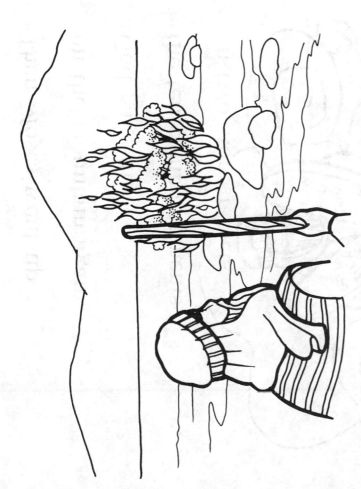

Moses grew up. He left Egypt

and became a shepherd.

In the desert near a mountain,

Moses saw a bush on fire.

"How strange," said Moses.

"The bush is on fire,

but it is not burning up!"

God spoke to the people.

He gave them ten commandments.

1. Have no other gods but me.
2. Do not worship idols.
3. Use my name for good.
4. Keep the seventh day a holy day.
5. Love and honor your parents.
6. Do not murder.
7. Be true to your husband or wife.
8. Never take what is not yours.
9. Always be honest.
10. Do not be jealous of what others have.

Then Moses went up

on the mountain again.

God gave him

the ten commandments

on two stone tablets.

54

Find the small verse number.

Find the big chapter number.

book / chapter: verse

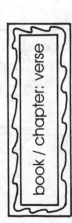

Find the page number.

Photocopy and cut apart the ten terrible troubles.

blood

frogs

gnats

flies

boils

cattle die

locusts

hail

darkness

firstborn die

God Cares

As a **baby in a basket**,
   fleeing Pharaoh's mean decree,
With the **fire** and **cloud** and
   parting of the wide Red Sea,
Moses didn't have to wonder.
   It was very plain to see.
God cared for Moses,
   and He cares for me.

He sent **manna** and **quail**,
   (yum, yum)
Water from a rock, (whoosh)
Ten Rules for living happily.
God cared for Moses,
   and He cares for me.

Tune: "Do Your Ears Hang Low?"

Unit 3

We Obey God Who Helps Us

Key Verse

"I have hidden your word in my heart."   Psalm 119:11, NIV

Unit Vocabulary

anoint
answer
battle
blast
bother
chosen
crash
explore
gates of Jericho
gathered
grain
grumbled
handsome
harp
land of Canaan
land of Moab
listen
palace
priests
special
spirit
tending
trumpets
voice
wheat

Unit Aims

By the end of the unit, learners will be able to

- tell five Bible stories about people who obeyed God.
- feel capable of finding verses in a Bible and reading *The Young Reader's Bible*.
- locate books, chapters and verses in their own Bibles.
- read (at their level) stories from *The Young Reader's Bible*.
- obey God.

Unit Projects

I Can Use My Bible Booklet

This project can continue over the five-lesson unit or be completed during one session.

Photocopy pages 8, 9, and 81 for the booklet. Work with the children to read the poems and fill in the blanks. They can color the pages.

Provide various colors of construction paper or lightweight poster board for the covers. Use a paper punch and yarn to fasten the booklet pages together. Children can copy the title and draw and color the cover for the *I Can Use My Bible* booklet.

Confident Readers

Provide a variety of children's Bibles for your more confident readers. Encourage the children to read the story from the Bible. Have them keep lists of new words. Later help them find similar words and ideas in *The Young Reader's Bible*.

	The Singing Bible (3 tapes)	Kids on the Rock (More Songs)	Follow the Leader (The Donut Man)	I'm a Helper (The Donut Man)	Good News (The Donut Man)
Lesson 11	Forty Years You'll Go				
Lesson 12	March Around Jericho				This Is the Day
Lesson 13	God Began a Nation				
Lesson 14				Speak Lord, I'm Listening	
Lesson 15	David				
Key Verse		Let My Words			
Unit Theme			I Will Arise		
All Lessons	The Books We Love the Best The Bible Book Is True	God's Word Is for Me			

The Singing Bible (3 tapes), ©1993 by Lightwave Publishing, Inc. Manufactured and distributed by Word Publishing, Dallas, TX 75234
Kids on the Rock! More Songs, ©1994 Gospel Light, Ventura CA 93006
The Donut Man (3 tapes): *Follow the Leader*, ©1990; *I'm a Helper*, ©1991; *Good News*, ©1991; Integrity Music, Inc., P.O. Box 16813 Mobile, AL 36616

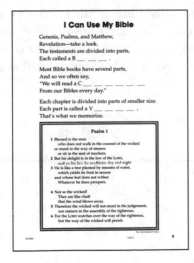

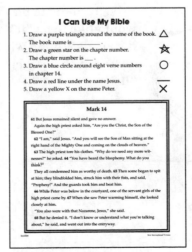

Key Verse Activities

Materials
- heart-shaped sugar cookies and frosting (or bread cut with heart-shaped cookie cutters and spreadable strawberry cream cheese)
- aluminum foil
- paper
- pen
- napkins
- plastic knives or craft sticks

Hidden in My Heart

Before class, print the memory verse on slips of paper and wrap each slip in aluminum foil. Place a foil-wrapped verse between pairs of cookies or bread hearts. Seal the hearts with three dots of frosting or cream cheese.

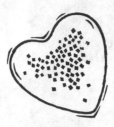

Tell the children, **There's something hidden in these hearts. Can you find it?** When they find the verses, read them aloud together. **What is God's Word?** (What He has said, the Bible.) **How can we hide it in our hearts?** (Remember what God has said.) **We'll practice saying the verse a few times, and then when you can recite the verse alone, you can frost the hearts and eat them.**

Materials
- clear acetate report covers or page protectors
- permanent marker
- scissors
- transparent tape
- glue stick
- paper punch
- several colors of tissue paper
- ribbon scraps
- Optional—large sequins, precut confetti, feathers, beads, other craft scraps

Confetti Hearts

Before class, cut two identical acetate hearts for each child. Print the memory verse on one heart of each pair. Tape together the bottom halves of the hearts.

In class, the children cut tissue paper into thin strips and shapes. Then they apply glue stick to the inside back edges of the acetate heart. Drop in tissue strips, craft scraps, sequins, etc. Glue the top of the heart closed. Punch a hole in the top of the heart and tie a ribbon through it for hanging. **Imagine that each of the pretty things in this heart are Bible verses. God wants our hearts to be full of His Word like that. If we keep learning and remembering Bible verses, our hearts will be full of God's Word.**

Materials
- a miniature paperback Bible
- red construction paper cut into identical hearts that are larger than the Bible
- cotton batting
- stapler

Bible, Bible, Who's Got the Bible?

Before class, staple together pairs of hearts stuffed with batting. Partially stuff and staple together one pair of hearts, leaving room to fit the miniature Bible inside.

God wants us to put His Word in our hearts. Pat your heart. What is God's Word? (What He says, the Bible.) Show them the Bible and put it between the two construction paper hearts that are partially stapled together. Staple the heart shut.

We're going to play a game called "Bible, Bible, Who's Got the Bible?" Who would like to be "It"? We'll stand in a circle with "It" in the middle and pass the hearts around while we say the memory verse three times. Then "It" will guess which heart has God's Word in it. We'll play until everyone has been "It."

Joshua and Caleb Obey God

Tell how two spies, Joshua and Caleb, obeyed God.
Choose a way to obey God.
Explain that "hiding God's Word in my heart" means learning Bible verses.

"I have hidden your word in my heart."   Psalm 119:11, NIV

① Get Ready to Read

Before class, print two sentences across the bottom of a sheet of white paper:
"They cut off a branch of a grapevine. It had one bunch of grapes on it"
(Numbers 13:23, ICB). Add eight 1½-inch diameter circles to represent grapes in a
bunch. Make a copy for each child.

Have the children color a stem and leaves on their sheet. Then have them
spread glue in each circle. Press the piece of purple yarn in a circular design to
make a grape. If children are not satisfied, the yarn can be pulled up and then
re-pressed into place.

**Today's Bible story is about a place where cows gave lots of milk, bees made
lots of honey, and grapevines grew lots and lots of grapes.**

Before class, prepare the table and measure the ingredients. As children arrive,
have them help combine and stir the ingredients. Then give each child a small
amount to roll into balls and roll the balls in the coconut or chopped nuts. Have
children place the cookies on a sheet of wax paper.

While making the cookies, say, **"Today's Bible story takes place in a place
people called 'The Land of Milk and Honey.' After the story everyone will get
to taste these milk and honey treats."**

Materials
- one sheet of white paper for each child
- eight 18-inch lengths of purple yarn for each child
- glue stick
- markers or crayons

Option
Give children a "taste" of milk and honey.

Milk and Honey Cookies
- 1/2 cup honey
- 1/2 cup peanut butter
- 1 cup powdered milk
- coconut or chopped nuts
- bowls, spoons, measuring cups and measuring spoons
- wax paper, paper towels
- plastic tub filled with water for washing hands

② Read the Bible Story

"Faith or Fear?"

Bring to class a jar of honey and a pitcher of milk. Talk about God's providing
honey from bees and milk from cows.

Tell the children that when people read about a place that is "flowing with
milk and honey," it makes them think of a very good place. **Do you think that
honey and milk would really be flowing in rivers, ponds, and lakes? When we
read the words, "a land flowing with milk and honey," we don't picture honey
in the rivers and milk in the ponds. Instead we picture a place where everything grows so well that the people always have enough to eat. What would
you like to have "lots of" where *you* live?**

Explain that "flowing with milk and honey" meant that the land was a very

Materials
- *The Young Reader's Bible*, pages 104-109
- photocopies of the Bible story (pages 271-273)
- *The Young Reader's Bible Audio Cassette* or a cassette on which you have recorded unit stories
- cassette player(s), earphones optional
- jar of honey and pitcher of milk
- word-bank list on poster board
- 18 index cards on which word-bank words are written
- photocopies of a nine-square grid
- tokens (coins or buttons), a handful for each child
- pencils, markers, or crayons

good place for growing crops. The grass would be so thick that cows, goats, and sheep would give lots of milk when they ate the grass. The land would make flowers grow so big and thick, that the bees would be able to make lots of honey.

Have the children turn to page 104 in their *Young Reader's Bibles* or use the photocopied story (pages 271-273). Use the following discussion to prepare to read the story aloud.

Look together at the first picture. Explain that the man in the white beard talking to the people is Moses. Recall the things that Moses had done (led the people from Egypt, received the Ten Commandments).

How many people are listening to Moses in the first picture? In the second picture, what are the men carrying? (grapes) **What is unusual about the fruit?** (the large size)

Discuss the four men in the next picture. (page 107) **What are they doing?** (talking together) **Are the men agreeing or disagreeing?** (some disagree) **How can you tell?** (by the frowns on their faces)

In the fourth picture, what do some of the men have in their hands? (rocks) **What might they do with the rocks?**

Listen

Have a child read the title of the story, "Faith or Fear?" Tell one group of children to listen to find out why some people were afraid. Have another group listen for names of people who showed they believed God. The children can follow along as you read the story.

Participate

Display the words *Canaan, Caleb, Joshua, Egypt, Moses.* Children can answer some of these questions by pointing to a name. **Who sent men to explore a new land?** (God told Moses to send twelve men.) **Name the land the men explored.** (Canaan) **Name the land the people had left.** (Egypt)

Have the listening groups report. **Who showed faith in God during this story?** (two men, Joshua and Caleb) **Why were some people afraid?** (People were stronger, their cities had walls around them.) **Who was afraid?** (the other ten men, the people)

Help children find the words in the story that show Joshua and Caleb's faith. ("The Lord will lead us. We should not be afraid.") Have them find the words that show the other men's fears. ("The people are strong; their cities have walls. It would be better if we went back to Egypt.)

Lead children to pray praise prayers. Praise God for keeping His promises, for providing all we need, and for leading us so we do not need to be afraid.

Before class, draw a 9-square grid on a sheet of paper. Photocopy one for each child in your group. (Save the nine-square grid to use in lesson 12.) Copy the word-bank list onto poster board and copy each word onto an index card. Put the index cards into a box.

Give each child a grid. Have the children choose nine words from the list to copy, putting one into each of their nine spaces. After children have copied a word into each square, play the game by drawing an index card from the box and calling out the word. If the children have that word written on their paper, they cover it with a token. The winner is the first to get three tokens in a row.

Read

Allow children time to read the story independently. Even children who can't read every word can look at the pictures and listen to the cassette. They can also color the Bible story pages.

Word Bank

Canaan, Joshua, milk, honey, Caleb, Egypt, Moses, faith, fear, Jericho, angel, trumpets, battle, seven, shout, walls, army, God

Options

• Most primaries copy slowly. If you prepare a variety of grids before class, you will have more time to play the game.

• Variations for the grid game include four corners, whole card, and diagonals.

• Call out a word and have the players find it on their grids. Then players work in pairs to find the word in a *Young Reader's Bible*. When they find a word in the Bible, they place a token on the sheet. (They can color it in if you don't plan to reuse the sheets.)

Snacks

If you used the milk and honey cookies recipe, serve those. Otherwise offer grapes and/or raisins, honey, and milk.

❸ Practice Using a Bible

Using My Bible

Have children find the table of contents in a Bible. **What is the first book in the Old Testament?** (Genesis) Spell the name. **On what page does the book of Genesis begin?** (answers vary)

Guide children to locate the book of Psalms by opening their Bibles to the middle. Pronounce the name *Psalms*. Spell the name. Talk about the silent letter *p*. Help the children conclude that we can easily find the books of Genesis and Psalms without using a table of contents. But that the table of contents list of book names and page numbers can help us find the first page of any Bible book.

Finding Bible Verses

Arrange children in pairs or groups of three. Provide each group with the Bible story and a Bible. Review the method for finding Bible references using the Reference Rhyme on page 32.

Help children locate Numbers chapter 13 in a Bible. Explain that you will name a verse number to find in chapter 13 and then you will read a few words.

Before class, print the Bible reference, Psalm 119:11, on each index card. Give each child a card. Have children trace over each letter and number of the reference using colored chalk. Say the Bible reference aloud together.

Review chapter and verse numbers. Large numbers (followed by two dots) are chapters, small numbers (after the dots) are verses. Give children time to help one another find the book of Psalms, chapter 119, verse 11.

When everyone has found the verse, have a volunteer read it aloud. Explain that "hiding God's Word in your heart" means memorizing Bible verses. **When I remember a verse, I have hidden it in my heart. It belongs to me because I know it from memory.**

Materials
- Bible for each child
- photocopies of the Bible story used earlier
- photocopies of page 32
- markers
- small index card, 1 per child
- crayons
- colored chalk

Numbers 13:2
You can find the word *explore*. It is the only word with an X. Have each child place a finger on the word explore in the Bible.

Numbers 13:23
Find the word *grapes* in a Bible. When children have located the word, read the verse aloud.

Numbers 13:27
Find the words *milk and honey*. Recall the meaning of this phrase.

Note
Some children will have trouble finding chapter 119, because they will begin with chapter one and just count one chapter at a time. Help them begin counting at Psalm 100.

❹ Share What We've Learned

Before class, print *fear* on one paper in large black letters. Color the background red or use red construction paper. On the other paper print, *faith*. Color the background green or use green construction paper.

The Bible stories show us how God helped people who obey Him. Who obeyed God in today's story? Who disobeyed God? What punishment did the people receive who refused to obey God? (They could not enter the Promised Land.) **Name people whom God wants us to obey.** Ask children to name some ways they can show their trust in God by obeying someone. **The Bible heroes Joshua and Caleb showed their faith by obeying God.** Some people have to overcome fear so that they can obey God.

Choose two children to be Joshua and Caleb. Joshua and Caleb stand at one end of the room. The rest of the class stands at the other end of the room. They begin to walk toward Joshua and Caleb.

Joshua and Caleb take turns holding up the *faith* or *fear* cards. If they hold up *faith*, the class continues to walk toward them. When they hold up *fear*, the children run back to their side of the room without getting tagged by Joshua or Caleb.

If they are tagged, they stand on the sideline and cheer, "Faith or Fear." Children who run to their side of the room when a sign isn't held up also join the group on the sidelines. Those who make it to Joshua and Caleb's side become taggers.

Materials
- *The Young Reader's Bible*
- two sheets of paper
- markers
- stickers with pictures of Bibles

Teaching at Home

Include the word-grid game in your family time. The words can be changed to fit any Bible story.

Reading tips
- Beginning with the numbers in this lesson, review number words.
- Point out the question mark in the title. Talk about what a question mark signals. Let children practice printing question marks.

Joshua 5, 6

Joshua Obeys God

Tell how Joshua and God's people obeyed God at Jericho.
Tell a way to obey God, even when it is difficult.
Copy and find a Bible reference.

"I have hidden your word in my heart."   Psalm 119:11, NIV

Materials
- modeling dough, enough for each child to have a handful
- wax paper
- one sheet of poster board or cardboard

① Get Ready to Read

Divide children into groups of three or four. Have children make "bricks" from their modeling dough on wax paper. Place the bricks on cardboard or poster board to make a wall.

In Bible times people usually built a wall around their city. The wall helped to keep them safe from robbers or enemy armies. The city of Jericho had a very strong wall. It was high, wide, and strong. The people of Jericho did not think that anyone could get inside their city because the wall was so strong.

In our Bible story today, we will find out that God is stronger than any wall.

Materials
- *The Young Reader's Bible,* pages 110-115
- photocopies of the Bible story (pages 274-276)
- photocopies of hand-drawn brick wall, two papers per child
- *The Young Reader's Bible Audio Cassette* or a cassette on which you have recorded unit stories
- cassette player(s), earphones optional
- poster board footprints
- taped marching music (Check your public library for a recording of "Joshua Fought the Battle of Jericho.")
- large cardboard blocks or boxes
- horns (paper towel tubes or kazoos)
- glue sticks
- scissors
- pencils, markers

② Read the Bible Story

"Seven Times and a Shout"

Before class, cut out shapes of footprints from poster board. On each footprint, print one of these words: *angel, march, tablets, commandments, priests, trumpets, seventh, shout.*

Securely tape the footprints to the floor. Have the children line up and march around, stepping on the footprints. Stop the music and have each player read the word he is standing on. Restart the music, have the children continue to march around, and then stop the music again. Continue until interest wanes.

Have children describe parades they have seen or participated in. Ask them to name reasons for parades.

Turn to page 110 in a *Young Reader's Bible* (or use a copy of the story). **On the first page of the story we see a picture of Joshua and an angel. What is unusual about the angel?** (clothing, sword, no wings) **In the next picture, what are the men and Joshua doing?** (marching around a wall) **How many men are leading the group?** (seven) **What are they doing?** (blowing horns) **How does the wall look different on the next two pages?** (wall is falling down)

Today, we will read about how this wall fell down.

Listen

Have a child read the title of the story, "Seven Times and a Shout." Tell the children to listen to find out how God helped Joshua. Some children can listen for the things that Joshua did. Read the story expressively.

When you have completed the story emphasize that the Bible stories we are reading show how God helps people who obey Him. **Who obeyed God in today's story?** (Joshua and the people) **What were the people trying to do?** (Go into the land God had told them was theirs.) **What did Joshua tell the people to do for the first six days?** (March around Jericho once a day for six days while carrying the Commandments.) **What were the priests to do?** (Blow trumpets.) **What were the people told to do on the seventh day?** (March around seven times and then shout.) **How was God helping the people?** (bring down the walls of Jericho)

What are the actions God's people used to obey Him? (marching, shouting) **Did it seem possible that God's plan would make the walls fall down? Is this a plan that you would have chosen? Do you think some people might have doubted that God's plan would work for conquering Jericho?**

Participate

Reinforce the Bible content by dramatizing the story. Have children help build a wall on the floor with large cardboard blocks (or use cardboard boxes you have collected). Have seven children carry horns and blow them while the other children follow them around the block wall.

Do this once and then stop and rest. Repeat this six times.

Finally, march around the blocks seven times and then have all the children shout. Have one child behind the wall knock it down when the children shout.

Before class, fill a piece of typing paper with eight to ten brick shapes to form a wall. Make two photocopies for each child.

Distribute scissors and one brick wall paper to each child. Have them cut apart their bricks. Collect the scissors. Then distribute the second sheet with pencils.

As you read the instructions, stop and spell out the word they are to find as you print it on your large paper wall.

Read

Recall why God's people had a parade. Then allow children time to read the story independently. Even children who can't read every word can color the pictures of the photocopied story as they listen to cassette.

Children can prepare and use word grids like those used in lesson 11. Some children can listen to "Faith or Fear?" They can reuse the word grids prepared last week.

❸ Practice Using a Bible

Using My Bible

Before class, cut out for each child a large numeral 7 from an index card. Print "Joshua" on the cutout seven.

Have children find the first page of the Old Testament in the Bible. **What is the first book in the Old Testament?** (Genesis) Have children find the middle of the Bible. **What book do we find in the middle of the Bible?** (Psalms)

Give each child a cutout "seven." Children trace over each letter using markers.

Turn to the table of contents. Help the children match up the word *Joshua* with the listing of Joshua in the table of contents. Let the children tell the page number on which the book of Joshua begins. Help them locate the book of Joshua.

Instructions
Find the word *Jericho* in the story. Copy it on one of the bricks, and glue it on your wall. The *CH* in *Jericho* make a K sound.

Find the word *trumpets* in the story. Draw a picture of a trumpet on one of the bricks and glue it on your wall.

Find two words in the story that begin with the letter S. Copy those words on two of the bricks and glue them on your wall.

Find the name of the man who was the leader for God's people. Copy his name on a brick and glue it on your wall.

Find the word that means Joshua and the people did what God told them to do.

Option
Prepare some walls with words already printed on them for those who struggle with printing.

Snacks
Provide bite-size crackers that can be stacked like a wall. Or give each child a paper plate containing a pile of marshmallows and a small scoop of peanut butter. Offer picnic-size plastic knives so children can build a wall.

Materials
• Bible for each child
• photocopies of Task Card #5 (page 111)
• numeral 7 cut from large index card, 1 per child
• scissors
• markers

Joshua 7

Finding Bible Verses

Have the children add 6:4 to the book name they traced on their 7s. Have the children read the Bible reference aloud together. Give each child a copy of Task Card #5. They can copy Joshua 6:4 onto the blank.

Guide children to locate Joshua chapter 6, verse 4, in their Bibles. Read the reference aloud. Have the children count the number of times they hear the word seven. (NIV has two *sevens* and one *seventh*.)

Direct them to look for verse 13, "Shout for the Lord has given you the city!" The first child to locate the verse should stand up and shout.

Direct the children to look for verse 20, "When the people gave a loud shout, the wall collapsed." **What words do you suppose the people shouted?** Accept their suggestions and choose a word you will all shout together. Close the Bibles and practice finding Joshua 6:4, 13, and 20. Have everyone shout the chosen word when the verse is found.

Recall how Joshua and the people obeyed, even when it was difficult. **God spoke directly to Joshua. Today we can read His Words in a book. Name the book.** (Bible) **We can trust God's Word to teach us the right things to do.**

Help them find the unit key verse, Psalm 119:11. Talk about people who help us understand God's Word. Remind them that when we hide God's Word in our hearts, we can say it from memory. Repeat Psalm 119:11 together. **How do we hide God's Word in our hearts?** (by memorizing verses and stories)

How will this memorizing help us obey God? (When we face a difficult situation we can remember what God says or how He helped Bible people. We will remember that God will help us, too.)

Offer a prayer, thanking God for telling us what is right to do and giving us people who will help us learn and understand it.

4 Share What We've learned

Materials
• cardboard blocks

Choose one or more children to act out each of the following **boldfaced** sentences. The remainder of the group should answer, "No, they shouted!" getting louder each time.

Did they knock down the wall? (*Swing arms like a golf club.*)
No, they shouted!
Did they poke holes in the wall? (*Pretend to ram a log through a wall.*)
No, they shouted!
Did they dig a tunnel under the wall? (*Pretend to shovel.*)
No, they shouted!
Did they climb a ladder over the wall? (*Act out climbing a ladder.*)
No, they shouted!

Provide the following active game to reinforce the Bible story content. Give each child one block. Meet in the center of the room and build a wall. Make sure there is one less block in the pile. Have children form a circle around the wall.

Have the children march around the wall until the leader shouts. Then everyone runs to grab a block and back to their place in the circle.

The child without a block becomes the shouter. After this round the child that was the shouter may return to the game and you will have a new shouter. Continue the game until everyone has been the shouter.

Encourage children to talk with you about what they have been learning. Focus the discussion by using questions based on the lesson and unit aims. See lessons 1-5 for guidance.

Teaching at Home

Let children use sidewalk chalk to make large footprints. Print vocabulary or words of the unit key verse in each footprint.

Reading tips
• Review the sound of *ar*. Use the words *march*, *army*, and *dark*.
• The word *city* reminds us that the letter *c* followed by *i* or *e* makes an *s* sound. Other examples include *police*, *celery*, *mice*.

Ruth Makes a Good Choice

13

Tell how people obeyed by sharing.
Choose a way to obey God by sharing with others.
Read and write Bible references and find the book of Ruth.

"I have hidden your word in my heart."   Psalm 119:11, NIV

1 Get Ready to Read

Give each child a white heart cut from construction paper. Have children draw pictures of their families. This may include grandparents, cousins, or anyone they include as family. If children do not want to draw, they may cut pictures from magazines to represent their families.

After children show their pictures to the class, tell them that the Bible story is about a very large family.

Materials
• large heart cut from white construction paper for each child
• magazines or clothing catalogs
• markers or crayons
• scissors

Option
See the reading tip at the end of this lesson.

2 Read the Bible Story

"Ruth's Rich Reward"
Before class, use a marker to print the following words on large cards:
Bethlehem, Judah, Moab, Ruth, Naomi, Orpah, Boaz, Obed, David.

Introduce the unusual people and place names. Help the children sound out the words. **The first three names are Bible places. Bethlehem is a city, and Judah is the area that city is in. Moab is an area outside of Judah. What city do we live in** (is nearby)?

What county do we live in? (Children might need some help.) **Name an area that is outside of our county.**

The last six names are Bible people who belonged to the same family. Let's take a moment to see the pictures you made of your families. Then we will find out more about this Bible family.

Have children share their family pictures.

Materials
• *The Young Reader's Bible*, pages 128-133
• photocopies of the two-page Bible story (page 76)
• photocopies of page 79
• *The Young Reader's Bible Audio Cassette* or a cassette on which you have recorded unit stories
• cassette player(s), earphones optional
• family pictures made earlier
• large cards
• 1" square pieces of fabric or felt
• cereal
• magazines
• large sheets of paper
• half sheets of paper
• glue
• markers, pencils, crayons

Listen

The people in today's story each pleased God and obeyed Him by sharing. Listen to find out what or how the person shared.

Divide your listeners into three groups to discover how people shared. One group listens for Naomi, one for Ruth, and one for Boaz. Have the children answer the following questions after you read the story. Point to each name as you mention it in the question.

How did Ruth share? (went to Bethlehem to be a friend to Naomi, shared the grain she picked up in the field)

How did Naomi share? (shared her home with Ruth)

How did Boaz share? (shared the grain from his fields with Ruth)

Give each child a copy of the Bible story excerpt (page 76). Distribute cereal, felt or fabric, and glue. Have children glue the cereal on the picture of Ruth gathering the grain, the felt or fabric on the picture of the baby.

While they glue the items, talk about the various ways people shared in the story.

Participate

Draw a vertical line in the middle of a large sheet of paper. Print the word *person* on one side and *place* on the other side. Use the name cards you displayed before the story. Say a name and have the children tell you whether the word names a person or a place. Put the card in the right column.

Distribute copies of page 79. Review the Bible story by reading all six sentences and crossing out two wrong sentences. Reread the four right sentences and color the pictures.

Play "Guess the Word," a variation of Hangman.

Have children list words from the story. Include *Bethlehem, Naomi, Ruth, grain, field, Boaz, marry, wife, Obed, grandfather, King David*. Then have children read each word aloud and recall its meaning.

Begin the game by mentally choosing a word from the word bank. On the large paper, draw as many blank lines as there are letters in that word.

Have the teams take turns guessing letters of the word. Keep a list of the letters as they are guessed, even if they are not in the word.

The team that guesses the word gets a point. Give each child a chance to guess a letter. If children need more of a challenge, cover the word list.

Read

Allow children time to read the story independently. Even children who can't read every word can enjoy looking at the pictures, listening to the story, and coloring the two-page excerpt.

Give each reader a half sheet of paper with the following written on the left hand side: Naomi, Ruth, Boaz, Moab, and Obed. If you have nonreaders, pair them with readers. Children point to the word as it is heard in the story. Players can make tally marks and count the number of times they hear each word.

③ Practice Using a Bible

Using My Bible

Before class, cut bread-shaped pieces from construction paper.

Give each child a bread shape. Have everyone use glue to print *Ruth* in the center of the bread shape. Then give each child a handful of the seeds or pasta to stick on the glue. When everyone has finished, have them say together the letters R-U-T-H. **The letters spell the word *Ruth*. The Bible has a book with the name Ruth—named after the same person in our Bible story. The story we read today is found in the Bible in the book of Ruth.**

Help the children use the table of contents to find *Ruth* in the Old Testament listing. Locate the page number on which the book of Ruth begins. Next, find the book of Ruth in a Bible. In lesson 12, children practiced finding the book of Joshua. Tell them that the book of Ruth is the book after Joshua.

Option

Before class, prepare stick-on name tags, one for each of the six key names in the story.
Have children wear the name tags you have prepared.
Arrange them to show the family relationships in the story.

Option

Pour flour into shallow pan. Let the children write key story words in the flour.

Option

Cue the cassette to the story from lesson 11 or 12. Allow children to follow along as they read the more familiar story.

Snacks

Serve whole grain crackers or whole wheat bread with jelly.

Materials

• Bibles
• photocopies of Task Card #6 (page 111)
• brown or tan construction paper
• unpopped popcorn, dried peas, beans, or pasta
• index cards
• scissors

Option

Give older children a handful of alphabet cereal or pasta letters. Have them find the letters to spell the name Ruth.

Finding Bible Verses

Give each child a copy of Task Card #6 filled in with the reference *Ruth 2:3* and the word *grain*. Work together to complete the task card.

Before class, print each Bible reference on an index card: Ruth 1:6 or 1:14; Ruth 1:3-5; Ruth 1:19; Ruth 2:3; Ruth 2:6; Ruth 4:13 or Ruth 4:17. Make a set of reference cards for each child or pair of children.

Have children open the Bible to the book of Ruth. Read each question aloud. After finding each answer, find the card with the reference written on it.

Locate chapter one and read the title of this chapter.

What did our story today tell us about how Naomi and Ruth were related? (Ruth was Naomi's daughter-in-law, Ruth 1:6 or 1:14)

What had happened to their husbands? (They had died, Ruth 1:3-5)

Find the name of the place Naomi and Ruth moved to. (Bethlehem, Ruth 1:19) **Put your finger on it.**

Locate chapter two and read the title. How did Ruth meet Boaz? (Ruth gathered grain in his field, Ruth 2:3)

Find the word that tells where Ruth was from. (Moab, Ruth 2:6) **Put your finger on it.**

Skip to chapter four. Read the title of chapter four. What did our story today tell us? (They had a baby boy and named him Obed, Ruth 4:13 or 4:17) **Find the baby's name and put your finger on it.**

Pray, thanking God for giving us the Bible so that we can read about His family.

4 Share What We've Learned

Before class, print out the following sentences on a large sheet of paper:
Ruth shared her friendship with Naomi.
Naomi shared her home with Ruth.
Boaz shared his grain with Ruth.
I can obey God by sharing _____.

Assist children in reading the sentences aloud. Let them take turns suggesting ways that they will share something during the coming week.

Talk about other things they have been learning and skills they have gained. Listening to their opinions will help you know where to place your teaching emphasis in the coming weeks.

If you did not use word cards earlier in the class, prepare these, one word per card: **Bethlehem, Judah, Moab, Ruth, Naomi, Orpah, Boaz, Obed, David.** Give each child a card.

If your card is the name of a place, line up on this side of the room. If your card is the name of a person, line up on the other side.

Let children move into place. Then have them read the word on their own card aloud. Collect the cards and pass them out again.

Then have players line up on one side of the room. Invite them to cross to the other side when they suggest a way that they can share with others.

Option
Younger children can trace the references.

Materials
• a large sheet of paper
• index cards made earlier

Teaching at Home

Help the children understand the relationships among your family members as you teach about Ruth.

Reading tip
Broaden child's vocabulary. Purchase a variety of grain. Handle the whole grain. Grind grain into flour. Bake simple bread. Name the kinds of grain. Read and follow recipes.

Samuel Hears God

Tell what Samuel did when God spoke to him.
Tell how we can be like Samuel.
Read Bible references and find Bible verses.

"I have hidden your word in my heart."   Psalm 119:11, NIV

❶ Get Ready to Read

Materials
- white construction paper
- photocopied and cut apart 2-by-2-inch squares on which phrases have been written, four squares for each child
- crayons
- scissors

Phrases to print on each square
Hannah prayed.
God answered.
God spoke.
Samuel listened.

Options
- Before the session have a parent of one of the children in your class record this week's story. Instruct the parent to keep this a secret from everyone. Have the lights turned off for children to listen to the tape. Explain that the person in the Bible story heard a voice in the dark, just like they will. Invite the children to listen carefully to the voice reading the story and try to guess who is speaking.
- Involve several parents in the story, selecting readers for Hannah, Eli, Samuel, the Lord, and the narrator. More children can be surprised to hear their parents' voices on the tape.

Materials
- *The Young Reader's Bible*, pages 134-139
- photocopies of the two-page Bible story (page 77)
- *The Young Reader's Bible Audio Cassette* or a cassette on which you have recorded unit stories
- cassette player(s), earphones optional
- a large sheet of paper
- word-sized poster board strips

Before class, copy one phrase on each square. Stack the 2-by-2-inch squares in order and staple them together. Some children might prefer to copy the phrases onto blank squares by themselves.

Give each child a piece of white construction paper, folded in half to make a booklet. The children will use a crayon to trace their hands on their booklets. Help them place their little fingers along the fold and keep all the fingers close together. Cut out the praying hands shape. Caution them not to cut on the fold along the edge of the little finger.

When they have cut out the booklet, give each child a set of phrase cards. Read the phrase cards together. Staple the phrase cards into the booklet.

We will find out more about these Bible people and what they did in our story today.

❷ Read the Bible Story

"A Voice in the Dark"
Talk about the words you will be reading in the Bible story—*Hannah* (spelled the same forward and backward), *Eli, Servant, message, prophet* (the PH makes an F sound).

Have you ever heard someone calling your name, but you did not answer? (discuss)

Assign three listening groups. Give each child or small group of children a question to answer while they read or hear the story. **How did God answer Hannah's prayer? To whom did God speak aloud? How did the person answer God?**

Listen and find out who speaks in the dark, who hears the voice, and who listens to the message.

Listen
Have the lights turned off for children to listen to the story. **In this Bible story, someone heard a voice in the dark, and we'll be listening in the dark, too.**

Have one child read the title of the story. Read the story or play the recording of the parents reading the story. If you use the cassette, encourage the children to listen carefully to guess who is speaking.

Participate

Before class, print one word or phrase on each strip of poster board: *Hannah, Eli, God, Samuel, praying, listening, speaking, praising God for answering prayer, bringing Samuel to serve God, taking care of Samuel.* Use the phrase cards to pantomime a review of the story.

Display the ten poster board strips and help the children read them. Then choose a person to pretend to be one of the characters. Select volunteers to choose the card naming a person and the card naming his or her action.

Gather the children around as you show and talk about the pictures in the story. Use these questions to review the story. Look at the first page of the story.

What is Hannah doing? (praying) **Who heard her prayer?** (Eli the priest, God)

What did Hannah ask for from God? (a son)

What did she promise God? (her son would serve God)

How did Hannah keep her promise? (She took Samuel to Eli at the temple when he was older.)

Turn to page 136. **Who are the people in this picture?** (Hannah, Samuel, Eli)

What do you think is happening? (Accept logical answers.)

Who heard a voice at night? (Samuel)

Who did Samuel think was calling him? (Eli)

Who was really calling him? (God)

What did Samuel say to God? (I am listening.)

Look at page 138. **What do you think Samuel is doing?** (He is talking to Eli in Eli's room.)

What is Samuel doing in the next picture? (listening to God)

How can *we* listen to God? (pray) **Where can we listen to God?** (anywhere)

Pray with the children.

Read

Give each child a copy of the story (page 77). Children can use crayons, markers, or colored pencils to color the pages.

As children work, encourage them to read the story independently at their own level. Even if children can't read every word, they can listen to the cassette, point to the words they know, and tell about the story by looking at the pictures.

❸ Practice Using a Bible

Using My Bible

Help children recognize Bible book names, chapter numbers, and verse numbers by pointing these out in a Bible.

Before class, make a large game grid on poster board. See the illustration on page 72

Divide the group into two teams. Use two kinds of coins or buttons for the X and O markers. Play tic-tac-toe. The team may claim a square with one of their markers when they "show and tell" in a Bible the word that appears in that square. For example, they can find the words *Old Testament* on a page. They can point to a chapter number or a verse number.

Finding Bible Verses

Before class, print the following message with a white crayon on white paper: *I am your servant, and I am listening.* Also, before class, fill in copies of Task Card #7 with the number *138* and the word *listening*.

Materials (cont.)
- praying hands booklet made earlier
- option: parent(s)'s recording of Bible story
- crayons, markers, or colored pencils

Snacks
Serve cookies on which you have written each child's name.

Materials
- *The Young Reader's Bible*
- Bibles
- photocopies of two-page Bible story (page 77)
- photocopies of Task Card #7 (page 111)
- white crayon
- white paper
- set of watercolor paints
- paint brushes
- cup of water
- paper towels
- 4-inch lengths of heavy cord
- construction paper
- markers
- scissors
- poster board
- game tokens such as buttons or coins

Options
• If your children are more advanced in finding Bible books, replace the ones listed on the game board with other Bible book names: Proverbs, Acts, Gospels, Prophets, etc.
• Make copies of the game board on sheets of construction paper or lightweight cardboard for children to take home.

Option
More confident readers can find 1 Samuel 3 in an NIV Bible. Help them locate verses 4-6. Let three children each read one verse. Then skip to verses 9 and 10. Does this sound like the words we have been reading in our *Young Reader's Bibles?*

Materials
• blindfold

Teaching at Home
Ask a relative, friend, or neighbor to record the Bible story. Allow the children to listen to the cassette-taped story and guess who is reading.

Reading tip
Tell about quotation marks. They signal when someone is speaking. Let children find quotation marks. Practice writing quotation marks.

Give each child watercolor paint and a brush to paint over the "blank" paper and discover the message. While the painted messages are drying, give each child a copy of Task Card #7 and the Bible story excerpt. Help children find the word *listening* on the Bible story page or in 1 Samuel 3:10 in an NIV Bible.

Before class, use a poster board pattern to trace copies of a telephone shape onto construction paper or other heavy paper. Print the Bible reference, 1 Samuel 3:10, on each telephone.

Have children cut out the telephone and glue a 4-inch length of heavy cord to the ear piece.

After the telephone pattern has been cut out and the paint on the message paper has dried, children can take turns reading Samuel's words aloud.

Have them trace over the Bible reference, 1 Samuel 3:10. Explain that the 1 in front of Samuel means that there is more than one book named Samuel in the Bible. Children can copy the words from the message paper onto their telephone bookmarks. Let them take the bookmarks home as a reminder of the Bible story.

Why did we use a telephone pattern to print the Bible reference? Did God call Samuel on the telephone? No, but Samuel heard God's voice without seeing him, just as when we talk on the telephone, we hear someone's voice without seeing a face.

Have children turn to the table of contents in the Bible.

How many books are named Samuel? (two)

How many books are named Kings? (two)

Help children find other books which have a 1, 2, or 3 in front of them.

Find 1 Samuel 3:10 in the Bible. Read the last part of the verse. Although the wording will be different, the meaning will be the same as the words on the message paper.

 ## Share What We've Learned

Emphasize the improvement you see in the children's Bible skills and reading skills. Take time now to encourage them to tell you what they have been learning. Help them recall skills they can do now that they could not do last month. Tell them that they will be able to read a Bible by themselves, even if it has no pictures to help them understand the stories.

Children have been learning to read many new Bible names. They have also been learning the names of others in the class. Perhaps some have made new friends. Help the children learn everyone's name.

Have children sit in a circle. Put a blindfold on one child who is "the listener." Have "the listener" stand in the middle of the circle. A child who is sitting in the circle calls out "the listener's" name. Give "the listener" three chances to guess who is calling him. If children are really good at this, allow the children in the circle to disguise their voice as they call out "the listener's" name.

The person you pointed to now becomes "the listener," even if "the listener" can't guess who was calling him.

Close with prayer, thanking God for each child by name.

15

God Tells Samuel to Anoint David King

Tell how God helped Samuel anoint David to be king.
Tell how God helps us do our special jobs.
Read Bible references and find Bible verses.

"I have hidden your word in my heart."   Psalm 119:11, NIV

① Get Ready to Read

Before class, make a pattern the shape of a prize ribbon. Distribute the paper, pencils, and scissors. While the children are tracing and cutting out the ribbons, have them name reasons people receive awards. Guide them to include ideas such as, did the best, did a good deed, made the team, etc.

Use a loop of masking tape on the back of each ribbon. Tape to the children.

While you are helping children pin or tape on their "awards," tell the children that they will be learning about a person who was chosen by God. **God chose this person for a special purpose. But this person did not receive an award that others could see. No one knew by looking that he had been chosen.**

Materials
• dark blue construction paper
• pattern for making a prize ribbon
• pencils
• scissors
• masking tape "loops" for attaching awards

② Read the Bible Story

"A New King for Israel"

During the week before the class, contact two children to help you introduce the story. One player will be the one who is to be "chosen." Secretly give this child a small sticker to keep hidden until this part of the class. Tell the child when to stick it on the palm of his hand. The other player will be the one who chooses. Tell this child to look at each child's palm to find a special sticker.

Have all the children line up and pass by the "chooser," asking, "Am I the one?" The chooser checks other's palms and answers, "No, you have not been chosen." Place the "chosen one" near the end of the line so that most of the children will pass by the "chooser" without being chosen.

Afterwards, explain how the child who was the chooser is like Samuel. **God sent Samuel to choose someone for a special job. Just as no one could tell who would be chosen from the line, Samuel could not tell by looking at a person whether or not he was the one chosen. Our chooser could not tell until it was revealed by the sticker in the hand. Samuel could not tell who was to be chosen either.**

Demonstrate the word *anoint* by rubbing a little oil on the back of each child's hand. Begin with the child who was chosen. As you rub the oil, say, **I choose you. I anoint you. Each one of us is special to God.** Touch each child with some

Materials
• *The Young Reader's Bible*, pages 140-145
• photocopies of the two-page Bible story (page 78)
• *The Young Reader's Bible Audio Cassette* or a cassette on which you have recorded unit stories
• cassette player(s), earphones optional
• stickers
• one child with a small sticker
• one child prepared to be the chooser
• cooking oil
• paper cups
• cotton swabs
• paper towels
• 5 strips of paper
• award ribbons made earlier
• crayons or colored pencils

oil. Give each one a sticker.

As we listen to this story, we will find out how Samuel learned who was to be chosen. We will see how Samuel anointed the chosen person.

Listen

We read a story about a young boy who heard God's voice. In this story the boy, Samuel, is grown up but he is still listening and obeying God. Today we will find out how Samuel obeyed God.

Form listening pairs. Pairs of children can listen for answers to these questions:

What did God tell Samuel to do to show who would be the next king? Where did Samuel go to find the next king? How many sons did Jesse have? Who played a harp for King Saul? How did the harp-playing help King Saul?

After reading the story, discuss the answers to these questions.

Participate

Before class, copy the five sentences written in the narrow column, one on each strip of paper or index card.

Mix up the order of the sentences and display them for the children to read. Help them sound out and read the sentences. Then give one of the sentences to each child or group of children. Instruct the children to listen for "their sentence" as the tape is being played. When they hear their sentence, they should place their strip or card on the table (or floor) so that the sentences line up in the correct order. Review the order and reinforce the reading by handing out the cards again and having children arrange themselves in the correct order.

Talk about the story using the pictures in a *Young Reader's Bible.*

Where was Samuel going and why? (Bethlehem—God had chosen the next king.)

Which man in the pictures did God choose to be king? (none)

How many sons did Jesse have? (8)

Where did Samuel find the new king? (caring for sheep)

How much oil did Samuel use to anoint David? What did it mean when Samuel poured oil on David's head? (God had chosen David.)

What did King Saul's helpers suggest to make him feel better? (music)

What would happen when David played music for the king? (He felt better.)

Display the word *anoint.* Help the children remove their award ribbons. Distribute cups of oil along with the cotton swabs. Have the children copy the word *anoint* on their ribbon, dipping the cotton swab in the oil to use as "ink." Talk about the Bible custom of anointing with oil. When directed by God, this action showed that God had chosen a person for a special job.

Read

Give each child a copy of the Bible story excerpt (page 78). Children can use crayons or colored pencils to color the pages. They can use cotton swabs to add oil to the picture of anointing.

Allow children time to read the story independently. Even children who can't read every word can listen to the cassette, look at the pictures, and retell the story.

❸ Practice Using a Bible

Using My Bible

Before class, print these Bible people's names on a large sheet of paper: *Joshua*

God told Samuel, "Go to Bethlehem and find Jesse."
Seven times God said, "This is not the one."
David was tending the sheep.
God told Samuel to anoint David.
David played his harp for King Saul.

Options
• Prepare multiple sentence strips for large groups. Divide into small groups of five or six to sort out the sentences.
• Give each child a cotton swab, the cup with a little oil, and a list of words to listen for. As you reread the story, the children mark each word with oil as it is read.
• Fill in Task Card #8 for children to use (140).

Snacks
Serve fruit and a small amount of a snack such as potato chips. Put the chips on napkins. Let the children see the oil absorbed into the paper.

Materials
• *New International Version* Bibles
• construction paper
• large sheet of paper
• markers
• cotton swabs
• dark-colored construction paper
• small amount of cooking oil in paper cups
• paper towels

and Caleb, Joshua, Ruth, Samuel, David. Then copy one Bible reference on the bottom of each sheet of construction paper. Draw the corresponding shape on each.

Numbers 13, 14—cluster of grapes
Joshua 5, 6—trumpet
Ruth—stalk of wheat
1 Samuel 1–3—candle or oil lamp
1 Samuel 16—harp

Choose one or more of the following activities using these visuals.

Have children find each Bible book and chapter. Have them tell you the name of the Bible person who goes with each paper. Choose five volunteers to copy the name of the Bible person onto the construction paper visual. Have children explain how each person obeyed God, or tell what God asked each person to do.

God helps us know how to do right in His book, the Bible. We can learn what the Bible people did, and we can follow their good examples to help us do right. We can memorize Bible verses to remind us how to do right and obey God. When we memorize God's Word, we can say that we have hidden His Word in our hearts. No one can see His Word when they look at us, but they can see the right things that we do. God's Word helps us obey Him.

Find and read the unit key verse, "I have hidden your word in my heart." Psalm 119:11, NIV. Pray, thanking God for helping us know right things to do.

Find Bible Verses

Use a *New International Version* Bible and have children find the first page of the book of 1 Samuel. Review the meaning of the numeral 1 in front of the book name, Samuel There are two books with the name Samuel. One (1) means it is the first of the two books.

Assist children in finding 1 Samuel 16:4 in their own Bibles. Help them use the table of contents if necessary. Two children can work together to find the reference.

What does this verse tell us about obeying? (That Samuel obeyed what God told him to do. When we obey God, we do what He wants us to do.)

How can you do what God wants you to do? What will you do?

Continue by having children turn to 1 Samuel 16:10, 11. These two verses should be easy for beginning readers to sound out and read with just a little help.

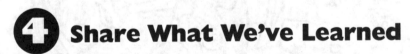

Share What We've Learned

Give each child a pencil and a copy of the crossword puzzle (page 80). Help children fill in the names. If you want to give your children more practice in finding verses, have them use an NIV Bible to find the verse which matches the word in the crossword puzzle. First, assist them in finding 1 Samuel 16. Then say the verse number or print it so that everyone can see it. Tell them what word they are searching for in the verse. Have them print the word in the blanks of the crossword.

Across
1. David—1 Samuel 16:13
3. Saul—1 Samuel 16:1
5. Bethlehem—1 Samuel 16:4

Down
2. Israel—1 Samuel 16:1
3. Samuel—1 Samuel 16:1 or 4
4. Jesse—1 Samuel 16:1 or 3

Children can assemble photocopies of pages 8, 9 and 81 into a booklet. See unit 3, pages 58 and 59.

Materials
• photocopies of page 80
• photocopies of pages 8, 9, and 81
• materials for making booklet (unit page)
• pencils

Options
• To simplify crossword, fill in the first letter of each word.
• Complete instructions for a tic-tac-toe game are provided in lesson 14. Children will enjoy playing and showing improvement in finding the Bible books listed.
• If children need more of a challenge, make new game sheets including names of other Bible books.

 Teaching at Home

Experience how music can change how we feel. Listen to different kinds of music and talk about feelings.

Reading tip
Look for proper names in this story. Notice that the capital letter signals a proper name. Practice writing common and proper names such as: *son/David; king/King Saul; prophet/Samuel.*

When they came to Bethlehem,
Naomi and Ruth were poor.

But God's law
allowed poor people
to pick up fallen grain.

Ruth gathered grain in a field
that belonged to a man
named Boaz.

Ruth was kind to Boaz.

He saw that Ruth was special.

He made plans to marry her.

Ruth became Boaz's wife,
and they had a son, named Obed.

When Obed was old,
he became the grandfather
of the great King David.

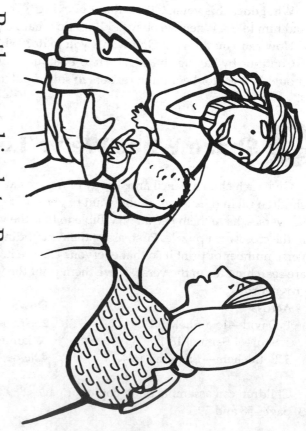

76

The voice called to Samuel
three times.

"It is the Lord," said Eli.

"If he calls you again, say,
I am your servant,
and I am listening."

God called Samuel again.

"I am your servant,
and I am listening," said Samuel.

God gave Samuel
a message for Eli.

As Samuel grew up,
God had more messages for him.
Everyone in Israel knew
that Samuel was God's prophet.

Jesse sent for David.

When David came,

God told Samuel,

"This is the one I have chosen.

Anoint him with oil."

Seven sons stepped forward.

Seven times God said,

"This is not the one."

"Do you have any more sons?"

Samuel asked Jesse.

"Yes," said Jesse.

"David is tending the sheep."

Find the Ruth Truth

1. Ruth promised Naomi, "I will go with you."
2. Ruth told Naomi, "Don't go back to Judah."

- **Read all six sentences.**
- **Cross out two wrong sentences.**

3. Boaz let Ruth gather grain for Naomi.
4. Ruth stacked grain for Boaz to sell.

- **Read four true sentences and color the pictures.**

5. Ruth married Boaz. They had a son.
6. One day their son would be David's grandfather.

Across

1. a shepherd, a king
3. king before David
5. David's city

Down

2. David's country
3. this prophet anointed David
4. David's father

David

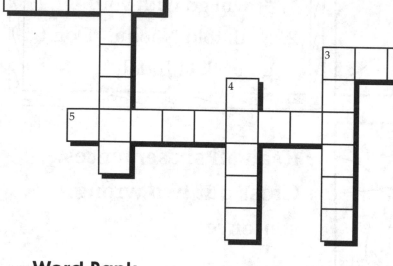

Word Bank

Bethlehem	David
Israel	Jesse
Samuel	Saul

Samuel and David

King Saul

King David

I Can Use My Bible

1. Draw a purple triangle around the name of the book. △
   The book name is _____ .

2. Draw a green star on the chapter number. ☆
   The chapter number is ___ .

3. Draw a blue circle around eight verse numbers ◯
   in chapter 14.

4. Draw a red line under the name Jesus. —

5. Draw a yellow X on the name Peter. ✕

Mark 14

61 But Jesus remained silent and gave no answer.

Again the high priest asked him, "Are you the Christ, the Son of the Blessed One?"

62 "I am," said Jesus. "And you will see the Son of Man sitting at the right hand of the Mighty One and coming on the clouds of heaven."

63 The high priest tore his clothes. "Why do we need any more witnesses?" he asked. **64** "You have heard the blasphemy. What do you think?"

They all condemned him as worthy of death. **65** Then some began to spit at him; they blindfolded him, struck him with their fists, and said, "Prophesy!" And the guards took him and beat him.

66 While Peter was below in the courtyard, one of the servant girls of the high priest came by. **67** When she saw Peter warming himself, she looked closely at him.

"You also were with that Nazarene, Jesus," she said.

68 But he denied it. "I don't know or understand what you're talking about," he said, and went out into the entryway.

New International Version

We Obey God
Who Answers Prayer

Key Verse

"The Lord listens when I pray to him."   Psalm 4:3, ICB

Unit Vocabulary

altar

break

broken

carved

cedar wood

celebrate

city of Jerusalem

destroy

enemies

favorite

feasted

jealous

King of Persia

nations

Nineveh

preach

rescue

sailors

storm

swallow

temple

tricked

troublemaker

wicked

wisdom

Unit Aims

By the end of the unit, learners will be able to

- tell five Bible stories about obeying God and praying.
- feel capable of finding verses in a Bible and reading *The Young Reader's Bible*.
- locate books, chapters and verses in their own Bibles.
- read (at their level) stories from *The Young Reader's Bible*.
- pray and obey God.

Unit Projects

Bible Story Neighborhood

People can find my house when I can tell them my address. One important skill for early readers is learning their addresses. The Bible Story Neighborhood will help children understand that Bible references are like addresses. They help us find verses in a Bible. In each lesson, children will read and locate two Bible references. After reading each verse, they will match the reference to the Bible Story Neighborhood house that tells the same message.

Make ten houses for the Bible Story Neighborhood. These can be as simple as drawing windows and doors and cutting angles off the corners of construction paper to form the roof line of a house. If you prefer, cut and fold paper to make three-dimensional houses or place toy village houses on a table. Paper houses can be put on a bulletin board. Title the display, "My Bible Story Neighborhood." Add two houses to the neighborhood each week or put up all ten houses and tape on two new envelopes each week.

Each lesson will give two Bible references to print on index cards. You'll make one index card for each child or pair of children. Each lesson will also include two Bible messages—print one message on each envelope. Tape one envelope on each house.

Temple-Builders Bulletin Board

Draw a large outline of a worship building on a sheet of butcher paper. Put pictures of the children or a class photo in the center.

Provide small colored index cards and markers. Each week, children report answered prayers, ways they served others, or skills they have mastered. Put the card on the building. Each card is a "building block."

	The Singing Bible (3 tapes)	Kids on the Rock (More Songs)	Follow the Leader (The Donut Man)	I'm a Helper (The Donut Man)	Good News (The Donut Man)
Lesson 16	Solomon				
Lesson 17	Elijah				
Lesson 18	Jonah and the Whale				
Lesson 19	Daniel				
Lesson 20			I Will Give My All		
Key Verse					
Unit Theme		Swim Upstream			
All Lessons	The Books We Love the Best / The Bible Book Is True	God's Word Is for Me			

The Singing Bible (3 tapes), ©1993 by Lightwave Publishing, Inc. Manufactured and distributed by Word Publishing, Dallas, TX 75234

Kids on the Rock! More Songs, ©1994 Gospel Light, Ventura CA 93006

The Donut Man (3 tapes): *Follow the Leader*, ©1990; *I'm a Helper*, ©1991; *Good News*, ©1991; Integrity Music, Inc., P.O. Box 16813 Mobile, AL 36616

Key Verse Activities

The Lord listens when I pray to him.
Psalm 4:3, ICB

Materials
- water in a transparent drinking glass or jar
- masking tape
- pen
- an effervescent antacid tablet (such as Alka-Seltzer)
- chalk

Rising Prayers

Have the children sit in a row. Lift the glass of water and tell the class, **Let's pretend the bottom of the glass is where we live.** Print "Earth" on a strip of tape at the bottom of the glass. **Let's say the space above the water is Heaven where God lives.** Print "Heaven" on tape above the water level. **This is you.** Draw a face on the effervescent tablet. Drop the tablet in the water. **If the bubbles are your prayers, what happens to them?** (They go straight up to Heaven.) *Important:* Immediately pour out the liquid so none of the children try to taste it while you are preoccupied.

Let's make a whisper chain. I'll whisper one word in someone's ear and you pass it down, whispering in each other's ears. The last person says the word aloud and I write it on the chalkboard. Repeat the process with each word of the memory verse. **You had to listen carefully to hear the words of the memory verse. God listens carefully to your prayers. He can even hear them when you pray silently.**

Materials
- tape recorder and blank cassette

Listening

Record each child saying, whispering, or singing (but not yelling) the memory verse and its reference. Then play back the tape and let everyone identify the voices. **Just as we enjoyed listening to everyone on the tape, God loves to listen to all of us, too. He wants to hear from us every day. What does He like to hear about?** (Let them respond and then emphasize that God likes to hear about *everything* that they care about, both happy and sad things.)

Materials
- a one-foot length of large, flexible plastic tubing (from a hardware store)
- a permanent marker

Totally Tubular

Before class, print the memory verse along the length of the tube.

Can you read what I have printed on the side of this tube? It's our memory verse. I'll read it to you and then we can all say it together. When we're praying, it's almost like we have a tube that goes directly to God.

Did you know that your voice sounds different to others than it sounds to you? With this tube, you can hear how your voice sounds to others. Let's practice saying our memory verse a few times. Then you can each take a turn reciting your memory verse into one end of the tube as you hold the other end of the tube at your ear.

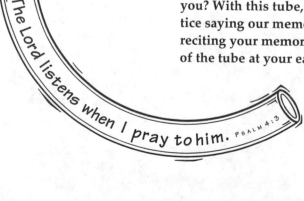

16

God Gives Solomon Wisdom

Tell how God answered Solomon's request.
Make a plan to pray every day.
Find the Old and New Testaments and Psalms.

"The Lord listens when I pray to him."   Psalm 4:3, ICB

❶ Get Ready to Read

Before class, cut and glue flat toothpicks into cross shapes. Make one for each child. Each child will also need graham cracker squares and a milk carton.

Cover a table with newspaper. To form building shapes, help children smear frosting on the sides and angled top of a milk carton. Stick graham crackers to the frosting on the sides . Split a graham cracker. Add for the roof. Next, have children dip gumdrops in the frosting and decorate their buildings.

What do we call the building where we worship God? (church) Give the children toothpick crosses to place on top of the church buildings they made.

Today we will read about King Solomon who built a beautiful place of worship for Israel called the temple.

❷ Read the Bible Story

"Solomon's One Wish"

Before class, print a definition of a vocabulary word (see narrow column) on a slip of paper. Print a sentence using the same vocabulary word on a second slip of paper. Put both slips of paper in a balloon. Inflate the balloon and print the vocabulary word on the inflated balloon.

Read the word written on a balloon. Ask if anyone can tell the meaning. Choose a volunteer to pop the balloon. Choose a good reader to read the meaning. Choose another reader to read the sentence. Continue with all the balloons.

Give each child a copy of the Bible story excerpt (page 100) and display page 159 in a *Young Reader's Bible*.

This king's name is Solomon. King Solomon wanted to obey God. How do you think King Solomon might be feeling in this picture? (puzzled, worried, sad)

Read pages 158 and 159. Have the children circle the word *wisdom* on their copy of the story. Emphasize that Solomon asked God for wisdom to be a good king. **Why did King Solomon look puzzled, sad or worried?** (He knew he needed wisdom and could not get it by himself.)

Materials
• newspaper
• graham crackers
• half-pint milk cartons
• flat toothpicks
• glue
• canned frosting
• gumdrops or other candy

Options
• Tour your church building and have someone answer questions about the building.
• Children can draw a place they would like to build to worship God, or a place they think of when they think of the word worship.

Materials
• *The Young Reader's Bible*, pages 158-163
• photocopies of the two-page Bible story (page 100)
• *The Young Reader's Bible Audio Cassette* or a cassette on which you have recorded unit stories
• balloons, one for each child plus four per teacher
• slips of paper
• markers

Vocabulary word examples
wisdom
knowing right from wrong (wise)
I use wisdom when I do right.
prayer
talking with God
Sorry, thank you, and please are kinds of prayer.
Solomon
the third king of Israel
King Solomon obeyed God and built a temple.
temple
the place of worship in Israel
Solomon worshiped at the temple.

Unit 4   **85**

Listen

Finish reading "Solomon's One Wish." Turn back to page 160. Reread the page with the children. Have them circle the name *King Solomon* and the sentence, *God was pleased with Solomon's prayer.*

Participate

How did Solomon show obedience to God? (He built a temple—a place for everyone to worship God and celebrate.) **How did King Solomon feel after the temple was finished? Why?** (Happy. The temple was finished.) **What would you ask God for if you were King Solomon?** (Every child has wished for something. Emphasize the wishing, not the value of the things wished for.)

The people came to the temple to celebrate and worship God. We celebrate and worship God when we come to church. Solomon obeyed God by building the temple for a place to worship.

Children can show the candy buildings and talk about the decorations they used. Make certain they understand that Solomon pleased God by building a temple. Explain that there are many other ways to obey God.

Use the following questions as a review. After the children give each answer, print it on a chalkboard. **How do we talk to God?** (pray) **What did King Solomon pray for?** (wisdom) **What did King Solomon promise?** (to obey God) **What other words have we learned from the story?** (temple, gold, wisest, etc.) **They had a big celebration when the temple was finished. When do we celebrate with balloons?** (birthdays, graduations) Give each child a balloon and marker. Each child chooses one word to copy onto a balloon. When balloons are ready, the children can bat them in the air. Try not to let any balloon touch the ground. After thirty seconds call out, **Stop!**

Each child grabs a balloon. Give children a chance to read or show you the word on the balloon they caught. Tell what the word reminds us about King Solomon.

Read

Have children color and read page 100 or a *Young Reader's Bible*. Children can listen to the cassette story and use facial expressions and hand motions to imagine Solomon's feelings.

❸ Practice Using a Bible

Using My Bible

Form teams of two or three. Try to place nonreaders with readers. Lay a broomstick on the ground. Tell the children to pretend that raising the broomstick is like building up the temple. The goal is to raise the temple (stick) above their heads. Use the game instructions in the narrow column.

When a team shows you that they have found the Bible section or Bible book given in an instruction, the team lines up behind the stick. Partners go under the stick when it is too high to jump over. Cheer for each team as they go over or under the stick. Make this a group effort, not a competition. Raise the stick about six inches after each instruction has been followed by every team. Everyone cheers together when the stick is moved.

Finding Bible Verses

Before class, prepare an index card for each child with one of the three parts of the unit key verse reference printed on it.

Option

If your children have limited writing skills, prepare the balloons before class and let them trace the words.

Snacks

Jell-O Jigglers gelatin snacks squares, or cheese squares, to represent blocks of the temple.

Materials
• Bible for each child
• two house shapes (unit page 82)
• index cards
• two envelopes
• broomstick or similar item
• a large sheet of paper
• marker

Instructions

Find the first book of the OT.
Find the first book of the NT.
Find the last book of the OT.
Find Psalms.
Find 1 Kings.
Find Psalm 4:3.

Explain that the set of cards completes a Bible reference. Bible references tell the name of the book, the number of the chapter, and the number of the verse or verses we want to find. Choose children to point to the Bible book name, the chapter number, and the verse number. Bible references are like addresses. Our home addresses tell where we live—where people can find us. Bible references tell where to find sentences in the Bible.

Next, give each child one of the cards you prepared before class. Tell the children that everyone has a part of a verse reference. At a signal, have the children search for two other parts to complete a reference. (A child who holds a *Psalm* card needs those holding *4:* and *3* cards.)

When three parts get together, they should stand in the correct order. Check each trio. One person from each match should copy the reference onto the large sheet of paper. Then let the trios break up and try to make a match with others.

Then come back together to find verses in the Bible. Use the Reference Rhyme (page 32) to remember how to find a verse from a reference. Help children find 1 Kings in a table of contents. Find the book, chapter (6), and verse (14).

Read the verse aloud. **The Bible tells us who built the temple. Read in the book of first Kings, chapter six, verse fourteen, the name of the King who built the temple. What was his name?** (Solomon)

Before class, display Bible Story Neighborhood Houses (see unit page).

Print *2 Timothy 3:16* on half of the index cards. Print *Psalm 4:3* on the rest of the index cards. Print *The Bible is God's Word* on one envelope. Print *God listens when I pray* on the other envelope. Attach one envelope to each house shape.

Children pair up. Each pair takes one of each Bible-reference index cards. They work together to look up and read the Bible verse and decide to which house the Bible reference belongs. Put the cards in the correct envelopes.

④ Share What We've Learned

Before class, prepare the game-path circle of heart shapes and squares, large enough to stand on. (You will need as many shapes as you have children, and up to half of the shapes can be hearts.)

Gather everyone in a circle to talk about what they have been doing and learning. Use the aims for this lesson as an outline for the kinds of questions you ask.

Begin a review game by playing music or singing as children march around the circle, stepping in the shapes. Children who are left standing on heart shapes when the music stops tell one way to obey God or one way God answers prayer.

Ask the children when we should pray. Tell them there are many ways to pray and many things to pray for, but that you will plan to pray for three things. Give each child a copy of page 103.

Do the maze that leads to "God, I thank You because . . . " **We want to thank God for things He does for us.**

Do the maze that leads to "God, I am sorry because . . ." **We want to tell God we are sorry when we do things He does not want us to do.**

Do the maze that leads to "God, please help . . . " **We want to ask Him for what we need, just as Solomon asked God for wisdom he needed to rule.**

Help the children print or draw something in each section for today's prayer. Encourage them to ask their family to pray every day.

Close with prayer. Ask the children to name things to pray about. Print them on a large sheet of paper. Save the paper to refer to from week to week. Ask God to give you and your children love for Him and hearts to obey Him.

Options
• If you have nonreaders, simply read the Bible reference, demonstrate finding the Bible verse, and then read the verse aloud.
• Refer to page 84 for ideas on teaching the unit key verse, Psalm 4:3.

Materials
• photocopies of page 103
• tape a game-path on the floor

Note
Send notes to parents encouraging them to set aside a time to pray together. Explain the three kinds of prayer they will be learning about (sorry, thank you, and please).

Teaching at Home

Build a model of the temple for a family project.

Reading tips
• Notice the suffix *ed*: died, asked, pleased, carved, covered, finished, prayed.
• Notice the word family *wise*: wise, wiser, wisest, wisdom.
• Emphasize initial consonant blend sounds: spoke, pleased, prayer (prayed), stone, promise

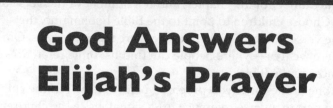

God Answers Elijah's Prayer

Tell about God's answer to Elijah's prayer.
Tell the differences among sorry, thank you, and please prayers.
Read Bible references and find Bible verses.

"The Lord listens when I pray to him."   Psalm 4:3, ICB

Materials
- two 2-liter plastic bottles
- water
- potting soil
- large seeds (bean seeds sprout easily)
- blue construction paper, one sheet per child, prepared before class
- sandpaper or tan construction paper for each child
- green construction paper for each child
- gardening magazines or seed catalogs
- dried weeds
- glue stick
- scissors

❶ Get Ready to Read

Prepare to read "The Lord, He Is God!" by talking about God's power over rain. Recall with the children that God planned for the weather. He provides both sunshine and rain. Sunshine and rain are needed for plants to grow. Animals eat plants and drink water from the earth. People use water and plants.

Before class, cut two 2-liter bottles in half.

Have the children help you prepare the bottles for planting.

Place water in the bottom of one bottle. Turn the top upside down with the cap removed. Fit it snugly into the bottle bottom. Its opening should reach into the water. Fill the top with potting soil and plant the seeds.

Do the same with the other bottle, except do not add water to the bottom bottle. Place both bottles on a sunny window sill.

Of course, the seeds in the bottle with the water will sprout and grow. If the soil you are using is damp, the seeds in the other bottle might sprout, but they will not grow into healthy plants.

Before class, fold in half one piece of blue construction paper for each child. On the top of the left side print, "Elijah Prayed." On the bottom right side print, "God Sent Rain."

Distribute sandpaper and a glue stick to each child. Instruct children to glue the sandpaper to the left side of the paper. They can add dried weeds to this side of the paper.

Distribute green construction paper and seed catalogs or gardening magazines. Children glue the green paper to the right side of the paper and add pictures of plants cut from the magazines.

Today, we will read about a time when it did not rain for three years.

Materials
- *The Young Reader's Bible*, pages 170-175
- photocopies of the Bible story (pages 277-279)
- *The Young Reader's Bible Audio Cassette* or a cassette on which you have recorded unit stories
- cassette player(s), earphones optional
- 8½- by-11-inch white paper
- scissors
- markers
- large sheet of paper
- sand (ground around altars)
- gold glitter (for King Ahab's clothes)
- brown grass (ground around altars)
- red tissue paper (for the fire)
- glue

❷ Read the Bible Story

"The Lord, He is God!"

Before class, fanfold (lengthwise) the 8½- by-11-inch papers with four folds, about 2 inches apart. Prepare patterns of a cookie-cutter figure with hands and feet touching the outside edges of the top section of each fanfolded paper.

Children will cut out the shape, being careful not to cut where the hands and feet meet the outside edge. When the children open up the paper, they should see five paper people connected at the hands and feet.

Print these words and definitions on a large sheet of paper:

Elijah—a man, a prophet who obeyed God

prophet—a person who says what God wants him to say

Baal—a false god, a god who isn't real

King Ahab—a bad king who didn't obey God

priests of Baal—men who taught people to worship a false God Baal

Read the words and talk about the meanings with the children. Clarify any misunderstandings. Tell the children to copy one vocabulary word on each paper-fold figure.

As you listen to the story, decide which people made God happy and those who did not please Him. You can assign two or three listening groups.

Listen

Before you read aloud "The Lord, He is God!" group children into three listening groups. All the children should smile when you read the word *Elijah*. Ask the children in other groups to frown when you read the words *Baal* or *King Ahab*.

Participate

Children read the vocabulary words written on their paper figures. Give each child a copy of the Bible story (pages 277-279). Have them find and circle the vocabulary words in the story.

Tell the children to draw a smile on the paper men who made God happy (Elijah and prophet). Tell the children to draw a frown on the paper men who made God sad (Baal, King Ahab, priests of Baal).

Indicate King Ahab (the man pointing). **Did King Ahab make God happy?** (no)

Show page 171 in the *Young Reader's Bible*. Let children find the picture of Elijah. **Did Elijah make God happy?** (yes)

Show page 173 in the *Young Reader's Bible*. Find the picture of the priests of Baal. **Did these priests who worshiped a false god please the true God?** (no)

Children can glue, sand, glitter, grass and red tissue paper to the Bible story pages to make them three-dimensional.

Before continuing, ask, **What did Elijah pray for?** (Everyone would know that God was God.) **How did God answer Elijah's prayer?** (God burned up the bull, the wood, stones, soil and water. Then, He sent rain. Baal could not do that.)

Read

As children read or listen to the cassette, ask them to think about what Elijah prayed and how God answered Elijah's prayer.

❸ Practice Using a Bible

Using My Bible

Have children separate the Old Testament from the New Testament. Find Genesis and Matthew. Open the Bibles to the center and find Psalms, then chapter four (4:), verse three (3). Choose someone to print the reference on a large sheet of paper. Choose someone to circle the Bible book name (Psalms). Underline the chapter—including the colon (4:). Draw a triangle around the verse (3).

Task Cards
#5. I Kings 18:22
#6. Matthew 28:20; obey
#7. 171; obey
#8. 170

Options
• Some beginning readers will not be able to read large enough numbers to find the page. Simply print I Kings, mark a Bible with a bookmark, and help them match the name with the name in the Bible.
• Readers can help nonreaders. The teacher or reader can demonstrate reading the Bible reference, finding the Bible verse, and reading the verse aloud. Allow nonreaders to place the Bible reference index cards with the correct house.

Materials
• photocopies of page 103
• markers
• index cards
• masking tape or sidewalk chalk

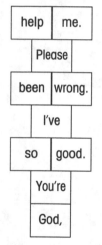

  Teaching at Home

Keep a weather chart. You can keep track of the temperature as well as the amount of rain or snow. Make a rain gauge to measure rainfall amounts.

Reading tips
• Make raindrop-shaped flash cards to review words that rhyme with rain.
• This is a good story to practice sequencing. Mount and display a child's pictures of the Bible story on construction paper. Put the pictures in story order. Print or dictate sentences about the pictures.

Finding Bible Verses

Before class, fill in Task Cards #5-8 (page 111).

Review the method for locating book, chapter, and verse in a Bible. Use the Reference Rhyme on page 32. Pair children and have them complete task cards.

Before class, attach the Bible Story Neighborhood Houses you made to a bulletin board or wall. (See unit page.)

Print *1 Kings 18:22* on half of the index cards.

Print *Matthew 28:20* on the other half of the index cards.

Print *One prophet against 450* on one envelope.

Print *Teach them to obey* on the other envelope.

Attach one envelope to each house shape.

Children pair up. Each pair takes one of each Bible-reference index cards. They work together to look up and read the Bible verse and decide to which house the Bible reference belongs. Put the cards in the correct envelopes.

 # Share What We've Learned

Read 1 Kings 18:22. **"Elijah said, 'I am the only prophet of the Lord here. But there are 450 prophets of Baal,'"** ICB. **Who won this contest? Why?** (Elijah. When Elijah prayed, it rained. Only Elijah served the true God.)

Divide the children into three groups. Assign each group one of the following phrases: 1) "The Lord, . . . 2) . . . He is God!" 3) . . . listens when I pray to him."

Point to group 1 and then alternately point to group 2 or 3. When you point, that groups repeats their phrase. First, they shout; next, they whisper.

Have everyone kneel and repeat the pattern. Then have each group stand up when they say their phrase. If the class enjoys this, have the groups use "high" voices and then "low" voices. They can stand on tiptoe and they can crouch low.

Before class, make a hopscotch court on your floor with masking tape or outside with sidewalk chalk. The court should have two single squares, side-by-side double squares, two single squares, side-by-side double squares, and finish with two single squares. Play hopscotch to help children remember how to talk to God with sorry, thank you, and please prayers. Line up in front of the course.

The first two squares and double squares are praise and thanks squares. Chant, "God, You're so good," as you hop through these.

The next squares are the "sorry" squares. Chant "I've been wrong," as each of you hops through two squares and land on the double.

Chant "Help me," for the final two "please" squares.

Children take turns hopping through the course. Chant as each child hops.

Gather everyone in a circle to talk about what they have been doing and learning. Use the aims for this lesson as an outline for the kinds of questions you ask. (See the unit project "Temple Bulletin Board.")

Were you able to pray every day this week?

Display the "Plan to Pray" (page 103) used last session.

What are three kinds of things to pray? (sorry, thank you, please)

What did Elijah pray? ("Let everyone know that You are God.")

Give each child a new copy of "Plan to Pray." (Some children will want to redo the mazes.

Pray together.

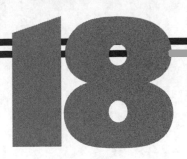

God Directs Jonah

Tell about God's answer to Jonah's prayer.
Report on their plans to pray every day.
Read Bible references and find Bible verses.

"The Lord listens when I pray to him." Psalm 4:3, ICB

❶ Get Ready to Read

Materials
- 18-by-36-inch colorful sturdy paper
- 18-inch pipe cleaners
- 36-inch length of string
- craft items to decorate the fish
- glue
- markers
- hole punch
- stapler

Before class, cut two 18-by-36-inch fish shapes, with extra tabs at the mouth, from sturdy paper for each child. (You can enlarge one of the fish shapes on page 104, adding tabs to the mouth.)

Have the children decorate their fish with markers. To hold the fish's mouth open, fold the tab at the mouth of one fish in, over a pipe cleaner. Staple.

Bend the pipe cleaner to form a circle and twist the ends together. Fold the other mouth tab over the pipe cleaner and staple. Staple the two fish sides together. Children can glue the fish sides together. They do not glue the tail or the mouth. Using a hole punch, make two holes directly across from each other just inside the pipe cleaner. Thread one end of a 36-inch piece of string through each side and tie around the pipe cleaner.

Today, we will learn how God used a fish to direct Jonah to do what was right.

❷ Read the Bible Story

Materials
- *The Young Reader's Bible,* pages 182-187
- photocopies of the two-page Bible story (page 101)
- photocopies of page 104
- *The Young Reader's Bible Audio Cassette* or a cassette on which you have recorded unit stories
- cassette player(s), earphones optional
- twelve-inch string for each fishing pole
- small magnet
- paper clips
- twelve goldfish-shaped crackers for each child
- markers, crayons
- scissors
- four index cards

"A Gulp and a Great City"

Have you ever ridden on a boat? Did you like it? What are some safety rules for riding on a boat? (Wear a life jacket. Do not run or lean over the side.) **Where would you like to travel on a boat?** If few of your children have had such experiences, show a video excerpt from a movie or television show of people in a boat.

Before class, print one vocabulary word on each index card.

Nineveh—a big city *wicked ways*—doing bad things
obey—do as you are told *change*—do something in another way

Show the index card with the word *change* written on it. Print the word *change* in the air, one letter at a time. Invite them to print each letter with you. Follow up in similar way with the word *obey*.

Show the card with the word *obey* written on it. Ask the children to touch their noses. Tell them they have just obeyed by doing what you asked. Give the children simple instructions to obey such as smile, raise your hands to the sky, fold your hands in your lap, or pat your head.

Show the phrase *wicked ways*. Explain that the words *wicked ways* mean doing bad things such as telling lies, taking things that are not yours, or disobeying parents.

Show the city name *Nineveh*. Help the children pronounce *Nineveh*.

Nineveh is a city mentioned in the Bible. Today we will learn more about this city and its people.

Listen

Read "A Gulp and a Great City" with suspense and enthusiasm in your voice and body language.

Give each child a copy of the Bible story (page 101). Instruct the children to find and circle the word *obeyed* every time it appears. Reread to find the instruction Jonah obeyed. Have the class underline, "Go to Nineveh."

Participate

Give each child twelve goldfish-shaped crackers. Tell the children to eat one cracker every time you read the word "Jonah." Read the story.

Did Jonah obey God? (not at first)

How did Jonah obey God? (by going to preach in Nineveh)

How can we obey God? (worshiping God, listening to our parents, telling others about Jesus, showing kindness to everyone, etc.)

Why do you think Jonah should have obeyed God? (God knew what was best for him.)

Could Jonah see what was going to happen on his trip? (no)

Could God see what was going to happen on Jonah's trip? (yes)

Before class, photocopy page 104. Cut apart one set of fish for every two or three children. Place a paper clip on each fish. Make a fishing pole for every two or three children by tying a magnet to the end of a string.

Give each child a copy of page 104. Read the sentences together. Number the fish in story order.

Place the fish on the table. Help children use their magnet to catch the first fish in the story sequence. Continue until all fish are caught and placed in order. Children can then color the fish.

Read

Children color and read page 101 or they can listen to the cassette and follow along with the story from a *Young Reader's Bible* .

❸ Practice Using a Bible

Using My Bible

Have the children work in groups to practice separating the Old Testament pages from the New Testament pages. Use a fish-shaped index card for a bookmark at the page labeled *New Testament*.

Next, help them find the book of Psalms, then chapter 4, then verse 3. Read the key verse together. Have the children place a bookmark in the page for Psalm 4:3.

Print Jonah 1:17 on the large sheet of paper. Choose a volunteer to circle the chapter, including the colon. Ask someone else to draw waves under the verse number.

Locate Jonah 1:17 by turning to the table of contents to find the book name. Let children tell you the page number that the book begins on in their own Bibles.

(These will vary.) Help the children turn to the correct page, then locate the large chapter number, then verse 17. Read, or choose a child to read Jonah 1:17. Have everyone place a bookmark at Jonah 1:17.

Which bookmark shows the book of Psalms? Which bookmark is in the space between the Old and the New Testaments? Talk about how we can easily find Psalms by turning to the middle of a Bible.

Finding Bible Verses

Before class, attach Bible Story Neighborhood Houses to a bulletin board or wall (see unit page).

Print *Jonah 1:17* on half of the index cards.

Print *Psalm 146:2* on the other half of the index cards.

Print *God sends a fish to swallow Jonah* on one envelope.

Print *I will praise the Lord all my life* on the other envelope.

Attach one envelope to each house shape.

Also fill in the Task Cards:

#5. *Psalm 146:2*   #6. *Jonah 1:17; Lord*   #7. *187; Jonah*   #8. *182*

Review the method for locating book, chapter, and verse in a Bible.

Pair up the children and have them complete the task cards.

While the children are still in pairs, work on the Bible Story Neighborhood. Each pair takes one of each Bible-reference index cards. They work together to look up and read the Bible verse and decide to which house the Bible reference belongs. Put the cards in the correct envelopes.

 Share What We've Learned

Gather everyone in a circle to talk about what they have been learning. Use the aims for this lesson as an outline for the kinds of questions you ask. Add cards to the unit temple project.

What do you think Jonah prayed for when he was inside the fish? (Get me out! Save me, etc.) **What kind of prayer is that?** (please)

Why would Jonah say he was sorry? (for running away and not obeying God)

What would Jonah thank God for? (for sending a fish to save him)

What do you think Jonah asked for? (dry land)

How did God answer Jonah's prayer? (First, He sent the fish. Then, He sent the fish to dry land to spit out Jonah.)

Could Jonah have prayed "sorry, thank you," and "please" prayers? (yes)

Did you pray every day this week? What are the three types of prayers we have been talking about? (sorry, thank you, please)

Before class, make a hopscotch court on your floor. Use the hopscotch squares to help children remember how to talk to God with sorry, thank you, and please prayers. See lesson 17, page 90 for game instructions.

Pass out the paper with the hopscotch pattern. Guide the children to print, draw, or tell something to print in each square. Their ideas should match the prayer ideas you talked about.

What can you thank God for? (Print—perhaps more than one word—in the "thank you" squares.)

Think of something you should tell God you are sorry about. (Print or draw in each of the "sorry" squares.)

What are you going to ask God? (Print in the "please" squares.)

Pray together.

Options

- The teacher or reader can demonstrate reading the Bible reference, finding the Bible verse, and then reading the verse aloud. Allow nonreaders to place the Bible reference index cards in the correct house.
- Refer to unit page 84 for ideas for teaching the unit key verse, Psalm 4:3.

Materials

- hopscotch shape drawn on 8½-by-11-inch paper, one per child
- masking tape, painter's tape, or sidewalk chalk
- markers

Options

- Give each child a copy of page 104 and the materials to make a fishing game.
- Weather permitting, take the children outside to fly their Great Fish Kites.

Note

Remove hopscotch tape immediately after class so that it leaves no marks.

 Teaching at Home

Visit a pet store (or aquarium) to look at saltwater fish. Visit a marina or boating supply store. Such trips can be great vocabulary builders.

Reading tip

Rhyming words can be practiced with boat-shaped cards (*coat, float,* etc.) or fish-shaped cards (*fish, dish,* etc.)

19

God Protects Daniel

Tell about God's answer to Daniel's prayer.
Report on their plans to pray every day.
Read Bible references and find Bible verses.

"The Lord listens when I pray to him."   Psalm 4:3, ICB

① Get Ready to Read

Materials
• paper plates
• paper fasteners (brads)
• markers
• scissors

Option
If you work with children with limited writing skills, make a list of things they name that frighten them. Have the children copy one item from the list onto their masks.

Before class, cut out the center from half of the paper plates. Discard the rim. Cut across the middle of the small circles in a sawtooth pattern, forming the mouths. Prepare to read "Daniel for Dinner?" by making lion faces.

Give each child two halves and one whole paper plate. Create a hinged mouth by fastening one side of both circle halves to the large plate with a brad. Children add features to make a lion's face.

Talk with the children about things that frighten them. Have each child open the lion's mouth and print something that frightens them.

Today, we will learn how Daniel trusted God to protect him.

② Read the Bible Story

Materials
• *The Young Reader's Bible,* pages 194-199
• photocopies of the Bible story (pages 280-282)
• *The Young Reader's Bible Audio Cassette* or a cassette on which you have recorded unit stories
• cassette player(s), earphones optional
• small, plain lollipops
• Tootsie Roll Pop lollipops
• two long poster board strips
• a spinner or dice
• lion faces made earlier
• large sheet of paper

"Daniel for Dinner?"

Before class, print each of the following sentences on one strip of poster board: *When I am __jealous__ of someone, I do not like them and I might treat them mean. When I __rescue__ someone, I save them from something bad.*

Hold up a Tootsie Roll Pop lollipop. **Who would like to have this lollipop? Why? What do you like about this Tootsie Roll Pop lollipop?** (The chocolate center; they're sweet, etc.)

Hold up the small lollipop. **Who would rather have this lollipop?** If lollipops were real, a small lollipop might be jealous of a Tootsie Roll Pop, because many children like Tootsie Roll Pops better than plain lollipops. Write *jealous* on the chalkboard.

Allow the children to talk about feeling jealous. Give an example of jealousy you have seen among children you teach. Clarify any misunderstandings and read the definition of the word *jealous* from the long poster board strip.

Name people who might rescue others. (police, firemen) Read the definition of the word *rescue* from the other poster board strips.

Show page 197 in the *Young Reader's Bible.* **What animal is pictured here?** (a lion) **What sound do lions make?** (roar) Let the children tell what they know about lions. Talk about the fact that lions are dangerous to people because lions eat meat, not plants.

What would you do if you saw a lion very close to you? Today, we will read about a man who had to spend a whole night with several lions!

Listen

Read "Daniel for Dinner?" with enthusiasm and expression. Tell the children to roar loudly every time they hear the word *lion* in the story.

Participate

Divide the group into pairs. On the large sheet of paper, make four simple faces: happy, sad, frightened, mean. Give each child a copy of the Bible story (pages 280-282). Children follow along as you reread the story. Stop occasionally, as you read a character's name. Ask each child to draw a face over the name—depending on how they think that person feels at that time.

Play "Teacher May I?" Children line up against the back wall of the room while you stand at the front. The objective for the children is to be the first to touch your hand. However, emphasize that it is most important to do right.

Players may only move toward you by asking, in turn, "Teacher, may I move two steps?" Roll one of the dice and respond according to the list in the narrow column.

Praise children who do not move when they must choose whether or not to pray. Talk about how hard it is to do right—especially if other people are getting ahead. Have children encourage one another to do right.

Play the game until someone reaches you.

Next, have children sit in a circle. Talk about how they felt when it was hard to do right. Ask them what helped them to do right.

Why do you think Daniel decided to pray when he knew he would be thrown in the lions' den? (He loved God; He wanted to obey God, etc.)

Recall things the children named that frighten them. They can hold the lion face and read what they wrote inside the lion's mouth.

Ask the children to roar like lions. Ask them to practice roaring: a happy roar, a sad roar, an angry roar, and a tired roar. Name children's fears. After each one, let children roar a sad, angry, or tired roar. **God protects us from the things we fear.** Let children roar a happy roar. Have them print the words *God protects me from* in front of the fear they listed on the lion face.

Read

Children can take turns reading "Daniel for Dinner?" or telling about the pictures as they listen to the cassette.

❸ Practice Using a Bible

Using My Bible

Have the children open their Bibles to the table of contents. Tell children to look for a Bible book name in the Old Testament that begins with a number. Have them tell you the numbers they find (1 and 2 Samuel, etc.)

Option

Make a lion's mane by cutting strips in a brown grocery bag or piece of heavy paper. Wrap around your face. Wear it as you read the Bible story.

Teacher Responses
• If you roll a one, four, or six, say, "Yes," and the children move forward two steps.
• If you roll a two or five, say, "No," and the children remain where they are.
• If you roll a three, say, "You must choose. If you move, you may not pray the rest of the day. If you choose to pray, you may not move." **Which is right to do?** (pray)

Snacks
Serve animal cookies and juice.

Materials
• Bibles
• two house shapes (see unit page)
• index cards
• two envelopes
• tape
• option: houses and Bible reference cards from lessons 16-18
• two pieces wrapped candy or treat per child
• small Bible reference strips—two matching strips per child

Bible References
Psalm 4:3; Matthew 28:20; 1 Kings 18:22; Jonah 1:17; Psalm 146:2; Daniel 6:11; 1 Thessalonians 5:17

Note
Be aware of dietary restrictions and substitute appropriately.

Options
• Make some references easy matches, different from all the others and easy to find in the Bible (e.g. Genesis 1:1, Psalm 100:1). Give these slips to those whose reading skills are not well developed. Make some matches very similar to the correct ones (e.g. Psalm 3:4; James 1:17), so that better readers must read more carefully.
• If you are working with only one or two children, tape all the reference pairs to pieces of candy and have the child find and match all of the pieces.
• Cut apart the reference (book/chapter and verse) and tape onto two pieces of candy. Challenge children to find matching pieces.

Materials
• photocopies of page 103
• markers

Teaching at Home

A trip to the zoo or to the library for books or videos about lions will expand children's appreciation of God's protection for Daniel.

Reading tips
• Note the change of y to i in words like *spy, spied; hurry, hurried.*
• Review the use of the question mark. Emphasize the change in how we read the three words "Daniel for Dinner?" because of the question mark.

Have them look in the New Testament list. Find a book that begins with a 1 and then the letters Th. Have them point to the name, *Thessalonians.* Read the word for them, emphasizing each syllable (Thes-sa-lo-ni-ans). Have the children clap five times as they repeat the word. Say the reference, 1 Thessalonians 5:17. Have the children repeat after you.
What is the chapter number? (5) **verse number?** (17)
How many books called *Thessalonians* are in the Bible? (2)

Finding Bible verses
Review with the children how to read a Bible reference. Use the Reference Rhyme on page 32. **Locate the book of 1 Thessalonians in the New Testament. Find chapter five and verse 17. Read the verse.**

Before class, print Bible references (narrow column) on strips of paper, two strips with the same reference for each child. Tape one reference slip on each treat of candy. Hide the treats in the room.

Give one Bible reference slip to each child. Tell the class that each person should look for a Bible reference that matches theirs exactly. They should not move candy with a Bible reference that does not match their own. When they find the match, they are to trace over the reference and then find the verse in their Bibles. Next, they bring the traced reference strip and Bible to you, and receive a second piece of candy.

Before class, attach Bible Story Neighborhood Houses to a bulletin board or wall (see unit page).
Print *Daniel 6:11* on half of the index cards.
Print *1 Thessalonians 5:17* on the other half of the index cards.
Print *Men found Daniel praying* on one envelope.
Print *Pray, continually* on the other envelope.
Attach one envelope to each house shape.

Have the children pair up. Each pair takes one of each Bible-reference index cards. They work together to look up and read the Bible verse and decide to which house the Bible reference belongs. Put the cards in the correct envelopes.

 Share What We've Learned

Gather everyone in a circle to talk about what they have been learning. Use the aims for this lesson as an outline for the kinds of questions you ask.

Continue adding to the unit bulletin board project. Children choose something they are proud they accomplished this week. Print the child's name and chosen task on an index card and add it to the bulletin board. Remember to add pictures of any new children.

Ask the children to name times when they like to pray.

Talk about "please" prayers. **What would Daniel say "please" about?** (He needed God's protection.) **What might we ask "please," for?** Have children word a "please" prayer for those who are *happy, sad, frightened, or mean.* (Be patient as children develop a willingness to pray for those who are mean to them.)

Talk about "thank you" prayers. **What could Daniel say "thank You" for?** (God closed the mouths of the lions.) **What can we say "thank You" for?** Work together to print a "Thank You" prayer statement.

Recall the unit key verse, "The Lord listens when I pray to him," Psalm 4:3, ICB. Pray together. Give each child a new copy of page 103. Encourage children to follow the prayer plan.

God Answers Nehemiah's Prayer

Tell about God's answer to Nehemiah's prayer.
Report on their plan to pray every day.
Read Bible references and find Bible verses.

"The Lord listens when I pray to him."   Psalm 4:3, ICB

❶ Get Ready to Read

Prepare to read "Remember and Obey" by building a wall. Give each child a copy of page 105 and markers. Have the children color the figures. As they work ask, **What do you think these people are doing?** (carrying rocks; building a wall; praying; looking for something) **Why do you think they would need to build a wall?** (for protection) **Why do you think the person is praying?** (sorry, thank you, please)

Children cut out the figures. Younger children can make smooth cuts around small details. Each child folds a piece of construction paper in half. Then demonstrate how to open it so that half lays flat on the table, and the other half stands straight up and forms a wall.

Children fold back tabs on the fold lines and tape the tabs onto the construction paper forming a pop-up picture.

Today we will learn about how God answered Nehemiah's prayer to build a wall to protect his city.

Materials
• photocopies of page 105
• scissors
• construction paper
• markers
• clear tape

❷ Read the Bible Story

"Remember and Obey"

Encourage children to talk about fences and walls. **Have you ever climbed on a fence or wall? Why do we build fences and walls? What would your home be like if the inside had no walls?**

The Bible story is about building a very important wall. Long ago, all cities had walls to protect the people from their enemies and wild animals.

Before class, print one vocabulary word on each of the seven index cards. Tape the index cards onto building blocks.

Jews—people of Israel who honored God's laws
Jerusalem—the most important city in Israel
afraid—scared
enemies—people who did not want the Jews to build the wall
laws—the Ten Commandments
remember—think about what God has done

Materials
• *The Young Reader's Bible,* pages 206-211
• photocopies of the two-page Bible story (page 102)
• *The Young Reader's Bible Audio Cassette* or a cassette on which you have recorded unit stories
• cassette player(s), earphones optional
• seven large building blocks
• dice
• markers
• seven large index cards

obey—do what God wants you to do

Recall that God's chosen people are called the Jews. Put the block with the word, *Jew*, on the table.

Tell them the city the people wanted to live in was Jerusalem. Place the *Jerusalem* name block on the table. Continue to build a wall with the vocabulary blocks, explaining the meaning of each word as you go.

Listen

With washable marker, draw a smile on one of your thumbs and a frown on the other. Have the children do the same with their thumbs. Help them as needed. Tell the children to give you a happy thumbs up when Nehemiah is happy and a sad thumbs down when he is sad.

Read aloud "Remember and Obey" from the *Young Reader's Bible*.

Participate

Talk about things that Nehemiah could pray "thank You" to God for. As you read the story again, have the children fold their hands as if to pray whenever they hear something for which Nehemiah could pray. (Nehemiah worked for the king. Nehemiah's brother visited him and reported the problems. Nehemiah knew God and could talk to Him. The king noticed Nehemiah's sadness, etc.)

Give each child a copy of the Bible story excerpt (page 102). **What kind of prayer is Nehemiah praying?** (please) Have children take turns pretending that they are Nehemiah. **What would their "sorry" prayer be about? What would their "thank you" prayer be about?**

Read

Children can read or listen to the cassette and color their Bible story pages.

❸ Practice Using a Bible

Using My Bible

Before class, copy one Bible reference (from the narrow column) on each index card. Group two or three children so that ability levels are relatively equal among the teams. Provide one set of cards for every group.

Each group of two or three children draws one index card, reads the Bible reference aloud, and locates the verse in a Bible. When they find it, they run to a designated area, arms linked with their partner(s), and form a wall with other groups already there.

Time the event from start to the last pair's arrival at the wall. Collect the cards and have another random drawing and race to build again. Encourage the children to beat their own collective time.

In small classes, find each reference and build by putting the reference cards on a wall.

Before class, place ten craft sticks side by side forming a solid square. Tape together along the top and bottom edges. Make enough squares so that you can give two squares to each child.

Print "Psalm 18:1" and "Mark 1:35" on the board. Direct the children to copy one Bible reference onto the taped side of each square—one letter or number per stick. Leave a blank stick for space between the book and the chapter number. (Mark 1:35 will have one leftover stick.)

Snacks
Fig bars will make a good building-block snack. Offer several simple snacks today to have a small celebration feast.

Materials
- Bibles
- two house shapes (see unit page 82)
- two envelopes
- stopwatch
- index cards
- wooden craft sticks, twenty per child
- masking tape
- markers
- index cards
- option: houses and index cards prepared for lessons 16-19

Bible references
Psalm 4:3
2 Timothy 3:16
Matthew 28:20
1 Kings 18:23
Jonah 1:17
Psalm 146:2
Daniel 6:11
1 Thessalonians 5:17
Psalm 18:1
Mark 1:35

Look up each verse and read it aloud. Direct the children to draw a picture of each verse on the untaped side of their squares. Show the children how to untape the squares.

Using one child's sticks as an example, mix up the craft sticks. Each child will have two 10-piece puzzles. One side of the puzzle forms a picture and the other a reference.

Encourage the children to take apart and put their puzzles together. Leave the Bible references written on the board to assist them. Put the puzzles in envelopes to take home and use.

Finding Bible Verses

Before class, attach Bible Story Neighborhood Houses to a bulletin board or wall (see unit page).

Print *Psalm 18:1* on half of the index cards.

Print *Mark 1:35* on the other half of the index cards.

Print *I love You, Lord* on one envelope.

Print *Jesus went and prayed* on the other envelope.

Attach one envelope to each house shape.

Children pair up. Each pair takes one of each Bible-reference index cards. They work together to look up and read the Bible verse. They then put the cards in the correct envelopes—the house for that Bible reference.

4 Share What We've Learned

Gather everyone in a circle to talk about what they have been learning. Use both the unit and the lesson aims to guide the questions you ask. Focus on the Bible knowledge and skills they have attained. Celebrate their achievements!

Complete the Temple Bulletin Board begun in lesson 16. Each child chooses a task learned or accomplished in the lesson. Print the child's name and chosen task on an index card. The child adds the card to the bulletin board. Add a wall around the temple. Use the objects on the bulletin board to review the lessons in unit four.

We obey God who answers prayer. Who obeyed God and built the temple? (Solomon) **How did God answer his prayer?** (God gave Solomon wisdom.)

Continue until all stories are reviewed.

Ask children to name three types of prayer you have been talking about (sorry, thank you, please). Label three building blocks, one type of prayer on each. Then stack the blocks. Tell the children that Nehemiah's wall was built one block at a time. But emphasize that the wall was first built with prayer.

Choose one building block. Label the six sides of the block as you name three kinds of prayer and give examples of each.

Talk about how we can say thanks to God. Name Bible people who said, "Thank You." Do the same with "sorry" and "please."

Let children take turns rolling the prayer block. When a block stops rolling, the child gives an example of the type of prayer named by the word or example on top of the block. For example, Jonah was *sorry* when he ran away from God.

Discuss prayer requests and pray together. Give each child a new copy of page 103. Children can fill in ideas about ways to pray sorry, thank you, and please prayers during the coming week.

Option

For children whose skills are very limited, place the cards in a Bible at the correct page. Children find the verse.

Materials
• markers
• three building blocks used earlier
• photocopies of page 103

 Teaching at Home

List jobs to be done. Estimate how many minutes, hours, or days it might take to finish the job. Keep track of the progress. You could practice making bar graph charts.

Reading tips
• Practice reading and writing some number words (to fifty-two).
• List opposites: *sad, happy; afraid, brave; broken, repaired.*
• Make up riddles to review proper names of people and places: *Nehemiah, Jew, Persia, Jerusalem, God, Moses, Miriam, Aaron.*

Solomon asked for only one thing.

"I need wisdom to be a good king," he said.

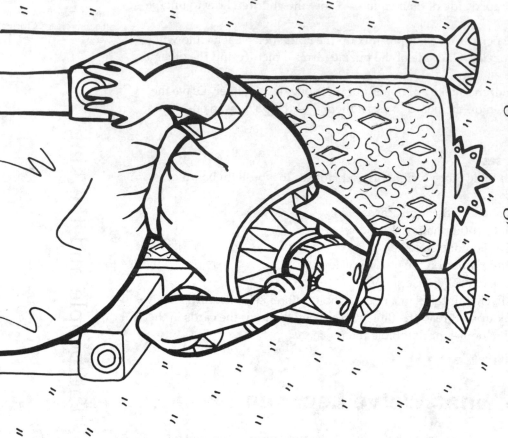

God was pleased with Solomon's prayer.

He made Solomon the wisest man who ever lived.

People from all nations came to listen to King Solomon.

100

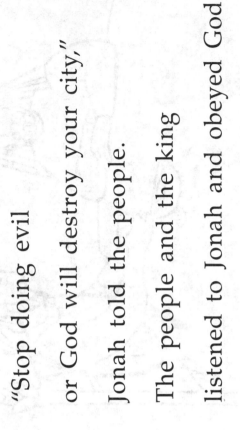
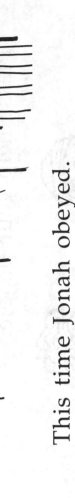

This time Jonah obeyed.

"Stop doing evil

or God will destroy your city,"

Jonah told the people.

The people and the king

listened to Jonah and obeyed God.

And God saved their city.

Inside the fish, Jonah prayed.

After three days, God told the fish

to spit Jonah out onto the land.

"Go to Nineveh," God told Jonah.

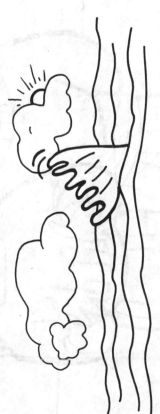

Nehemiah's brother came to visit.

"The city of Jerusalem
has broken walls
and burned gates," he said.

"The people are sad and afraid."

"Please, God," prayed Nehemiah.
"Please help your people."

"Why are you so sad?"
the king asked Nehemiah.

"My city has broken walls
and burned gates," said Nehemiah.

"The people are sad and afraid."

"You may go and help them,"
said the king.

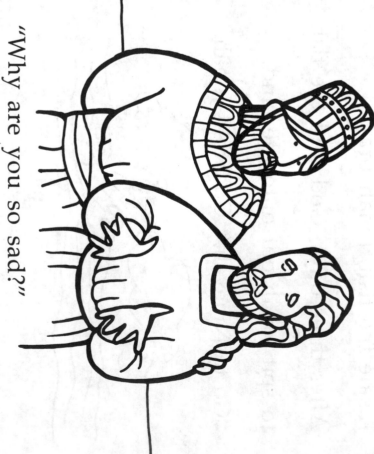

Plans to Pray

Follow each maze path. Write something to pray.

1

God, I thank You because

2

God, I am sorry because

3

God, please help

I will talk to God every day.

Fishing for Facts

What happened first? What happened last?
Number all the fish in story order.

1 God said, "Go!"

Jonah prayed.
The fish spit him out.

Jonah said,
"No!"

A great fish
swallowed
Jonah.

God sent
a storm.

6 Jonah said,
"Yes!"

Jonah obeyed God.

Pop-Up Wall

construction paper

Photocopy page for each child. Children color, cut out, fold and tape each piece to folded construction paper.

fold

fold

God's people rebuilt the wall.

fold

fold

Old Testament Celebration

Remember Old Testament stories.
Practice finding verses in the Old Testament.
Recognize Old Testament vocabulary words.

Materials
- streamers and tape
- twelve balloons
- construction paper
- photocopies of activity charts, page 109
- markers
- paper punch
- yarn, twine, or curling ribbon
- stickers (optional)

Option
Bible costumes for everyone to wear (sheets or towels with strips of cloth to hold them in place)

Get Ready to Celebrate

Before class, prepare twelve balloons by printing one letter on each: **O-L-D T-E-S-T-A-M-E-N-T**. Also, fold colored construction paper in half widthwise and staple along the sides. Print each child's name at the top. Glue an activity chart cut from a photocopy of page 109 to the folded construction paper. Punch holes near the top corners of each paper. Tie the ends of a 32-inch piece of yarn, twine, or curling ribbon to both holes.

Today's lesson celebrates the completion of a study of Old Testament stories. To encourage a festive atmosphere, decorate the room. The fun setting can be maintained and the lesson aims will be accomplished using activity tables. You will need three tables or areas to offer three activities each. You will need at least one adult or teen helper to assist at each table. Children can choose the order in which they will do the table activities.

Divide into three groups. Follow this three-step lesson plan, allowing twenty minutes for each step:

1 Children choose a table at which to begin (blue, red, yellow). They complete their choice of three activities offered at that table. The class gathers for Group Time 1.

2 Next, children complete their choice of activities at a different table. The class gathers for Group Time 2.

3 Children complete their choice of activities at their last table. The class gathers for Group Time 3.

Remember What We've Learned

Can you guess why we have balloons and streamers in our room today? (We're having a party.) **Who can read what the letters on the balloons spell?** (Old Testament)

We learned that the Bible is divided into two parts, the Old Testament and the New Testament. We've been reading stories from the first part of the Bible, the Old Testament, so we're having a party to celebrate.

Each of you will get to choose from nine fun activities. You can wear this small activity chart. When you complete an activity, we'll mark that box (or give you a sticker for it). Each time you complete the activities at a table, our class will gather as a group for some fun.

Snacks
Serve party cupcakes and ice cream or frosted muffins and frozen yogurt. See Group Time 2.

A–Make Old Testament stick pictures and put them in Bible order.

Before class, print these instructions on blue construction paper: *Color the Bible pictures and glue them onto craft sticks to make puppets. Trace the Bible names. Place the pictures on the time line in order.*

Also, cut apart the pictures from the photocopies. Each child will need one set of pictures. Those with good cutting skills can cut their own.

Next, print Bible names on the shelf paper in this order: *Adam, Noah, Abraham, Joseph, Moses, Ruth, David, Daniel.* If you wish, you can print the Bible names in order on each child's envelope (four names on each side).

In class, children color the stick puppets. Then, have them match the stick-puppet names with the names on the shelf-paper time line. When finished, let the children store the puppets in their envelopes. They can practice putting the names in Bible order using the list you wrote on the envelope.

B–Match Bible people and stories.

Before class, print these instructions on blue construction paper: *Place each word balloon so that it matches a Bible person.*

Also, print each of the following clues on a word balloon cut from brightly colored paper: *I was the first man God created. • I believed God when He said there would be a flood. • God promised me a very large family. • God helped me know the meaning of Pharaoh's dreams. • I was a baby in a basket. Later, God helped me rescue my people. • I promised to stay with my mother-in-law, Naomi. • When I grew up, I became a king. • I prayed even when it was against the law.*

If children need help, read the word balloon clues aloud and talk about them.

C–Match Bible people to the pictures in a *Young Reader's Bible.*

Before class, copy these instructions on blue construction paper: *Place each Bible person bookmark in The Young Reader's Bible with the story it matches.* Also, cut strips of colored paper to make bookmarks and cut out sets of Bible people from the photocopies of page 109. Help them glue people cutouts to bookmarks.

D–Spin arrows and find a verse.

Before class, prepare a poster. Draw three large circles (trace a dinner plate). Divide two circles into six segments. Put one number (1 – 6) on the chapter circle. Choose six numbers (1 – 10) to print on the verse circle. Divide the other circle in half. Put one Bible book name (Genesis, Psalms) in each segment of the circle. Cut arrows from poster board. Label them: *book, chapter, verse.* Attach the appropriate arrow to the center of each circle.

Also, print these instructions on red construction paper: *Spin each arrow. Find a book, chapter, and verse to look up in your Bible. Say the reference.*

In class, read the directions aloud and show how to spin the arrows. Read the book, chapter, and verse the arrows point to. Explain that this is the reference to find in the Bible. Review using the Reference Rhyme (page 32).

If the children need more help, open the Bible to the page on which the reference is found. Let the children point to the verse.

E–Toss the dice and find a verse.

Before class, print these instructions on red construction paper: *Toss the dice. Look up that chapter and verse in Genesis. Say the reference.*

In class, helpers can give this example: "If you roll a two and a six, look up Genesis chapter 2, verse 6 or chapter 6, verse 2."

If the children need help, read the directions aloud and show how to find Genesis and the chapter. Let the child find the verse.

Blue Table
Review Old Testament stories. (A, B, C)

Materials
- blue construction paper
- photocopies of page 109
- scissors
- craft sticks
- glue stick
- shelf paper for a time line
- envelopes

Materials
- blue construction paper
- brightly colored paper for word balloons
- photocopies of page 109
- *The Young Reader's Bible*

Materials
- blue construction paper
- photocopies of page 109
- strips of colored paper
- markers
- *The Young Reader's Bible*

Red Table
Locate Old Testament verses. (D, E, F)

Materials
- poster board
- paper fasteners (brads)
- red construction paper
- Bible
- photocopies of page 32

Materials
- red construction paper
- a pair of dice
- Bible

Materials
• red construction paper
• dominoes (or index cards drawn
  to look like dominoes) in a bag
• Bible

F–Count domino dots and find a verse.

Before class, print these instructions on a sheet of red construction paper: *Pull a domino out of the bag. Find the chapter and verse in Psalms. Say the reference.*

In class, helpers can use this example: "If your domino has five dots and three dots, you would look up Psalm 3:5 or 5:3."

If the children need help, read the directions aloud, give the example and show how to find Psalms and the chapter. Let the child find the verse.

Yellow Table

Recognize vocabulary.
(G, H, I)

Materials
• yellow construction paper
• slips of white paper
• hat
• Scrabble word-game tiles, alphabet macaroni or cereal, or letters
  written on small index cards cut
  in fourths

G–Match letters to make Bible words.

Before class, print these instructions on yellow construction paper: *Pull a word out of the hat. Find letters to make each word.*

Also, on each slip of white paper, print one Old Testament vocabulary word (from the lists on the unit pages). Put the papers in a hat.

After the children make the word using the matching letters, guide the conversation about the meanings of the words.

Materials
• yellow construction paper
• cassette player with earphones
• cassette tape on which you have
  recorded a message
• pencil and paper

H–Listen to a riddle and write Bible word.

Before class, prepare a cassette tape. (Making a backup would be wise.) Read these instructions onto the cassette:

"Here's a riddle for you. I'm a word that means ___ . *(Tell the meaning of a vocabulary word.)* What word am I? Print your guess. *(Pause.)* I'll give you a hint. *(Spell the word slowly.)* Please turn off the tape player now."

Repeat with enough vocabulary words so that children in each group can each listen for one definition.

Print these instructions on the yellow construction paper: *Listen to the riddle and print the word.* Copy the list of words on construction paper as well.

In class, each child will listen to one riddle. Help children put on earphones and turn on the tape. When they have printed a word, turn off the tape and praise them. If they can't print the word that was spelled, ask them what the word was and print it for them. Let them copy or trace the letters you wrote.

Materials
• yellow construction paper
• small snack crackers
• a can of aerosol cheese
• paper plates
• pen
• list of Old Testament vocabulary
  words (for teacher or helper
  use)

I–Snack on a Bible Word.

Before class, print these instructions on the yellow construction paper: *Unscramble the crackers to find one of your Bible words.*

In class, print letters of an Old Testament vocabulary word with aerosol cheese on individual crackers. Move the crackers out of order and let the children put them back in order. If they need help, tell them the word and let them try to put the crackers in order. If they can't figure out the order, print the word on the paper plate so they can match the crackers to printed letters. Let them eat the crackers.

Group Time Celebrations

1 Stick Puppet Stories
Let the children take turns telling Old Testament stories with stick puppets or have them hold up the puppets while you read from a *Young Reader's Bible*.

2 Snack
Serve party cupcakes and ice cream or frosted muffins and frozen yogurt. Top each cupcake or muffin with a candy decoration letter or one written with frosting to spell O-L-D T-E-S-T-A-M-E-N-T.

3 Singing
Sing songs the children have especially enjoyed.

Adam · Noah · Abraham · Joseph

Moses · Ruth · David · Daniel

Photocopy one activity card for each child, cut out, outline with blue, red, and yellow markers, and glue to construction paper. Add a ribbon so the card will hang around the child's neck.

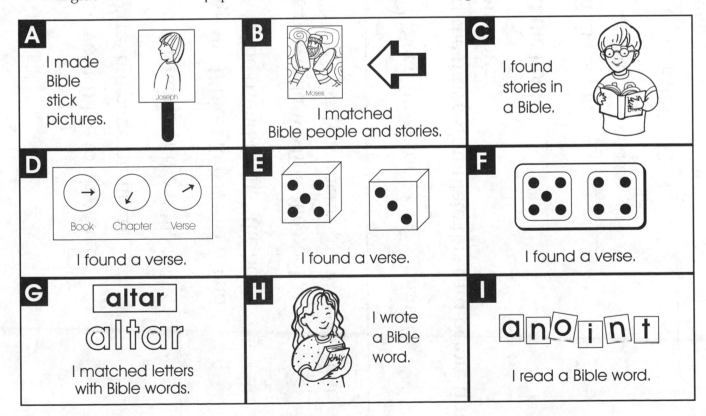

A I made Bible stick pictures.

B I matched Bible people and stories.

C I found stories in a Bible.

D Book Chapter Verse
I found a verse.

E I found a verse.

F I found a verse.

G altar
altar
I matched letters with Bible words.

H I wrote a Bible word.

I anoint
I read a Bible word.

1

Copy this Bible book name on every line.

Where can we find the book, _____ ?

Circle: Old Testament   New Testament

Find _____ in your Bible.

2

Open your Bible to any page.
Write the page number. _____

Copy the name of the Bible book. _____

Close the Bible. Give it to a friend.
Ask the friend to find the book.

Where would we find the book, _____ ?
Circle: Old Testament   New Testament

3

Find _____ in the table of contents.

Write the number of the first page. _____

Write the number of the last page. _____

Where can we find the book, _____ ?

Circle: Old Testament   New Testament

4

Set a timer for _____ minutes.

Start the timer. Complete this card before time
runs out.

Find the book, _____ .

Find the book,
chapter _____ , verse _____ .

Close your Bible. Find _____
again.

Photocopy Task Cards. Cut apart. After you fill in a copy, cover it with clear adhesive plastic. Save for skill-building practice.

5

Copy this Bible reference. ______________

Find the verse in your Bible.

Draw or tell about it.

6

Copy this Bible reference. ______________

Find ______________ in your Bible.

Read the verse. Find the word ______________ .

Draw or tell about it.

7

Find page _______ in *The Young Reader's Bible.*

Look at the picture.

Find ________________ .

Read about it in the story .

Draw or tell about it.

8

Find page _______ in *The Young Reader's Bible.*

Read the story with a friend.

Act out the story together.

We Worship Jesus Because He Is the Son of God

Key Verse

"Jesus is the Son of God."   1 John 4:15, NIV

Unit Vocabulary

cousin
different
engaged
follow
hurry
impossible
innkeeper
killed
King of the Jews
kingdom
Passover Feast
please
praise
prophet
quietly
servant
shepherds
slavery
stable
tenderly
thought
warning
wrapped

Unit Aims

By the end of the unit, learners will be able to
• tell Bible stories of Jesus' childhood.
• feel confident in finding verses in a Bible and reading *The Young Reader's Bible*.
• locate books, chapters and verses in their own Bibles.
• read (at their level) stories from *The Young Reader's Bible*.
• worship Jesus because He is the Son of God.

Unit Projects

Lights, Camera, Action

A committee can be lots of help as you work with the children on this unit-long video or photo project. Committee members can gather props (listed in each lesson) and help plan and carry out the project during class. At the end of the unit, show the video at a family outreach or fellowship gathering.

Recruit someone to operate a video camera or take photographs. Recruit several helpers to assist children with their Bible costumes and to guide them as they act out their parts. Check each lesson for the props that they need. Encourage adults to interact with the children, helping them identify and express emotions.

It would be best to begin by reading the story aloud yourself so that you can pace your reading to children's actions. Later, play the story from *The Young Reader's Bible Audio Cassette* to make the production sound professional.

Look, Listen, and Read

When children become familiar with the stories, play a searching game. Fast forward and rewind the cassette at random and play one or two sentence segments. Challenge the children to find the page in *The Young Reader's Bible* from which the sentences come. Make this a time for children to enjoy the story and become familiar with the Bible story book.

	The Singing Bible (3 tapes)	Kids on the Rock (More Songs)	Follow the Leader (The Donut Man)	I'm a Helper (The Donut Man)	Good News (The Donut Man)
Lesson 22	Starry Sky				
Lesson 23	Starry Sky				
Lesson 24	Starry Sky				
Lesson 25					
Lesson 26					
Key Verse		Christmas Angels			
Unit Theme			We Have Come to Glorify		
All Lessons	The Books We Love the Best The Bible Book Is True	God's Word Is for Me			

Note: The Donut Man *Christmas* tape would be useful for this unit.
The Singing Bible (3 tapes), ©1993 by Lightwave Publishing, Inc. Manufactured and distributed by Word Publishing, Dallas, TX 75234
Kids on the Rock! More Songs, ©1994 Gospel Light, Ventura CA 93006
The Donut Man (3 tapes): *Follow the Leader*, ©1990; *I'm a Helper*, ©1991; *Good News*, ©1991; Integrity Music, Inc., P.O. Box 16813 Mobile, AL 36616

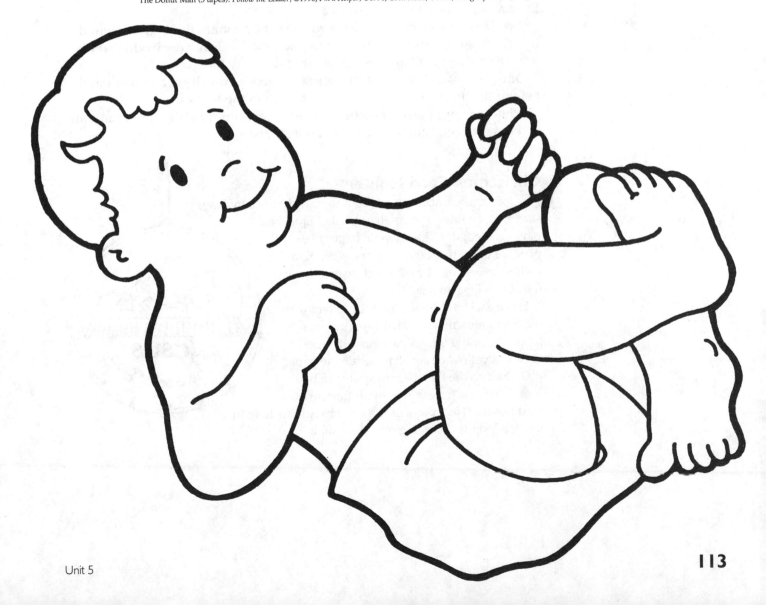

Key Verse Activities

Jesus is the Son of God.
1 John 4:15, NIV

Materials
- strips of yellow paper
- a pen
- tape

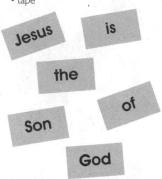

Materials
- four full 2-liter bottles
- four index cards
- tape
- small artificial wreaths or Styrofoam rings that will fit over a bottle
- cups

Materials
- paper plates
- scissors
- stapler
- paper punch
- yellow paper
- baby Jesus pattern, page 113
- tan cardstock
- glue stick
- pencil
- red and green markers
- ribbon or yarn scraps for hanging

Manger Hay Game

Before class, print one word of the memory verse on each strip of yellow paper. Make a complete set of strips for each student. Hide the strips around the room (tape them under chairs, behind chair legs, on the chalk tray, and so on). Print the memory verse on the chalkboard.

Ask the class, **What is a manger?** (a box for an animal's food) **The manger Jesus slept in may have been filled with soft yellow hay that animals eat. I've hidden pretend hay** (strips of yellow paper) **around the room that has the words of your memory verse on it. Let's have a race to see who can find six pieces of hay to complete the words of the memory verse in order. To stay in the game, you must never be holding more than six pieces of "hay." Re-hide unneeded pieces, or trade with someone to complete your verse.**

Wreath Toss Game

Before class, print one of the following phrases on each of the index cards: "Jesus is," "the son," "of God," "1 John 4:15." Tape the index cards to the bottles. Put a masking tape line on the floor.

Ask, **Do you know why we have wreaths at Christmas time? They remind us that God's love is like a circle; it never ends. God so loved the world that He sent His only Son. Who does our memory verse say that is?** (Jesus.)

Once each of you can recite the memory verse, you will get a turn to stand behind the line and throw a wreath onto each of the bottles.

Whoever rings the most bottles can help serve cups of soda. Pour from a liter that has not been knocked down or beware of the foam!

Christmas Card Holder

Before class, trace and cut from cardstock the baby Jesus shape. Cut some paper plates in half. Staple one paper plate half to each whole paper plate. With pencil, lightly print the memory verse. Cut the yellow paper into 4-by-7½-inch rectangles and fold them lengthwise.

Have each child trace over the letters with red and green markers. Let them cut one long side of the folded paper into fringes. Glue the yellow paper strip inside the paper plate half so the fringe shows. Glue in baby Jesus. Punch a hole in the top of the Christmas card holder. Tie a piece of ribbon through the hole to make a loop for hanging on a doorknob.

Mary Believes God's Message

22

Tell how Mary learned that Jesus is the Son of God.
Worship Jesus in a song.
Find and read in the Bible that Jesus is the Son of God.

"Jesus is the Son of God."   1 John 4:15, NIV

① Get Ready to Read

Children act out the story and make the first segment of a unit-long video.

Read the story from pages 226-231 of the *Young Reader's Bible*. Look at the pictures and talk about the story. **How do you think Mary felt when the angel came? When she heard the angel's news? How do you think the angel felt about his news?** List the emotions children name.

Tell the children they will make a video of the story. Ask children to volunteer for the parts of Mary, Joseph, and the angel Gabriel. Other children can be director (helps decide where characters stand and prompts them with their lines), announcer (announces the title of the story on camera), narrator (choose a good reader), or prop directors (help put on costumes and decide how props are to be arranged).

When all jobs are assigned, practice acting out the story. Encourage children to use the list of emotions made earlier to help them be creative in their actions. To simplify the production, have a narrator read all speaking parts. Practice and then use the video camera to film the children acting out the story.

Materials
- *The Young Reader's Bible*
- costumes and props (towels tied on with cloth strips for head coverings, sandals, bathrobes, white robe or sheet for angel, blanket, baskets, clay pots)
- video camera and blank tape

Option
If you cannot locate a video camera, take photos using an instant camera. If you are working with only two or three children, use a nativity set. Allow the children to create the different scenes of the stories. Take pictures of each scene. Mount the pictures on poster board or in a scrapbook. Help the children choose a sentence or two from the Bible story to print beneath each picture.

② Read the Bible story

"Mary Meets an Angel"
Have you ever heard some good news? What was it? How did you feel? What did you do? Tell about hearing some good news. Encourage children to share. Perhaps some have heard good news about a new baby brother or sister, a visit from grandma or grandpa, a special vacation, or someone who had been sick getting better. Talk about their reaction to the news. Explain that someone got some very good news in today's story.

Show the pictures from pages 226-231. Identify Joseph, Mary, and the angel. **What do you think the angel is telling Mary?**

Before class, print the following names on poster board strips: *Mary* (in red marker), *Joseph* (in blue marker), *angel Gabriel* (in green marker).

Display the names. **These are the people in today's story.** Read the names together. Have a child point to each name as the children say them with you.

Materials
- *The Young Reader's Bible*, pages 226-231
- photocopies of the two-page Bible story (page 130)
- *The Young Reader's Bible Audio Cassette* or a cassette on which you have recorded unit stories
- cassette player(s), earphones optional
- poster board
- red, blue, and green crayons, markers or colored pencils

Listen

Read the story aloud to the children. Ask them to listen for the names listed on the poster board strips.

What did the angel tell Mary? (You will have a baby boy.) **What would Mary name her baby boy?** (Jesus) **What would be special about baby Jesus?** (He is the Son of God.)

Participate

Divide the children into two groups. One group will be Mary. The other group will be the angel. The angel group will wave and say, "Hello, Mary!" every time they hear their name. The Mary group will bow their heads and say, "I love God!" every time they hear their name. Call out the names several times as the groups practice their actions. Then read the story again. Pause to allow the groups to do their actions at the appropriate times.

Read

Give each child a copy of the Bible story excerpt (page 130). Display the poster board strips with the names *Mary, Joseph,* and *angel Gabriel.* Ask children to use red, blue, and green crayons or pencils to circle the names as they find them in the story. They should circle Mary's name in red, Joseph's in blue, and Gabriel's in green. Children may also color the Bible-story pictures. As they work, they can listen to the cassette. Even children who can't read every word can look at the pictures and tell the story.

❸ Practice Using a Bible

Using My Bible

Distribute the bookmarks from page 133.

Children cut out the bookmark and choose pictures to cut, color, and glue onto the blank back of the bookmark to decorate it. Help primaries fold the bookmark back along the dotted line and glue it together.

Place all the completed bookmarks on the sticky side of a large sheet of clear adhesive. Carefully place another sheet of clear adhesive on top of the bookmarks, sticky side down. Smooth the two sheets together. Cut apart the bookmarks.

Allow children to trim the plastic around the edges of their bookmarks. If you wish, use a paper punch to make a hole in the top of each bookmark and help children loop yarn through the hole to make a tassel.

Have children put their bookmarks in their Bibles at the first page of the New Testament. **Hold the part of your Bible that is the Old Testament. Now hold the part of your Bible that is the New Testament. The New Testament tells us about Someone whom people worshiped and obeyed. Whom did people worship and obey?** (Jesus, God's Son.)

In the New Testament, we can read about how Jesus came to earth. The New Testament also tells how people worshiped and obeyed God and His Son, Jesus, and how the church told others about Jesus.

Finding Bible Verses

Remind (or ask) them how to find the Old Testament (open to front; look for Genesis and mark it with the bookmark). Find Psalms and move the bookmark (open to middle of Bible). Find the New Testament and move the bookmark.

Option

Play a game to help children review the story. Print and show the following words: *big news, Son of God, loved God, afraid, Jesus.* Group children in pairs, including at least one confident reader in each pair.

Point to and call out one word or phrase at a time from the story. Have the reader pairs find it in the story. As soon as each pair has found the word or phrase, they should stand. When all children are standing, the sentence in which the word is found can be read aloud.

Snacks

Serve fresh fruit and bite-sized pieces of angel food cake.

Materials

• *The Young Reader's Bible*
• Bible for each child
• photocopies of pages 32, 130, 133
• photocopies of Task Card #1 (page 110)
• markers or colored pencils
• index cards
• glue stick
• scissors
• clear adhesive plastic

Next, give each child a copy of Task Card #1. Let them copy the Bible book name, *1 John*, and mark Old or New Testament.

Print 1 John 4:15 on a large sheet of paper. Use the Reference Rhyme (page 32) to recall how to find Bible verses. Find 1 John 4:15 in their Bibles. Read the verse aloud together.

What does the Bible tells us about Jesus? (Jesus is the Son of God.)

Give each group of two or three children a Bible and a copy of the Bible story excerpt (page 130). Use the Reference Rhyme to find Luke 1:31-37 in their Bibles.

Before class, print these words on index cards to give to each small group of children: *Jesus, Son of God, great, angel, kingdom, impossible, Holy Spirit.* Assign each group one or two of the words to find in both the *Young Reader's Bible* and a Bible.

When all groups have found all their words, choose volunteers to read from both the story and the Bible the sentences in which the words are used. Help children to conclude that the stories in the *Young Reader's Bible* tell about real events from the Bible.

Explain that the unit key verse also tells why Jesus is special. Have children open a Bible to the table of contents. Work together to find the books with the name John. Find first, second, and third John. Turn to 1 John 4:15. (Suggest that children begin near the end of the Bible.) **Read the verse to find out why Jesus is special.** (Jesus is the Son of God.)

4 Share What We've Learned

Gather everyone in a circle to talk about what they have been doing and learning. Use the aims for this lesson as an outline for the kinds of questions you ask.

What special thing did the angel Gabriel tell about Jesus? (He is the Son of God.) **I'm so glad that Jesus is the special Son of God! Let's sing a song to worship Jesus.** Make this singing time a fun time of celebration for your children.

Sing the following words and do motions to the tune of "Jingle Bells."

We love You. We love You, *(Cross arms and hug self.)*
Jesus, Son of God. *(Raise hands in air, look upward.)*
Oh what fun it is to worship Jesus, Son of God. *(Clap hands, jump up and down.)*
We love You. We love You, *(Cross arms and hug self.)*
Jesus, Son of God. *(Raise hands in air, look upward.)*
Oh what fun it is to worship Jesus, Son of God. *(Clap hands, jump up and down.)*

If you have time, allow children to choose favorite familiar tunes and sing "Jesus is the Son of God" or "We will worship Jesus" to the tunes. Some suggestions are: "Three Blind Mice," "Old Mac Donald," "London Bridge."

What new words did you learn today? What did you learn about Mary? about Jesus? about the angel? Allow children to share and express growing confidence in their developing skills and knowledge.

If children enjoyed the game played during the Bible story, repeat it now, or allow children to "read" the Bible story again from the *Young Reader's Bible*. Give children the copies of reproducible page 130 if they were not used earlier. Allow children to color the pictures and read the words.

Options
• If you have less-advanced readers, work together as a group. Ask the children to find in a Bible only the first four words listed—*Jesus, Son of God, great, angel*. When the children have pointed to a word, you read the sentence aloud for them as they follow along.
• Refer to unit page 114 for a choice of ideas for teaching the unit key verse.

Materials
• photocopies of the two-page Bible story (page 130)
• crayons or markers

Teaching at Home

Recruit family and friends to make your own video project.

Reading tip
Review using capital letters on people's names and names of cities (proper nouns): *Mary, Joseph, Lord, Nazareth, Gabriel, God, Jesus, Holy Spirit.*

Jesus Is Born in Bethlehem

Tell how the special Son of God was born.
Worship Jesus with a picture or a sentence.
Read Bible references and find Bible verses.

"Jesus is the Son of God." I John 4:15, NIV

Materials
- *The Young Reader's Bible* or photocopies of the Bible story (pages 283-285)
- costumes and props (towels tied on with cloth strips for head coverings, sandals, bathrobes, doll wrapped in blanket, box filled with straw)
- video camera and video tape used last session

Option
If you are making a scrapbook or poster board scene of photographs, continue the one begun last session. Children can create the scenes of the story using nativity figures. Take pictures of each scene. Mount pictures on poster board or in a scrapbook. Help children choose a sentence from the Bible story to print with each picture.

Materials
- *The Young Reader's Bible*, pages 238-243
- photocopies of the Bible story (pages 283-285)
- *The Young Reader's Bible Audio Cassette* or a cassette on which you have recorded unit stories
- cassette player(s), earphones optional
- scissors
- crayons or colored pencils
- straw or dried grass
- glue
- large piece of paper

❶ Get Ready to Read

Children will make another segment of the video begun in lesson 22. See the instructions for that activity on page 115.

Give each child a copy of the Bible story (pages 283-285). Read the story as the children follow along.

How do you think Mary and Joseph felt while they were on their long journey? How do you think they felt when the innkeeper said there was no room for them? How do you think they felt when baby Jesus was born? Make a list of emotions the children name.

Tell children they will make a movie of the story. Ask children to volunteer to be Mary, Joseph, and the innkeeper.

When all jobs are assigned, practice acting out the story. See the notes in lesson 22. Practice as long as time permits, then use the video camera to film the children acting out the story.

❷ Read the Bible Story

"One Night in Bethlehem"

Before class, print the words *Mary, Joseph,* and *Jesus* on a large piece of paper.

Ask the children to tell you about trips they have taken. **How did you travel?** (Walk, ride in car, bus, train, airplane.)

Point to the words *Mary, Joseph,* and *Jesus* and explain that these people also took a trip. Ask the children to say the names with you. **Which of these people were in our story last session? What happened to them?**

Look again with the children at the pictures in the Bible story (pages 283-285). **Where do you think Mary and Joseph are going? Why do you think they are traveling? Do they look happy or sad? Why do you think they are sad? happy? Listen to find out.**

Listen

Read the story aloud, asking the children to follow along, pointing to the names *Mary, Joseph,* and *Jesus* as you read them. If you prefer, the girls can stand when you read *Mary*, boys when you read *Joseph* and have everyone fold their arms as if rocking a baby when the name *Jesus* is read.

Play the video made earlier.

Where were Mary and Joseph going? (to Bethlehem)

Why were Mary and Joseph going to Bethlehem? (to be counted)

What sad thing happened when they got to Bethlehem? (They couldn't find a place to stay.)

What wonderful thing happened in Bethlehem? (Baby Jesus was born.)

Participate

Before class, make photocopies of pages 283-285—each page on a different color of paper (or use a colored pencil to color-code papers after copies are made). Cut each page into six puzzle pieces. Hide all the pieces in different places in your classroom.

Divide into three teams. Assign each team a color. Teams should collect only puzzle pieces of their color. When they have found six pieces, they can assemble the puzzle and practice reading together the words on their page. Discuss the pages the teams found.

Who has a page that tells about a problem Mary and Joseph had in Bethlehem?

Who has a page that tells why Mary and Joseph went to Bethlehem?

Who has a page that tells about the special Son of God who was born?

Read

Children can use crayons or colored pencils to color the Bible story pages. Provide glue and straw or dried grass for the feeding box and the floor around the feeding box.

❸ Practice Using a Bible

Using My Bible

Before class, print numbers 1-8 on eight pieces of paper. On another set of eight papers, print the following instructions, one instruction on each paper.

1. Choose an Old Testament book that begins with "J" and find it in your Bible. Print the book name.

2. Choose a New Testament book that begins with "P" and find it in your Bible. Print the book name.

3. Find the last book in the Old Testament. Print the book name.

4. Find the last book in the New Testament. Print the book name.

5. Find the first book in the New Testament. Print the book name.

6. Find the first book in the Old Testament. Print the book name

7. Print the name of any Old Testament book on your paper. Find the book in your Bible.

8. Print the name of any New Testament book on your paper. Find the book in your Bible.

Post the eight papers in eight different areas of your classroom.

Divide the children into groups of two or three. Include a good reader in each group. (If you have more than eight groups, make more stations.)

Give each group a numbered sheet of paper to assign stations—each group at a different station. The groups will complete the instructions at their station, writing the Bible book they find on their paper after the correct number. When you

Options
• If you have twelve or more children, make two photocopies of pages 283-285 and divide the class into six teams.
• If you are working with only one child, use only page 285.

Snacks
Serve birthday cake or cupcakes to celebrate Jesus' birthday.

Materials
• Bible for each child
• *The Young Reader's Bible*
• photocopies of the Bible story (pages 283-285)
• photocopies of page 134
• crayons or colored pencils
• photocopies of Task Card #2 (page 110)
• paper
• large sheet of paper

Option
For early or nonreaders, simply read each instruction and help children complete them. Encourage children to help each other.

say "Scramble!" the groups must hurry to another station. Only one group may be at a station at a time. Groups may not repeat stations.

When each group has completed the eight stations, gather and discuss the Bible books the groups found. Help children pronounce names as needed.

Finding Bible Verses

Give each child a copy of Task Card #2. Have them work in pairs. Each pair will complete a Task Card for the partner to use. A child will open the Bible and copy the page number and book name. The other child will find the book in the Bible. Then, the children will switch roles.

Print **Hebrews 4:12** on a large sheet of paper. Ask the children to read the reference with you. Review what each part of the reference means—**Hebrews** (Bible book); **4:** (chapter number); **12** (verse number).

Help children find the reference in their Bibles. First, help them look up the page number in the table of contents to find the book of Hebrews. Then help them find the big number 4 for the chapter, and the small number 12 for the verse. Read the verse.

What does this verse tell us about the Bible? Read the first part of the verse aloud together, "God's word is alive and working."

Work together to find Luke 2 in their Bibles. Give each child a copy of page 134. Ask children to find the words on the page in the first seven verses of Luke 2. When they find a word, they should print the verse number in the blank space and color in that part of the picture on the page. For example, for the word *Mary*, the child would print *5* in the blank verse space and color Mary in the picture.

When children have completed the activity, review the words to the unit key verse, 1 John 4:15, "Jesus is the Son of God."

 ## Share What We've Learned

Before class, use a permanent broad-tipped marker to draw a simple manger (feedbox) on the plywood. Use the shape on page 134 to guide you.

Gather everyone in a circle to talk about what they have been learning. Use the aims for this lesson as an outline for the kinds of questions you ask.

What was special about the baby born to Mary? (He is Jesus, the Son of God.)

How do you feel about Jesus? (Encourage children to express their love for Jesus.)

What new words did you learn to read today? What verses did you find by yourself in the Bible? What did you read about in the Bible?

Praise children for their efforts and their knowledge.

Distribute construction paper and other materials and ask children to draw a picture or print a sentence to show their love for Jesus. Help children who need ideas. They could print "I love you, Jesus." They could draw a picture of themselves hugging Jesus. They could draw a picture of something Jesus made that they like, such as trees or snow.

When children have completed their pictures, gather around the manger board. Explain to the children that they can pretend they are bringing their pictures to the baby Jesus' manger (feeding box) to show their love for Him. Ask children to bring up their papers one at a time and tell about them as you attach the papers to the manger board. End the activity with praise prayers.

When each child has shared, sing the words and do the motions to the tune "Jingle Bells" learned in lesson 22 page 117.

Answers, page 134
Mary—2:5
Joseph—2:7
manger or feeding box—2:7
strips of cloth—2:7
baby—2:6

Options
• If you have nonreaders, read the Bible reference, demonstrate finding the Bible verse, and then read the verse aloud.
• Refer to unit page 114 for ideas for teaching the verse.

Materials
• poster-size sheet of plywood
• permanent markers
• construction paper
• pushpins
• scissors
• crayons or markers

Option
Allow children to draw their pictures outside, using sidewalk chalk. Or decorate a large window in your classroom with their pictures, using paint made for use on glass.

Note
Keep the manger board to use in lesson 25.

 Teaching at Home

Talk about each child's birth. Find newborn pictures. Talk about the family changes.

Reading tip
Talk about the use of quotation marks. Let children practice reading the two-way conversation on pages 238 and 239 of the Young Reader's Bible. Make sure children know that no one reads words not in quotation marks. Highlight the spoken words with different colors of markers.

Angels Tell Shepherds Jesus Is Born

Tell how the shepherds heard that Jesus is the Son of God.
Worship Jesus by telling about Him.
Find and read in Hebrews that the Bible is the Word of God.

"Jesus is the Son of God."   1 John 4:15, NIV

① Get Ready to Read

Children will make another segment of the video begun in lesson 22. See the complete instructions and an optional activity in that lesson.

Read the story aloud. **How do you think the shepherds felt when they saw an angel? How do you think the angels felt about the news they told? How do you think the shepherds felt when they saw baby Jesus?** List emotions the children name.

Tell children they will continue to make a video of the story. Ask children to volunteer to be the shepherds, the angels, and Mary and Joseph. When all jobs are assigned, practice as long as time permits, then use the video camera to film the children acting out the story.

Materials
- *The Young Reader's Bible*
- costumes and props for acting out the Bible story (costumes and props used last session, costumes for the shepherds, canes or sticks to use as staffs, white sheets or robes for the angels)
- video camera and video tape used last session

② Read the Bible Story

"Good News of Great Joy"

Before class, print the words *Mary, Joseph, Jesus,* and *shepherds* on a large sheet of paper.

Point to the names and explain that these are the people in today's story. Ask the children to say the names with you.

Which of these people was in our story last session? What happened to them? Recall the story. Explain that today's story tells about shepherds. **What is a shepherd's job?** (take care of sheep)

Show children the walking cane and explain that a shepherd carried a stick shaped with a curved end called a staff. Use a stuffed animal to demonstrate how a shepherd used the curved end of the staff to rescue a sheep who fell down a hill or to pull a sheep back into line who wandered away. Allow the children to take turns using the "staff" to rescue the "sheep."

Show a *Young Reader's Bible* pages 244 and 246. Give each child a copy of the Bible story (pages 286-288). Talk about shepherds holding sheep.

Have you ever been afraid at night? What frightened you? What did you do?

Look at the picture on page 244 in the *Young Reader's Bible*. Explain that the shepherds saw something at night. **Look at the picture. Why do you think the**

Materials
- *The Young Reader's Bible,* pages 244-249
- photocopies of the Bible story (pages 286-288)
- *The Young Reader's Bible Audio Cassette* or a cassette on which you have recorded unit stories
- cassette player(s), earphones optional
- walking cane (staff)
- eight stuffed animals
- paper
- crayons or colored pencils
- transparent tape
- happy-face stickers
- large sheet of paper

shepherds are afraid? What do you think the angel is telling the shepherds?

Listen

Let's pretend to be the shepherds in the story. It is night, so the shepherds are resting. Children can lie down.

Some shepherds are holding sheep. Children hold stuffed animals. Read the story aloud expressively to the children as they rest like the shepherds did.

Participate

Divide children into two groups. One group will be shepherds. The other group will be angels. Read through the story slowly, asking children to follow along. Every time you come to the word *shepherd* or *shepherds*, the shepherd group should bow down on the ground. Every time you come to the word *angel* or *angels*, the angel group should raise their hands in the air and say, "Glory to God!"

Play the video made earlier. Then compare the facts to the predictions the children made.

What kind of news did the angel have? (good news of great joy) **What did the angel tell the shepherds?** (Today a Savior has been born in Bethlehem.) **Who was the Savior?** (Jesus, the Son of God) **What did the shepherds find in Bethlehem?** (They found Mary, Joseph, and baby Jesus just as the angel had said.)

Before class, print the following words on separate pieces of paper: *sheep, bears, angel, Bethlehem, baby, cow, joy, sad.* Tape each piece of paper to a stuffed animal. Immediately before the activity, display the stuffed animals with the words clearly visible in various places—on the floor, under chairs, on the table, on a shelf, in a box, and so on.

Shepherds must care for their sheep. We will pretend to be shepherds. Our sheep are these stuffed animals. Display the animals.

Only five sheep have words from today's story on them. These five sheep are the sheep that should be rescued. Children decide which sheep have words from today's story on them. They may look at the story. Then they take turns rescuing the sheep with the story vocabulary by using the staff (walking cane).

The five words from the story are: *sheep, angel, Bethlehem, baby, joy.* When the sheep have been rescued, ask children to retell the story using the five words.

Read

Children can use crayons or colored pencils to color the Bible story pages. Children can put happy-face stickers by the pictures of the people who worshiped God in the story (shepherds, angel who told good news, other angels). As children work, they can listen to the cassette. Encourage them to read the story independently at their own level. Even if children can't read every word, they can point to the words they know and tell about the story.

❸ Practice Using a Bible

Using My Bible

Have the children sit on chairs holding their Bibles. Call out names of Bible books. Children should find the book in their Bibles. If the book is in the Old Testament, they should stand up. If the book is in the New Testament, they should sit on the floor. Practice several times by simply calling out "Old Testament" or "New Testament" and having children do the appropriate action.

Recall that the Old Testament books tell us that people worshiped and obeyed

Options
• Instead of stuffed animals, used rolled up towels or small pillows. Children's imaginations and your enthusiasm will make almost anything work as a "sheep."
• Let children find and circle answers to "Who?" questions. For example, "Who watched the sheep? came to visit? was afraid?"

Snacks
Spread out a blanket. Pretend to be shepherds eating lunch. Serve string cheese, raisins, and milk.

Materials
• *The Young Reader's Bible*
• Bibles
• photocopies of the Bible story (pages 286-288)
• a highlighter marker
• large sheets of paper

God. The New Testament books tell us that people worshiped and obeyed God and His Son, Jesus. **What do people who worship and obey Jesus do after they hear about Him?** (Tell others.)

Finding Bible Verses

Before class, print *Hebrews 4:12* on a large sheet of paper.

Ask the children to read the reference with you. Review what each part of the reference means—**Hebrews** (Bible book); **4:** (chapter number); **12** (verse number).

Guide children to find the reference in their Bibles and read the verse. Recall the Reference Rhyme (page 32) for help. **Where can we read the words of God?** (in the Bible)

Print **Luke 2:8** on a large sheet of paper. Ask children to copy the reference on paper and use the steps above to find it in their Bibles.

Before class, highlight photocopies of pages 286-288 for (at least) every two children. On each copy, highlight the following phrases: *Good news of great joy! A Savior has been born. You will find the baby wrapped in cloths. Glory to God.* Print the same four phrases on a large sheet of paper. Leave space after each phrase to print the reference.

Using their Bibles, ask children to find verses 8-20 in Luke 2. Distribute the highlighted photocopies to pairs of children. Ask them to find the highlighted phrases in Luke 2, verses 8-20, in their Bibles. As children tell you the reference, print it beside each phrase. (Good news of great joy—Luke 2:10; A Savior has been born—Luke 2:11; You will find the baby wrapped in cloths—Luke 2:12; Glory to God—Luke 2:14.)

When children have completed the activity, review the words to the unit key verse, 1 John 4:15, "Jesus is the Son of God."

Options
• For nonreaders, work as a large group. Print the following words on poster board—*news, born, baby, God.* Help children find one word at a time and then decide which verse the word is in.
• Refer to unit page 114 for ideas for teaching the verse.

4 Share What We've Learned

Materials
• index cards
• manger board from lesson 23
• slips of paper

Gather everyone in a circle to talk about what they have been doing and learning. Use the aims for this lesson as an outline for the kinds of questions you ask. Talk with the children about their new skills.

What new Bible words did you read today? What Bible verses did you find by yourself? Whom did you read about in the Bible? Praise children for effort.

What was special about the baby the angels and shepherds saw? (He is Jesus, the Son of God.) **What did the angels and shepherds tell about Jesus?** (He is Savior. He is Christ the Lord. He was wrapped in strips of cloth. He was in a manger—a feeding box.)

What can you tell about Jesus? (Children can name facts from the previous sessions' stories, or other things they know about Jesus.)

Before class, print one of the following instructions on each index card—*Say it loud; Say it soft; Say it low; Say it high, Say it fast; Say it slow; Say it happy; Say it sad; Say it mad.*

Ask each child to think of one thing to tell about Jesus.

Choose and read an index card. Have the children say (in unison) one thing they thought to tell about Jesus in the manner described on the index card just read. Then show the card that says, *Say it happy.* Pray praise prayers in happy voices. If time permits, continue until all cards are used.

Sing the words to "Jingle Bells" with the actions described in lesson 22.

Children can print something they have learned to do or something they can tell about Jesus on a slip of paper. Put the paper on the manger box.

Teaching at Home

Find out more about shepherds' work. Using pillows or stuffed animals as sheep, let children be shepherds, caring for their sheep.

Reading tip

Focus on punctuation marks, especially the exclamation point. Let children find the six statements with exclamation points. Read them with enthusiasm.

Wise Men Worship Jesus the King

Tell how the wise men showed Jesus is the Son of God.
Worship Jesus with gifts that honor Him.
Read Bible references and find Bible verses.

"Jesus is the Son of God."   1 John 4:15, NIV

1 Get Ready to Read

Materials
- *The Young Reader's Bible*
- photocopies of the two-page Bible story (page 131)
- costumes and props (towels tied on with cloth strips for head coverings, sandals, bathrobes, gold or glitter crowns and costume jewelry for the wise men and King Herod, ornate containers for the wise men's gifts)
- video camera and video tape used last session

Children will make another segment of the video begun in lesson 22. See that lesson for complete instructions and options.

Read the story from pages 250-255 of the *Young Reader's Bible*.

How did King Herod feel when the wise men asked him about Jesus? How do you think the wise men felt when Herod told them where Jesus was? How do you think they felt when they saw Jesus? How do you think Mary and Joseph felt when they saw the wise men's gifts? List emotions children name.

Tell children they will make a video of the story. Ask children to volunteer to be the wise men, King Herod, and Mary and Joseph.

2 Read the Bible Story

Materials
- *The Young Reader's Bible*, pages 250-257
- photocopies of the two-page Bible story (page 131)
- *The Young Reader's Bible Audio Cassette* or a cassette on which you have recorded unit stories
- cassette player(s), earphones optional
- a large sheet of paper
- poster board
- scissors
- markers
- glitter
- glue
- a long thin board (lath) or a yardstick
- small cards
- crayons or colored pencils

"Follow That Star!"

Before class, print the words *Mary, Jesus, King Herod,* and *wise men* on a large sheet of paper.

Point to the words and explain that these are the people in today's story. Ask the children to say the names with you. **Which of these people was in our story last session? What happened to them?** Briefly recall what happened in previous stories.

What kings have you read about in stories? Have you heard about any real kings? Do we have a king in our country?

Today's story is about a good king and a bad king. Listen to find out who is a bad king in the story. Who is a good king?

Listen

Read the story aloud expressively to the children.

Play the video made earlier. Then discuss the story and compare the facts to the predictions the children made. Talk about good and bad kings (wise men and Herod).

Why did the wise men decide to find Jesus? (They saw a special star.)

How did the wise men know where to find Jesus? (They asked King Herod.)

How did the wise men show they knew Jesus was special? (They bowed to Him. They gave Him special gifts.)

Participate

Before class, cut a star out of poster board and decorate it with glitter. Attach the star to a stick. On small cards, print the following words: *The East, Jerusalem, star, King Herod, King of the Jews, Bethlehem, Jesus' house, gifts, a dream.* Set up a path in your room. Attach the cards along the path on chairs, on the wall, on shelves, and so on.

Today, we will pretend to be the wise men following the star. When the star stops, we stop. You hold the star in the air and lead them along the path. Each time you come to a card with a story word on it, stop. Have the children read the word and tell something about that word from the story. Allow a different child to talk each time.

Read

Give each child a copy of the Bible story excerpt (page 131). Children can use crayons or colored pencils to color the pages and glue glitter on the star. As children work, they can listen to the cassette. Encourage them to read the story independently at their own level. Even if children can't read every word, they can point to the words they know and tell about the story.

Practice Using a Bible

Using My Bible

Before class, fill in six copies of Task Card #3 with one of these Bible book names: *Esther, Numbers, Ephesians, Jude, Proverbs, Ezra.*

Allow children to take turns choosing a Task Card and reading aloud the instructions for the group. The group will call out the answers and the children will print them on the Task Card. Continue until all six Task Card #3 copies are used.

Finding Bible Verses

Before class, print location names in large letters on five different sheets of paper: *Cousin Elizabeth's house, field, feeding box* or *manger, temple, house.* Attach the papers to the wall in the room. On each index card, print one word and reference: *Mary (Luke 1:46, 47); angels (Luke 2:14); shepherds (Luke 2:20); Simeon (Luke 2:28); Anna (Luke 2:36, 38); wise men (Matthew 2:11).*

Why is the Bible a special book? (The Bible contains the message of God.)

Guide children to find Hebrews 4:12 in their Bibles and read the verse. They have been finding this verse since lesson 23, so they should be able to use the table of contents to find Hebrews. Recall the Reference Rhyme (page 32), if necessary, to find the chapter and verse.

When baby Jesus was born, many people knew He was special. Today we will play a game so we can discover people who worshiped God for the special baby Jesus. Divide children into six groups and give each group an index card. Have the groups find the Bible verse on their card. **Read to find out where the person worshiped Jesus and how the person worshiped Jesus.** The group then goes to stand by the paper that tells the place where their person worshiped.

When all groups are standing at the correct place, ask each group to tell who their person was and how they worshiped Jesus.

Option

If you have very young readers or children who are very familiar with the Christmas stories, play a quiet game. You will point to a page in a *Young Reader's Bible,* and then you will act out one of the people mentioned on the page. They will decide who you are portraying, and they will point to that name on the page. Children can work in pairs to help younger children.

Example: page 244—sheep—get on your hands and knees and pretend to bleat; page 245—shepherds—put your hands over your face and look frightened; page 247—angels—fold your hands together and pretend to happily sing; page 248—shepherds—hurry along searching around for something; page 249—Mary and/or baby—cradle your arms as if holding a baby.

Snacks

Serve star-shaped cookies or crackers and milk.

Materials
• *The Young Reader's Bible*
• Bibles
• six photocopies of Task Card #3 from page 110
• five sheets of paper
• six small index cards

If you have fewer than six groups, repeat the process.

When children have completed the activity, review the words to the unit key verse, 1 John 4:15, "Jesus is the Son of God."

Materials
- manger board from lesson 23
- Christmas bows

 # Share What We've Learned

Gather everyone in a circle to talk about what they have been doing and learning. Use the aims for this lesson as an outline for the kinds of questions you ask.

Allow children time to express confidence in their new skills. **What new Bible words did you learn to read today? What Bible verses did you find? What did you read about in the Bible?** Praise children for their efforts and their knowledge.

What was special about the baby the wise men saw? (He is Jesus, the Son of God.) **How did the wise men show they knew Jesus was special?** (They brought Him precious gifts of gold, frankincense, and myrrh.)

What gifts can you give to Jesus? (Children can name actions they do which please Jesus; giving gifts to those in need is like giving to Jesus.)

Ask each child to think of a gift to give to Jesus this week. The gift can be an action that will please Jesus or something given to someone that will please Jesus. Display the manger board made in lesson 23. Recall with the children how they worshiped Jesus by drawing or telling how special He is. Now they will worship Jesus by giving gifts to Him. Allow each child to choose a bow to add to the manger board. As the children add the bows, they should share the way they will give. Sing the words and actions the children have learned to "Jingle Bells."

 Teaching at Home

Find out more about the lands of the east from which the wise men came. Visit a planetarium to learn about the changing night sky.

Reading tips
- Practice adding or removing the suffix *ed* to story words: wanted, called, killed, followed, bowed, stopped.
- Find synonyms for some of the story words: saved, kept; began, started; end, finish; street, road; city, town; searched, looked; talking, speaking; taller, bigger; wiser, smarter.

Jesus Talks to Teachers in the Temple

Tell who learned that Jesus is the Son of God.
Worship Jesus in a prayer.
Read Bible references and find Bible verses.

"Jesus is the Son of God."   1 John 4:15, NIV

❶ Get Ready to Read

Children will make another segment of the video begun in lesson 22. See the instructions in that lesson.

Read the story from pages 256-261 of the *Young Reader's Bible*.

How do you think Mary and Joseph felt when they couldn't find Jesus? How did the teachers and other people who heard Jesus' answers feel? How do you think Mary and Joseph felt when they found Jesus? How do you think Jesus felt? List emotions children name. Ask children to volunteer to be Jesus, the teachers in the temple, and Mary and Joseph.

❷ Read the Bible Story

"Taller and Wiser"

Before class, print the words *Mary, Joseph, Jesus,* and *teachers* on a large sheet of paper.

Point to the words and explain that these are the people in today's story. Ask the children to say the names with you. **Which of these people have been in our stories? What happened to them?** Briefly recall what happened in previous stories.

Have you ever been lost? How did you feel? What did you do? What happened to you? Today we'll find out that Mary and Joseph looked for Jesus because they thought He was lost.

Ask children to help you set up camp in the room. Explain that Jesus' family may have "camped out" when they went to Jerusalem, as you are pretending to do. Pile sticks to make the pretend campfire in the middle of your camp. Children can spread out sleeping bags around the fire, and set up pots and pans near the fire. When the camp is completed, invite children to sit in a group around the campfire.

Listen

Give each child a copy of the Bible story excerpt (page 132) or have them find page 256 in the *Young Reader's Bible*. Read the story aloud expressively as the children follow along.

Materials
- *The Young Reader's Bible*
- photocopies of the two-page Bible story (page 132)
- costumes and props (towels tied on with cloth strips for head coverings, sandals, bathrobes, paper rolled over dowel rods or pencils to make scrolls)
- video camera and video tape used last session

Options
• If you are making a scrapbook or poster scene of photographs, complete the one begun in lesson 22. Since nativity figures will not depict the scenes of the story, take photos of the children acting as the characters in Bible costumes.
• If you are working with one child, the child can be Jesus and you can be the teachers and one of His parents. Be creative in making scenes with the characters available.

Materials
- *The Young Reader's Bible*, pages 256-261
- photocopies of the two-page Bible story (page 132)
- *The Young Reader's Bible Audio Cassette* or a cassette on which you have recorded unit stories
- cassette player(s), earphones optional
- items to "make camp" in your room (sleeping bags, pots and pans, sticks for pretend campfire, paper to protect floor)
- index cards
- treat (stickers, candy, or erasers)
- a large sheet of paper
- crayons or colored pencils

Participate

Play the video made earlier. Then compare the facts to the predictions the children made.

Why did Jesus stay in the temple for so long? (God is His father. It was God's house. He probably loved talking about His father, God.) **How do you think Mary and Joseph felt when they found Jesus?** (Relieved, happy. Maybe also confused or upset about why He would not have told them where He was.) **What did Jesus do after His parents found Him?** (He went home and obeyed them.)

Before class, copy each of the five clues from the narrow column on a piece of paper. Roll the pieces of paper tightly and hide them separately.

Tell children that they will help find Jesus as Mary and Joseph did. Ask them to find the five rolled-up pieces of paper. When they have found the papers, let them decide as a group the word and letter answer to each question. (Jerusalem, Egypt, surprised, understood, Son) As they discover each letter, print it on a piece of paper. Put the letters in order. They will spell the name *Jesus*. Congratulate them for finding Jesus!

Play another game to review the facts of the Bible story.

Before class, print each of the following questions on an index card. Answers are in parentheses.

How old was Jesus? (twelve) *To what feast did Jesus go in Jerusalem?* (Passover) *Where did Mary and Joseph find Jesus?* (temple) *Who was Jesus with?* (teachers of the law) *Whose house did Jesus say he had to be in?* (His Father's house) *Where did Jesus go after Mary and Joseph found him?* (home with them) *How did Jesus keep growing?* (taller and wiser)

Think of places to hide the question cards. Think of a clue that will lead children to a place where a question card is hidden. For example, "Go to the place where we sharpen our pencils."

Before children arrive, hide the cards in the places corresponding to the clues. At the last place, hide a small treat, such as stickers, candy, or erasers.

Tell the children that they will search just as Mary and Joseph did for Jesus. Read the first clue. When children find the card and answer the question, read the next clue. Continue until all questions are answered and the treat is found.

Read

Help children find words (on Bible story page 132) that tell about Mary and Joseph looking for Jesus. Then ask children to circle the words that tell what Jesus did when Mary and Joseph found Him. Color the picture of Mary and Jesus hugging. As children work, they can listen to the cassette.

❸ Practice Using a Bible

Using My Bible

Call out the following phrases and ask children to hold the part of the Bible the phrase describes: the Old Testament, the New Testament, or the whole Bible. Answers are in parentheses for your reference.

It tells how people worshiped and obeyed God. (whole Bible)
It tells how people worshiped and obeyed Jesus. (New Testament)
It tells how God created the world. (Old Testament)
It tells about the walls of Jericho. (Old Testament)
It tells about how people told others about Jesus. (New Testament)
It tells about David and Goliath. (Old Testament)

Clues

1. Name the first letter of the city where Jesus and His parents visited. (page 256)
2. Name the first letter of the desert country where God saved His people from slavery. (page 256)
3. Name the first letter of how the temple teachers felt as they listened to Jesus. (page 258)
4. Name the first letter of what Jesus knew about God and His ways. (page 258)
5. Name the first letter of Jesus' place in the family (to Mary and to God). (page 258)

Option

If you have a large group, make two sets of questions. Set up two different sets of clues and hide them in different rooms. Divide children into two teams. See who can complete their search first.

Snacks

Serve graham crackers and peanut butter with water or juice.

Materials

• *The Young Reader's Bible*
• Bibles
• index cards
• photocopies of Task Card #4 (page 110)

It tells about how Jesus was born. (New Testament)

If you have time, continue naming other Bible events that your children are familiar with.

Finding Bible Verses

Before class fill in one copy of Task Card #4 with the Bible reference ***Hebrews 4:12.*** Fill in a second copy of Task Card #4 with the Bible reference ***Luke 2:49***. Photocopy both versions of Task Card #4 so each child can have his own set.

Give each child the Task Card and a Bible. If you have practiced each week, children should easily find Hebrews 4:12. Offer clues about Luke 2:49 if necessary. Recall the Reference Rhyme on page 32.

Which Bible reference tells us about the Bible, God's Word? (Hebrews 4:12)

According to the Bible, where did Jesus say He had to be? (in His Father's house) **Which verse gives this answer?** (Luke 2:49)

Before class, print four words on each index card.

Card One—***Passover, three, amazed, obedient***

Card Two—***twelve, teachers, searching, grew***

Ask the children to leave their Bibles open to Luke 2. Have them find verses 41-52 in chapter 2. Divide into two teams. Give each team a blank piece of paper and a card with four words on it.

Challenge the teams to find the words on their paper in the verses in Luke 2. They should print the reference for each word on the blank piece of paper.

When teams have finished, they should exchange answer papers with the other team and look up the four references on the other team's paper.

Review the unit key verse, 1 John 4:15, "Jesus is the Son of God."

Answers for Card One
Luke 2:41; Luke 2:46; Luke 2:47; Luke 2:51

Answers for Card Two
Luke 2:42; Luke 2:46; Luke 2:49; Luke 2:52

4 Share What We've Learned

Gather everyone in a circle to talk about what they have been doing and learning. Use the unit and lesson aims as a guide for your questions.

What was special about the child Jesus? (He is the Son of God.) **How did the teachers of the law know Jesus was special?** (His answers about God surprised and amazed them.) **How do you know Jesus is special?** (Children offer ideas.)

Explain that one way to worship Jesus is by praying to Him and telling Him He is special. **What are some different ways that people look when they pray?** Allow children to tell or demonstrate ways people look when they pray.

Act out with the children some different prayer positions—bow head and fold hands, kneel, lay prostrate on floor, raise hands and look upward, and so on. **How does God expect us to look when we pray?** (Discuss.)

We pray in many ways—ways that help us remember how powerful God is and help us think about Him. God does not look on only our appearance—what we look like as we pray. He cares about our feelings and thoughts, and He listens to the words we say and thoughts we think.

Read the ideas and praise statements and talk about the pictures children have put on the manger board. Ask children to get ready to pray in a position that helps them to think about God and how powerful He is. Have children say sentence prayers, telling Jesus why He is special, or why they love Him.

Help the children answer the questions and fill in the blanks on page 135. When they have completed their pages, hug them and put stickers at the top of their papers. Express your pride and pleasure in what they have learned.

Sing the words with actions to "Jingle Bells" the children have learned.

Materials
- photocopies of page 135
- manger board from lesson 24
- stickers

Option
Have nonreaders draw a picture of a Bible story or a new thing they learned about Jesus on page 135. As the children work on their pictures, have them tell you why Jesus is special and name some new words they have learned.

Teaching at Home

Hiding games can easily be played by one child. Invite a few friends or engage the whole family in the fun.

Reading tips
- This story offers several multi-syllable words: Passover, Jerusalem, understood, slavery. To help children count syllables in a word, have them rest their chins on a hand and say the word. They can count how many times their chins move.
- Review the use of the question mark in this story. List question words to watch for in reading: *who, what, where, when, why, how.*

Gabriel had big news for Mary.

"You are going to have
a baby boy," he said.

"You will name him Jesus.

He will be great,

and his kingdom will never end."

"How can this be?" asked Mary.

"I don't have a husband."

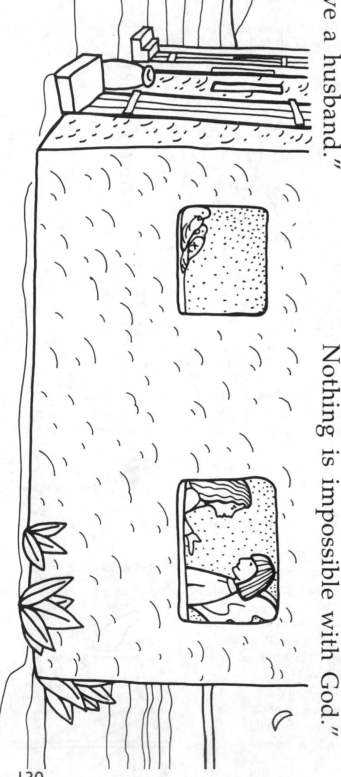

"God's Holy Spirit will come

upon you," said the angel.

"That is why the baby

will be called the Son of God.

And your cousin Elizabeth

is having a child,

even though she is old.

Nothing is impossible with God."

The wise men left for Bethlehem.

"Look!" they said.

"There is the star again."

They followed the star

until it stopped

right over the house

where Jesus was.

The wise men went inside.

They saw Jesus

with Mary, his mother.

They bowed down

to worship him

and gave him precious gifts.

Mary and Joseph went back
to Jerusalem.

They looked up and down
the streets of the city.

They found Jesus at the temple,
talking with the teachers.

Everyone who listened
was surprised.

Jesus understood so much
about God and his ways!

"Son," said Mary,
"why have you made us
search for you?"

"Why were you looking for me?"
asked Jesus.

"Didn't you know I had to be
in my Father's house?"

Then Jesus went home
with Mary and Joseph
and always obeyed them.

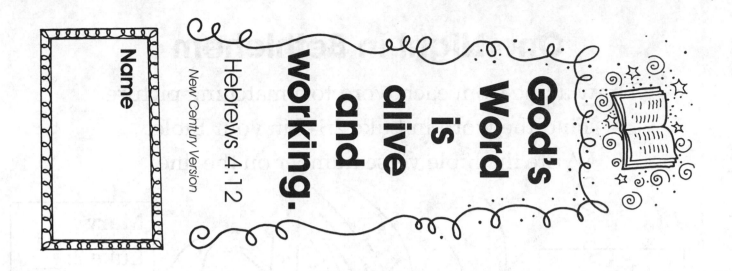

Name

New Century Version

Hebrews 4:12

God's Word is alive and working.

---

fold

The Bible is God's Word.

Jesus is the Son of God.

I love Jesus.

God loves me.

God made everything.

God made Heaven for me.

One Night in Bethlehem

Draw a line from each word to a matching picture.
Find the word in Luke 2:1-7 in your Bible.
Write the Bible verse number on the line.

Joseph
Luke 2:___

Mary
Luke 2:___

manger or box
Luke 2:___

cloth or cloths
Luke 2:___

baby
Luke 2:___

★ You do good work! ★ You did it! ★

★ Great effort! ★ I'm proud of you!

Some GREAT Things I Know

I know Jesus is special because

Here are some new words I can read.

Here is a Bible verse I can find.

Here is a Bible story I can read.

Here is a new thing I learned about Jesus.

Unit 6
We Worship Jesus;
He Does Great Things

Key Verse
"Lord, you have done such great things!"   Psalm 92:5, ICB

Unit Vocabulary
afternoon
alive
amazed
believe
carrying
crowd
danger
five thousand
forgive
grave clothes
heal
howled
leftovers
loaf (loaves)
lowered
mountainside
names of disciples
resurrection
roaring
twelve
wake/woke

Unit Aims
By the end of the unit, learners will be able to
- tell five Bible stories about the great things Jesus can do.
- feel confident in finding verses in a Bible and reading *The Young Reader's Bible*.
- locate books, chapters and verses in their own Bibles.
- read (at their level) stories from *The Young Reader's Bible*.
- worship Jesus who does great things.

Unit Project
Jesus Does Great Things Posters
Provide a large sheet of poster board for each child. Use a broad-tip black marker to divide each poster into five sections. If new children attend in subsequent weeks, draw lines dividing poster boards into fourths or thirds. Half-sized poster-board pieces will work for children who come only the last two lessons of the unit.

Children will make an undersea scene and scenes of friends lowering a man through the roof, a stormy sea, bread and fish, and an open tomb (for Lazarus). Provide a wide variety of art materials so children can be creative as they prepare their posters. See "Get Ready to Read" in each lesson for more detailed instructions for each poster section.

	The Singing Bible (3 tapes)	Kids on the Rock (More Songs)	Follow the Leader (The Donut Man)	I'm a Helper (The Donut Man)	Good News (The Donut Man)
Lesson 27	Twelve Guys		We're Following Jesus; Peter Was a Fisherman		
Lesson 28	Who Do You Say I Am?				
Lesson 29	Who Do You Say I Am?				
Lesson 30	Who Do You Say I Am?			Sing a Song of Praise	
Lesson 31	Who Do You Say I Am?				
Key Verse		You Hear My Heart			
Unit Theme		Jesus Came to Town			Lord of All
All Lessons	The Books We Love the Best The Bible Book Is True	God's Word Is for Me			

The Singing Bible (3 tapes), ©1993 by Lightwave Publishing, Inc. Manufactured and distributed by Word Publishing, Dallas, TX 75234
Kids on the Rock! More Songs, ©1994 Gospel Light, Ventura CA 93006
The Donut Man (3 tapes): *Follow the Leader*, ©1990; *I'm a Helper*, ©1991; *Good News*, ©1991; Integrity Music, Inc., P.O. Box 16813 Mobile, AL 36616

Key Verse Activities

Materials
- frozen juice lids
- permanent marker
- wide satin or gift wrapping ribbon cut into 24-inch lengths
- four colors of narrow ribbon cut into 4-inch lengths
- masking tape

Deserving a Medal

Before class, print "I know Psalm 92:5" on the juice lids. **Sometimes people get medals when they do great things. Who has done the greatest things of all?** (God.) **What are some things He has done?** (Created the world and everything in it, sent His son, answered our prayers, and more.) **God deserves a medal more than anyone.**

Today you will get a medal when you memorize Psalm 92:5. At the beginning of each of the next four lessons, if you can still remember the verse perfectly, you will get ribbons to add to your medal.

At the beginning of each of the four subsequent lessons, the children will tape the end of a wide ribbon to the back of the medals. They wear their medals in class until the last lesson of this unit, and then they wear the medals home.

Materials
- used paper
- marker
- chalk
- a laundry basket

Snowstorm Game

Before class, wad sheets of paper so the used sides are on the inside of the wads, and the outside surfaces of the wads are fairly smooth. Print one of the following words on the outside surface of each wad: "Lord" "you have" "done such" "great things!" "Psalm 92:5." For each child, there should be a set of five wads. Drop them in a laundry basket.

In class, print the memory verse and reference on the chalkboard. **Does it look as if there will be a snowstorm outside?** (Pause.) **There will be one in here! In a minute I'll throw "snowballs" around the room. Wait until I say "go" and then gather "snowballs" until you have five that make up the memory verse. Try to line up five snowballs in order so that you can read the verse.**

Materials
- corrugated cardboard
- markers
- X-Acto knife or opened scissors
- transparent tape

Stand-up Paintings

Before class, prepare an example to display.

Even if you haven't seen Jesus heal someone instantly, He has made you well when you were sick. Even if you haven't seen Jesus calm a storm, He has kept you safe while it thundered outside. Although you haven't seen Him feed thousands from two fish and five loaves of bread, you have always had food. Even if you haven't seen Jesus raise anyone from the dead like Lazarus, He will bring you back to life someday if you believe in Him.

Draw a picture of something God has done for you. I'll make parts of your drawing stand up. Let children draw and color a scene. Cut through the top layer of cardboard around parts of the drawings. Carefully pull up the pieces so they will stand. Use tape to repair any small tears.

The Fish Finder

Tell what amazing thing Jesus did.
Choose a way to worship Jesus.
Find the Old and New Testaments and the Gospels.

"Lord, you have done such great things!"   Psalm 92:5, ICB

1 Get Ready to Read

Children will begin work on posters that show great things that Jesus can do. Divide each sheet of poster board into five sections. Children choose a section of their poster to complete today. They will make a picture of the sea with fish in it—the fish that only Jesus knew where to find. The children will color the water. Then they will cut many fish out of construction paper and glue them in one area of the water. Last, they will glue clear plastic wrap over their picture to make it look as if it is underwater.

2 Read the Bible Story

"Jesus' Team of Twelve"

Before class, print the names *Jesus, Peter, Andrew, James,* and *John* on a large sheet of paper.

Point to the words and explain that these are the people in today's story. Ask the children to say the names with you. **Which of these people were in earlier stories?** (Jesus) **How old was Jesus when He went to the temple?** (twelve years old) Recall the story.

Allow children to examine a fishbowl and fish. Then cover the fishbowl with a cloth or piece of paper. Ask the children to tell you where the fish is in the bowl. Tell them whether each guess is correct or not. **How can you tell where the fish is in the bowl?** (They cannot tell unless they can see the fish.)

Today, we will read about something Jesus did after He had grown up. We know that Jesus can do amazing things because He is the Son of God. In today's story, Jesus found some fish that He couldn't see. Where do you think Jesus finds some fish? Why do you think Jesus needs to find fish? Allow children to predict what they think will happen in the story.

Listen

Read the story aloud from a *Young Reader's Bible*.

What great thing did Jesus do? (He helped Peter and Andrew catch many fish.) **Why were Peter and John amazed?** (They had fished all night and caught nothing.) **Why could Jesus do such an amazing thing?** (He is the Son of God.)

Why couldn't Peter and Andrew find fish in the lake? (They couldn't see or

Materials
• poster board for each child
• construction paper
• scissors
• glue
• markers or colored pencils
• clear plastic wrap

Options
• Let children name games or other activities where you need a team. Tell what players are called. Jesus' team were called disciples.
• Let children copy this sentence filling in their own names: "_____ is on Jesus' team!"

Materials
• *The Young Reader's Bible,* pages 268-273
• photocopies of the two-page Bible story (page 154)
• *The Young Reader's Bible Audio Cassette* or a cassette on which you have recorded unit stories
• cassette player(s), earphones optional
• small fishbowl with fish in it
• paper or a cloth to cover the bowl
• netted produce bags
• fish-shaped crackers
• fishing tackle worm
• tracing paper
• a large sheet of paper
• construction paper fish
• markers

Option
If you don't have a fish and fishbowl, fill a deep bowl with water that is colored with a mixture of food coloring. Drop a bottle cap or other object that will not show up easily in the bowl, swirl it around, and ask children to guess where it is.

Option

Tell the children they will pretend to be fishermen like Peter and Andrew. Give each child a "net" and march purposefully to an area of the room where you will fish. **How do you think the fishermen felt when they first started to fish?** (Hopeful that they would catch some fish. Probably had lots of energy.)

Pretend to cast out nets and bring them back in. As the fishermen work, sing a song together to the tune of "Frere Jacques."

Each time you sing the song, insert different children's names for "Peter" and "Andrew" and have the children tell whether or not they have caught any fish.

After you have fished a while, tell children it is almost daylight and you have caught nothing. **How do you think the fishermen felt about working all night without catching anything?** (tired, discouraged, sad, or angry) Slowly and wearily walk back to the other area of your room dragging the nets.

"We are fishing. We are fishing.
All night long. All night long.
Peter, have you caught some fish?
Andrew, have you caught some fish?
All night long. All night long."

Snacks

Serve fish-shaped crackers and juice.

Materials
• *The Young Reader's Bible*
• Bible for each child
• photocopies of Task Cards #1 and #2 (page 110)
• a three-ring folder with four sheets of paper for each child
• colored pencils
• poster board

know where the fish were.) **Why could Jesus find fish?** (He is the Son of God.) **Why did Jesus find fish for Peter and Andrew?** (To help them because they had tried all night. It also helped them know He is the Son of God.)

Participate

Before class, print the following words on construction paper fish—*nets, catch, water, fish, break, boats, full, sink.*

Designate an area of the floor to be the "lake." Scatter the paper fish in the lake area. Place a masking tape line at the edge of the "lake" for the children to stand behind. Divide into two teams. Children will take turns throwing a worm from behind the line. If the worm lands on a fish, their team has "caught" the fish. The team must say a sentence from the story, using the word on the fish. If their sentence is correct, they keep the fish. If they cannot say a sentence, the fish is thrown back in the lake. Continue until all fish are caught.

Give each of the hardworking fishermen several fish-shaped crackers as you talk about how the fishermen in the story felt. **How do you think the tired fishermen felt when Jesus asked them to go back out on the water?** (hopeful that something would happen; reluctant to go back to work again) **How do you think the fishermen felt when they found fish?** (excited, happy, full of energy, surprised)

What did Peter, Andrew, James, and John do when they saw the amazing things Jesus could do? (They left everything and followed Jesus.)

Give each child a copy of the two-page Bible story (page 154). Read the names of the twelve men Jesus called. Invite the children to repeat each name after you.

Count the followers listening to Jesus. Give each child a piece of tracing paper. Children can trace Jesus and then draw themselves and eleven friends.

Read

Let children listen to the cassette story as they read the Bible story and color the Bible story pictures.

❸ Practice Using a Bible

Using My Bible

Ask children to hold the part of the Bible that is the Old Testament. **What does the Old Testament tell us about?** (how people worshiped and obeyed God)

Ask children to hold the part of the Bible that is the New Testament. **The New Testament tells us something about worshiping and obeying God too. What does the New Testament tell us about?** (how people worshiped and obeyed God and His Son, Jesus, and how people told others about Jesus)

Give each child a copy of Task Card #2 and ask the children to work in pairs to complete the cards. Each pair will complete two cards—one card done by each child for the other.

Finding Bible Verses

Before class, print the names *Matthew, Mark, Luke, John* on poster board. Give each child a copy of Task Card #1. Have children copy one book name on their Task Card #1. Read the cards aloud. Make certain that at least one person has each of the four books.

Ask children to open their Bibles to the table of contents. Explain that four books of the Bible tell us stories about Jesus' life. **Which testament do you think books with stories about Jesus would be in?** (Children should guess New

Testament because it tells how people worshiped and obeyed Jesus.) Children can circle the *New Testament* on their Task Card.

Next, help children find the book name in their table of contents.

These four books are called Gospels. Print *Gospels.* **The word *Gospel* means "good news." Why do you think books about Jesus' life would be called books of good news?** (The news about what Jesus did is good news for everyone.)

Give each of the children a three-ring folder and paper. Explain that they will make Gospel folders to help them learn special things about each book.

As you read, print each word of the key verse, *"Lord, you have done such great things!"* on the board. Explain that the notebook will tell about the great things Jesus did. Ask the children to copy the key verse on the cover of their folders. (Print the key verse on folders for younger children. Some children might be able to trace the letters.) Then ask children to print the name of one of the Gospels on each of four sheets of paper.

Have you heard the name Matthew before? (He was one of Jesus' team of twelve.) Explain that Matthew was a tax collector who left his job to follow Jesus. Ask children to decorate their Matthew page to remind them of Matthew. (They could draw a picture of Matthew sitting at his tax table or following Jesus.)

Explain that the four Gospels tell many of the same stories about Jesus. Parts of the stories about the fish and Jesus' team of twelve are in all four Gospels.

Before class, print each reference on an index card: *Matthew 4:18-22; Mark 1:16-20 and 3:13-19; Luke 5:1-11 and 6:12-16; John 1:35-42.*

Divide class into four groups and give each group one Bible reference card. A group member (or an adult reader) reads the verses. Each group decides what to tell about the part of today's story told in their Gospel. Only Luke tells about the great catch of fish; only Mark and Luke tell about Jesus' choosing the twelve.

Ask children to draw a picture of a great catch of fish on the Luke page and Jesus and His disciples on the Mark page. On the page for John they can draw a picture of two fisherman disciples (Andrew and Peter). Children should put their four book pages in order in their folders. Collect the folders to use next session.

4 Share What We've Learned

Gather everyone in a circle to talk about what they have been learning. Use the aims for this lesson as an outline for the kinds of questions you ask.

What new Bible person did you learn about today? (Peter or any of the other men Jesus called) **What new thing did you learn about the Bible?** Allow children to share and express enthusiasm in their developing skills and knowledge.

What great thing did Jesus do for Peter and Andrew? (catch lots of fish) **Why was what Jesus did so great?** (Only Jesus could help them find fish.) **Why can Jesus do great things?** (He is the Son of God.)

Give each child a copy of page 157. Ask children to choose a way they will worship Jesus for the great things He does. They may fill in any one of the four sections on the paper.

When children have completed their personal worship papers, have a group worship time. Ask several children to show the pictures they drew. Ask some children to share the great thing they will tell about Jesus. Allow children to suggest one or two songs the group can sing to Him. Then ask one or two children to say the prayers they wrote for Jesus.

Materials
• photocopies of page 157

Option
Refer to unit page 138 for ideas for teaching the unit key verse, Psalm 92:5.

 Teaching at Home

A trip to the fishing department of a store will be a vocabulary builder. Net fishing, however, will have to be investigated at the library.

Reading tip
Pronouncing the names of Jesus' team of twelve should provide ample challenge.

The Fixer Upper

Tell about the great and amazing healing Jesus did.
Choose a way to worship Jesus.
Read Bible references and find Bible verses.

"Lord, you have done such great things!"   Psalm 92:5, ICB

Materials
- *The Young Reader's Bible*
- posters begun last week
- extra pieces of poster board
- scissors
- glue
- markers or colored pencils
- sandpaper

1 Get Ready to Read

Children will continue to work on posters that show great things that Jesus can do because He is the Son of God. Children not present last week will need a blank piece of poster board divided into four sections. Children can choose which section of the poster they will complete this week. They should fill the section with a roof made from sandpaper glued to the poster board. They should leave out a section in the middle of the roof. They can add Jesus, the lame man, and his four friends after hearing the Bible story.

Materials
- *The Young Reader's Bible,* pages 274-279
- photocopies of the Bible story (pages 289-291)
- *The Young Reader's Bible Audio Cassette* or a cassette on which you have recorded unit stories
- cassette player(s), earphones optional
- large sheet of paper
- craft sticks
- small twigs
- clay
- glue
- newspaper
- leaves or leaf shapes cut from construction paper
- stepladder
- eight strips of paper
- slips of paper
- tape
- toy figure for each team
- basket or other container
- crayons or colored pencils

2 Read the Bible Story

"Inside and Out"
Today's story tells what happened to the roof of a house. Have you ever built a playhouse? What did you use to build it? What did you use to make the roof? Would it have been easy to make a hole in your roof?

Explain to children that roofs in Bible times were probably made using boards with branches laid across them. A thick layer of clay covered the top. Show children the supplies you have brought and ask them to help you make a roof. Children should lay the craft sticks on the newspaper like boards for the roof. Then they should lay the twigs across the craft sticks and glue them in place. Finally, children can press clay onto the top of the roof.

Before class, print the words **Jesus, forgive,** and **sins** on a large sheet of paper.

Point to the words and ask the children to say them with you. **Today's story tells about the roof of a house and how some people got from outside to inside. It also tells about how Jesus can change people on the inside as well as the outside.**

Listen
Read the story aloud expressively to the children.
How could the sick man's friends make a hole in the roof? (Refer to the roof the children made. They probably dug through the clay and removed some of the branches between the boards.)
What two things did Jesus do for the man who couldn't walk? (He forgave the man's sins. He made the man walk.) **What are sins?** (things we do that dis-

obey God) **What does it mean to forgive?** (to forget the wrong thing; not to make someone be punished for the wrong thing)

Who can forgive the wrong things we do? (God, Jesus) **Who else can forgive our sins?** (no one)

Why did people think it was amazing for Jesus to forgive the man's sins? (Only God can forgive sins.) **Why was it so amazing for Jesus to make the man walk?** (Doctors couldn't heal him.)

Participate

Before class, print the eight phrases on eight strips of paper.

Set up a ladder and tape the strips of paper to the steps of the ladder. Place two numbered strips on each step of the ladder.

Play a review game. Divide into two teams. Place a toy figure for each team on the bottom step of the stepladder. Teams take turns answering clues. Each time a clue is answered correctly, the team will move up one step. If a team misses an answer, they may look in their books for the answer and wait until their next turn to try again. The first team to reach the top of the ladder wins.

Before class, print words and phrases on separate slips of paper. Put the slips of paper in a basket or other container.

Next, have the teams take turns drawing slips of paper. The team should decide how to show what the person or group did or how they felt in the story by moving only their faces. The other team will guess the person or group. If this is too difficult, children can show an action.

Complete the unit poster art. Children can add Jesus, the lame man, and his four friends. In the cutout roof section of the poster, children should draw Jesus talking to the man on the mat.

Read

Give each child a copy of the Bible story (pages 289-291). Children can use crayons or colored pencils to color the pages and glue real or paper leaves to the roof. As children work, they can listen to the cassette. Encourage them to read the story independently at their own level. Even if children can't read every word, they can point to words they know and tell about the story.

❸ Practice Using a Bible

Using My Bible

Ask children to follow your instructions and show you the parts of the Bible.
Open your Bible to the Old Testament.
Open your Bible to the New Testament.
Open your Bible to the book of Psalms.
Open your Bible to the table of contents.
Continue. Call out the name of a Bible book. Children look up the book name in the table of contents and then find any page of the book in the Bible. As soon as a child finds the book, he should stand, show the book in his Bible, and tell whether it is in the Old Testament or the New Testament.

Finding Bible Verses

Before class, on photocopies of the top of page 158, fill in the blanks with the words or numbers in the narrow column on page 144. (Make enough photocopies of the filled-in pages for each child to have one.)

Phrases for paper strips for the ladder
1. place where Jesus was teaching
2. what the sick man was lying on
3. how many friends carried the sick man
4. why the friends couldn't reach Jesus
5. where the friends went to get to Jesus
6. what Jesus forgave the man on the mat
7. what Jesus told the man on the mat to do
8. how everyone felt when Jesus healed the man

Words and phrases for game
Jesus, crowd of people, four friends, teachers of the law, man who could not move before Jesus made him well, man who could move after Jesus made him well

Suggestions
Jesus—look up to Heaven or bow head; **crowd of people**—move head as though straining to see; **four friends**—bend head over as though looking down a hole; **teachers of the law**—lift noses in air and look disapproving; **man who could not move (before)**—close eyes, look sad, in pain; **man who could move (after)**—smile from ear to ear

Snacks
Serve vanilla wafers and milk.

Materials
• *The Young Reader's Bible*
• Bible for each child
• Gospel folders begun in lesson 27
• extra paper for the folders
• colored pencils
• photocopies of three filled-in copies of the top of page 158

Copy #1
Find the word *sins*. Look in
Matthew 9:2. Look in Mark 2:5.
Look in Luke 5:20.
Copy #2
Find the word *teachers*. Look in
Matthew 9:3. Look in Mark 2:6.
Look in Luke 5:21.
Copy #3
Find the word *mat*. Look in
Matthew 9:6. Look in Mark 2:11.
Look in Luke 5:24.

Options
• For more help, mark the pages
in three Bibles where each of the
three references is found.
• Refer to unit page 138 for ideas
for teaching the unit key verse,
Psalm 92:5.

Give each child a copy of a filled-in photocopy of page 158. Ask the children to work in pairs. Assign each pair one or two words to find in three Gospels. Ask the pairs to use slips of paper to mark the places in their Bibles where the words are found. Watch carefully how children approach this task. It will help you know how much help they need. If they are frustrated by the task, do one word at a time and find each of the three Bible verses together.

Distribute the Gospel folders begun last week. Read the key verse from the folder cover. Review the information. **Name the four Gospels.** (Matthew, Mark, Luke, John) **What do the Gospels tell about?** (good news about Jesus; stories about Jesus' life) **Who was Matthew and what did he write about?** (Matthew was a tax collector who became one of Jesus' followers. He wrote to tell people that Jesus is the Son of God, the Savior promised in the Old Testament.)

Ask the children to turn to the folder page for the Gospel of Mark.

Was Mark one of Jesus' team of twelve? (no)

Explain that Mark is mentioned later in the New Testament. Many people think that Mark wrote things he heard Peter preach. Peter was one of Jesus' team of twelve. Mark's book is the shortest Gospel. Ask the children to decorate a Mark folder page to remind them of some special things about Mark. They could draw something "short." They could draw Mark standing next to Peter.

Remind children that the four Gospels tell many of the same stories about Jesus. Print the following references from today's story on a large sheet of paper: *Matthew 9:1-8; Mark 2:1-12; Luke 5:17-26.* Give each child three pieces of paper. Have the children copy each Bible reference onto a piece of paper. Children can draw a scene from the Bible story on each reference page.

Give children time to put the reference pages in their folders with the appropriate Gospel.

Materials
• photocopies of page 157

4️⃣ Share What We've Learned

Gather everyone in a circle to talk about what they have been doing and learning. Use the aims for this lesson as an outline for the kinds of questions you ask.

What great things did Jesus do for the man who couldn't walk? (He forgave the man's sins. He made the man walk.) **Why was what Jesus did so great?** (Only God can forgive sins. Doctors couldn't make the man walk. Only Jesus could.) **Why can Jesus do great things?** (He is the Son of God.)

Give each child a new copy of page 157. Ask children to choose a way they will worship Jesus for the great things He does. They may fill in any one of the four sections on the paper. Encourage them to choose a section different from the one they chose last session.

When children have completed their personal worship, have a group worship time. Ask several children to show the pictures they drew about Jesus. Ask some children to share the great thing they will tell about Jesus. Allow children to suggest one or two songs the group can sing to Jesus. Then ask one or two children to say the prayers they wrote for Jesus. Encourage them to tell about their worship ideas at home.

What new words did you learn today? What new thing about the Bible did you learn? Allow children to share and express joy in their developing skills and knowledge.

🏠 **Teaching at Home**

Build comparative vocabulary by putting objects of varying weight in paper sacks. Let children sort them by heavy, heavier, heaviest. Add food coloring to water. Let child talk about dark, darker, darkest or light, lighter, lightest (in both examples). What if the friend had been heavier? What if the house had been taller? What if Jesus were not the greatest?

Reading tip
Talk about spelling comparatives such as heavy, heavier, heaviest; tall, taller, tallest; great, greater, greatest.

A Fair-Weather Forecast

29

Tell the great and amazing thing Jesus did.
Choose a way to worship Jesus.
Read Bible references and find Bible verses.

"Lord, you have done such great things!"   Psalm 92:5, ICB

❶ Get Ready to Read

Continue to work on posters that show great things that Jesus can do because He is the Son of God. See lessons 27 and 28. Children not present the last two sessions will need a blank piece of poster board divided into three sections.

Tell about some times when you were in a thunderstorm. How did you feel? What did you do?

Children can choose which section of the poster they will complete this session. Ask children to draw a dark, stormy sky and huge waves on a stormy sea on the poster. They should use glue and glitter or the glitter paint to draw streaks of lightning on their picture.

Materials
- *The Young Reader's Bible*
- posters begun in lesson 27
- extra pieces of poster board
- glue and glitter or glitter paint
- markers or colored pencils

❷ Read the Bible Story

"Wild Winds and Waves Obey"

Show children the weather forecast in a newspaper. **What do these pictures tell us about the weather?** Explain that in today's story, the men didn't have a forecast. They had to decide what the weather would be like in other ways. Ask children to pretend that they are fishermen in Bible times. They have to decide what the weather will be like. If possible, take the children outside briefly, or open several windows in your room.

What does the sky look like?
What does the air feel like?
What does the air smell like?
What do you think the weather will be like today?

Explain that the fishermen in today's story decided that the weather would be calm. They could sail across the lake. But they were wrong. A storm came up while they were in the middle of the lake. It was a very bad storm.

What do you think the fishermen did?

Listen

Read the story aloud expressively to the children.
How do you think it felt to be on the boat in the storm? (wet and cold, hard

Materials
- *The Young Reader's Bible*, pages 292-297
- photocopies of the Bible story (pages 292-294)
- *The Young Reader's Bible Audio Cassette* or a cassette on which you have recorded unit stories
- cassette player(s), earphones optional
- newspaper pictures of a weather forecast
- large inflatable beach ball
- five cardboard boxes, large enough to put the beach ball inside
- masking tape
- foil stars or other star stickers
- ten pieces of paper
- markers
- crayons or colored pencils

to keep your balance, scary, confusing)

What did Jesus have to do to make the storm stop? (He told the storm to stop and it did!) **Can weather forecasters make a storm stop?** (No. They can only predict what the weather will be like. They can't change the weather.)

What great thing did Jesus do? (He stopped a storm.) **Can you make a storm stop? Why was what Jesus did so amazing?** (No one but God could tell the weather what to do.) **Why can Jesus do such amazing things?** (He is the Son of God.)

Participate

Before class, fold the top edges of the cardboard boxes to the inside. Print the following words in large letters on separate pieces of paper: *boat, lake, sleep, storm, wind, danger, woke, drown, still, obey.*

Tape two word papers to two adjacent sides of each cardboard box. Put the boxes randomly several feet apart in the classroom. The corner between the two pieces of paper should face forward, so children can see and read both words as they play. Make a masking-tape line on the floor an appropriate distance from the boxes.

Children will take turns trying to throw a beach ball into one of the boxes. When the ball lands in a box, they may choose a word on the box. Work together to find and read a sentence from the Bible story about that word. Once a word has been used, it may not be used again. Depending upon the skill of the children, you may wish to give each child several tries to get the beach ball in a box during each turn.

Read

Give each child a copy of the Bible story (pages 292-294). Children can use crayons or colored pencils to color the pages. Then they can add foil stars or star stickers to the pages that show a calm night sky. As children work, play the cassette story. Encourage them to read the story independently at their own level. Even if children can't read every word, they can point to words they know and tell about the story.

❸ Practice Using a Bible

Using My Bible

Before class, write Bible book names on slips of paper. Suggested names: *Genesis, Psalms, Isaiah, 1 Kings, Mark, Revelation, Acts, 1 Peter, Colossians.* Place the slips of paper in a container.

Ask children to work in pairs. Give each pair a copy of Task Card #3. Ask the pairs to draw a slip of paper from the container. One child in each pair should fill in on the card the Bible book name they chose. They then can follow the instructions to complete the card. If you have time, have children put the slips of paper back in the container, choose again, and do the activity a second time. Any pair that draws the same Bible book name should put the slip of paper back and choose again.

Finding Bible Verses

Before class, on photocopies of the top of page 158, fill in the blanks with these words or numbers from the narrow column on page 147. Make enough photocopies of the filled-in pages for each child to have one.

Option
Play the game in teams, taking turns throwing the beach ball.

Snacks
Serve blue Jell-O Jigglers gelatin snacks cut in boat shapes, juice.

Materials
- *The Young Reader's Bible*
- Bibles
- photocopies of Task Card #3 (page 110)
- slips of paper
- Gospel folders used in the last two sessions
- extra paper for the folders
- colored pencils
- photocopies of four filled-in copies of the top of page 158

Options
- For more help, mark the pages in three Bibles where each of the three references are found.
- Refer to unit page 138 for ideas for teaching the unit key verse, Psalm 92:5.

Distribute the Gospel folders begun in lesson 27. Read the key verse together and then review the information they have in their notebooks so far.

What does the word *Gospel* mean? (good news)

Why are Matthew, Mark, Luke, and John called books of "good news"? (because they tell stories of Jesus)

What have you learned about Matthew and Mark? (Allow children to share information they remember. Read this section in lessons 27 and 28 to find information on Matthew and Mark.)

Ask the children to turn to the folder page for the Gospel of Luke. Explain that Luke was a doctor. He was a good friend of the apostle Paul. Luke also wrote the book of Acts. Ask the children to decorate their Luke folder page to remind them of some special things about Luke. They could draw a picture of a doctor. They could print the name *Acts* to remind them that Luke wrote the book of Acts.

Remind children that the four Gospels tell many of the same stories about Jesus. Give each child three pieces of paper for their folders.

Print these Bible references on a large sheet of paper and have the children copy one reference on the top of each paper: *Matthew 8:23-27; Mark 4:35-41; Luke 8:22-25.*

Give each child a copy of a filled-in photocopy of page 158. Ask the children to work in groups of two or three. Make sure children in each group have the same filled-in copy. Assign each group one word to find in all three Gospels.

Ask the pairs to use slips of paper to mark the places in their Bibles where the words are found. Watch carefully how children approach this task. It will help you know how much help they need. If they are frustrated by the task, do one word at a time and find each of the three Bible verses together. When the groups have found their words, ask them to read the sentence in which the word is found in each book. Ask the children to print the words on their reference pages. Children can draw a picture on each page to remind them of the Bible story.

Give children time to put the new reference pages in their folders behind the appropriate Gospel.

 ## Share What We've Learned

Gather everyone in a circle to talk about what they have been doing and learning. Use the aims for this lesson as an outline for the kinds of questions you ask.

What great thing did Jesus do in today's story? (He stopped a storm.) **Why was what Jesus did so great?** (No one but God can tell the weather what to do.) **Why can Jesus do great things?** (He is the Son of God.)

Give each child a new copy of page 157. Tell children to choose ways they will worship Jesus for the great things He does. They may fill in any one of the four sections on the paper.

When children have completed their personal worship, lead the group outside if weather permits, or stand on a covered porch or entrance. Ask the children to name something about the weather for which they are thankful. They can name something Jesus did in the Bible or something about the weather today. When everyone has shared, shout together "God, You are great!"

What new words did you learn today? What new thing about the Bible did you learn?

Copy #1
Find the word *boat*. Look in Matthew 8:24. Look in Mark 4:37. Look in Luke 8:23.

Copy #2
Find the word *drown*. Look in Matthew 8:25. Look in Mark 4:38. Look in Luke 8:24.

Copy #3
Find the word *calm*. Look in Matthew 8:26. Look in Mark 4:39. Look in Luke 8:24.

Copy #4
Find the word *obey*. Look in Matthew 8:27. Look in Mark 4:41. Look in Luke 8:25.

Option

For early or nonreaders, work as a large group to find the words in the Gospels. Mark the page in three Bibles where the three references are found. Guide the children to find the word on the page by looking at the reference. Then read the verse for them.

Materials
• photocopies of page 157

Teaching at Home

Continue to add to the Gospel folder. Purchase a reference Gospel harmony. Some study Bibles include this help. Whenever you read from a Gospel together, make it a practice to read other Gospel accounts of the same event. Record them in the family Gospel folder.

Reading tip

Practice reading exclamations or commands and questions with lots of drama. Let children find them in the story and then practice writing exclamations, commands, and questions.

The Fantastic Feast

Tell what great and amazing thing Jesus did with one boy's lunch.
Choose a way to worship Jesus.
Read Bible references and find Bible verses.

"Lord, you have done such great things!"   Psalm 92:5, ICB

❶ Get Ready to Read

Materials
- *The Young Reader's Bible*
- posters begun in lesson 27
- extra pieces of poster board
- construction paper
- scissors
- glue or tape
- markers or colored pencils

Children will continue to work on posters that show great things that Jesus can do because He is the Son of God. Children not present the last three sessions will need a half piece of poster board divided into two sections.

Children can choose which section of the poster they will complete this session. Children will cut out circle shapes for loaves of bread and fish shapes to glue onto the section. Then they will cut out strips of paper and weave them together and glue them over the top of the section to make a basket. (If you have limited class time, cut strips of construction paper ahead of time for children to weave together and glue.)

❷ Read the Bible Story

Materials
- *The Young Reader's Bible*, pages 298-303
- photocopies of the two-page Bible story (page 155)
- *The Young Reader's Bible Audio Cassette* or a cassette on which you have recorded unit stories
- cassette player(s), earphones optional
- a lunch packed in a paper bag or lunch box (sandwich, some crackers, an apple, a box of juice)
- seven index cards
- props and costumes for acting out the Bible story
- small basket shapes cut from woven place mats, burlap or other coarsely woven cloth, or construction paper
- glue
- crayons or colored pencils

"Enough for Everyone"
Show children the lunch you brought. **What would happen if you all forgot your lunches and we had to share my lunch? Would we get very much to eat?**

If you wish, divide the sandwich into tiny bites and give each child one. Explain that in the story today, a very large group of people had only one small lunch about the size of yours to eat, but Jesus was there.

What do you think happened when it was time to eat? Listen to find out.

Listen
Read the story aloud expressively to the children.

How do you think the people felt when they saw only one small lunch was all they had to eat? (hungry, tired, didn't think they'd get even one bite) **What did Jesus tell His disciples to do?** (Give the lunch to the people.) **What happened when they gave the food to the people?** (There was enough for everyone.) **How much was left over?** (twelve baskets)

What great thing did Jesus do? (He fed over five thousand people with one boy's lunch.) **What was amazing about what Jesus did?** (Only God could make a little food feed so many—with leftovers!) **Why could Jesus do such an amazing thing?** (He is the Son of God.)

Participate

Before class, on separate index cards, print the following words: *busy, boat, bring, boy, bread, broke, baskets.*

Play a game. Have each of seven children hold a word card. Work together to find the words in the Bible story. Have the seven children stand in the order the words appear. When the children are in order, choose someone to read a sentence from the story or tell what happened next as you point to each word in order.

Before class, gather props for acting out the story—a basket with five pieces of bread and two construction paper fish; one or two large clothes baskets for collecting leftovers; items for Bible-times costumes (towels and strips of cloth for head coverings, bathrobes)

Assign roles to act out the story. Necessary characters include Jesus, the boy, two disciples, and several people to be the crowd. Additional characters may be a sick man, a woman and her son.

Choose two good readers to read the story, or read the story yourself.

Give children props and costumes and discuss how to act out the story. Designate the middle of your classroom as the lake. The story will begin on one side of the lake. Then Jesus and His disciples will go across the middle of the lake and the crowd of people will run around the outside of the lake to the other side. When actions have been decided, read or have good readers read the story as the characters act it out. If you have time, reassign roles and act out the story again.

Read

Give each child a copy of the two-page Bible story (page 155). Children can use crayons or colored pencils to color the page and cut out and glue extra baskets onto the picture. As children work, play the cassette story.

③ Practice Using a Bible

Using My Bible

Ask the children to sit in a large circle with their Bibles. Give each child a blank copy of Task Card #3. Ask each child to open a Bible to any page and print the Bible book name on the first line of the Task Card. You may wish to ask children to try to find a book in the Bible that they have never heard of or have not found before. They should then find that book in their Bible's table of contents.

When children have completed that step, pass the Task Cards to the left and complete the second line on the card. Children should pass the Task Card to the left two more times. Each time they complete one of the four lines on Task Card #3, they are working on a different card. When the activity is completed, talk about the Bible books they found in the Old and New Testaments.

Finding Bible Verses

Before class, cut apart the four puzzles on page 159. Cut each puzzle in half and put the halves in an envelope. Make enough for every child to have one set of eight puzzle pieces.

Help children find John 6:1-13 in their Bibles. They should read the words printed on the top of each puzzle-piece figure. Match the puzzle-piece top with a bottom picture of a basket that goes with the words. Next, using their Bibles, they can find the verse that tells the words or the ideas of the words on each puzzle piece. Matching the puzzle pictures, they can print the correct Bible reference

Snacks
Serve hard rolls and tuna. (Or cook fish to taste.)

Materials
• *The Young Reader's Bible*
• Bibles
• photocopies of Task Card #3 (page 110)
• Gospel folders
• extra paper for the folders
• colored pencils
• photocopies of page 159
• envelopes
• a large sheet of paper

Here is a boy with 5 loaves and 2 fish.
John 6:9
Jesus held the bread and gave thanks.
John 6:11
Everyone had enough to eat.
John 6:12
They filled twelve baskets with leftovers.
John 6:13

Option
For early or nonreaders, print in the correct Bible references before you photocopy the page. Then have them match the pictures, say aloud the Bible reference and find the verse in a Bible. You can read each verse aloud for them.

on the line on the bottom of the matching picture.

Give the children their Gospel folders and read the key verse together. Review the information in the folders.

What are the four books about Jesus' life called? (Gospels)

Name the four Gospels. (Matthew, Mark, Luke, John)

What have you learned about Matthew, Mark, and Luke? (Allow children to share information they remember. Read this section in lessons 27-29 to find information on the three books.)

Ask the children to turn to the folder page for the Gospel of John.

Was John one of Jesus' team of twelve? (yes)

Explain that the Gospel books, Matthew, Mark, and Luke, are most alike. John also tells about Jesus, but his Gospel is different from the other three.

John never names himself in his Gospel. Instead, he calls himself "the disciple whom Jesus loved." Ask the children to decorate a John folder page to remind them of John. They could draw a picture of the other three Gospel books together, and then draw a picture of the book, John, by itself to remind them that it is different. They could draw a picture of John and Jesus together to remind them that he calls himself the disciple whom Jesus loved.

Remind children that the four Gospels tell many of the same stories about Jesus. Print the following references from today's story on a large sheet of paper and ask the children to copy references from each book onto a separate sheet of paper: *Matthew 14:13-21; Mark 6:30-44; Luke 9:10-17; John 6:1-13.* Ask the children to find the references in their Bible and print some words they recognize from each reference on the correct page. If you have time, the children can draw a picture on each page to remind them of the Bible story.

Add the pages to the folders in the correct places.

Share What We've Learned

Gather everyone in a circle to talk about what they have been doing and learning. Use the aims for this lesson as an outline for the kinds of questions you ask.

What great thing did Jesus do in today's story? (He fed more than five thousand people with one boy's lunch.) **Why was what Jesus did so great?** (No one but God could make such a little food feed so many.) **Why can Jesus do great things?** (He is the Son of God.)

Before class, print one of the following Bible references on each slip of paper: *Deuteronomy 10:21; 2 Samuel 7:22; Psalm 47:2; Joel 2:21; Romans 16:27; 2 Corinthians 1:3; Revelation 7:12.*

Give each child a new copy of page 157. Ask children to choose a way they will worship Jesus for the great things He does. They may fill in any one of the four sections on the paper.

When children have completed their personal worship, have a group worship time. Sit in a circle. Pass around the basket and ask each child or pair of children to take a slip of paper and find the Bible verse printed on the paper. Children should practice reading the verse and ask you for help with any unfamiliar words. If a verse is too long or difficult, help them choose a few words to read.

When the children have practiced their reading, have a praise time. Children or pairs will take turns reading their verses. In between each reading, the entire group will say the key verse, Psalm 92:5, together.

When all verses have been read, ask children who are willing to say a sentence prayer to Jesus, thanking Him for a great thing He did!

Option

Children take the pages out of their folders and work in pairs to play a Gospel folder game. Each pair needs one folder to play. Give these instructions and see who can complete each first.

Hold up the page about the book written by a doctor.

Put all the references in Matthew in order.

Find three pages with Bible references for the story of Jesus' stopping the storm.

Hold up the page about the book written by a tax collector.

Put all the references for John in order. (There is only one.)

Hold up the page for the shortest Gospel.

Find four pages with Bible references for the story of Jesus' feeding the people.

Have children reorganize their folders.

Materials
• photocopies of page 157
• slips of paper in a basket or other container

 **Teaching at Home**

Gather food items and read the nutrition labels and serving sizes. Look at a food pyramid and talk about the foods Jesus multiplied.

Reading tips
• Write words and numerals for 5,000 and for 12. Practice reading and writing large numbers.
• Find the examples of compound words in the story (*afternoon, leftovers, mountainside*). Make up more compound words. Practice dictionary skills by looking up each invented word to see whether or not it is a word.

A Faithful Friend

Tell the great and amazing thing Jesus did.
Choose a way to worship Jesus.
Read Bible references and find Bible verses.

"Lord, you have done such great things!"   Psalm 92:5, ICB

❶ Get Ready to Read

Children will continue to work on posters that show great things Jesus can do because He is the Son of God. Children not present the last four sessions will need a smaller piece of blank poster board.

Children should cut a cave shape from construction paper and glue it to the last section. They can also cut out a paper stone and glue it to the side of the entrance as though it has been rolled back. Then they should draw the figure of Lazarus coming out of the cave. Tape strips of cloth to cover him.

Materials
- *The Young Reader's Bible*
- posters begun in lesson 27
- extra pieces of poster board
- gray or brown construction paper
- strips of cloth
- scissors
- glue or tape
- markers or colored pencils

❷ Read the Bible Story

"Lazarus Lives Again"

Before class, print the names *Jesus, Mary, Martha,* and *Lazarus* on a large sheet of paper.

Point to the names and explain that these are the people in today's story. Ask the children to say the names with you. Display page 334 in a *Young Reader's Bible.* Look at the picture.

Who do you think the women and the man are? What is wrong with the man? Why do the women look sad?

Talk about times when people call the children by name. **When do people call out your name?** (calling attendance, calling in from play, called on in class, called over by friends) **Who calls out your name?** (friends, parents, teachers)

Listen to find out whose name Jesus called out. Listen to hear the very special reason.

Listen

Read the story aloud expressively to the children.

Why do you think Jesus waited to go to Lazarus? (We don't know for sure. He probably knew that He would bring Lazarus back alive.)

What did Jesus say? ("Lazarus, come out!")

What great thing did Jesus do? (He made Lazarus come back alive after he was dead.) **What was so amazing about what Jesus did?** (Dead people stay dead. Only God or His Son could bring someone back to life.) **Why can Jesus do such amazing things?** (He is the Son of God.)

Materials
- *The Young Reader's Bible,* pages 334-339
- photocopies of the two-page Bible story (page 156)
- *The Young Reader's Bible Audio Cassette* or a cassette on which you have recorded unit stories
- cassette player(s), earphones optional
- paper plates
- markers or crayons
- scissors
- craft sticks
- tape
- a large sheet of paper

Participate

Give the children the paper plates. Ask each child to make a sad face on one side of the plate and a happy face on the other side of the plate. If you have time, children may cut eye holes in the plates. Tape a craft stick as a handle on the bottom of each plate.

Tell children you will read through the story again as the children hold their happy/sad plates in front of their faces. If the words you are reading are sad, the children will show the sad face. If the words you are reading are happy, the children will show the happy face.

If your children are good readers, do the activity again with the children reading or taking turns reading the story aloud while you hold up the happy or sad face.

Read

Give each child a copy of the two-page Bible story (page 156). Ask children to circle the words *dead* or *died* in black. They should circle the words *live* or *life* in their favorite color and color Jesus' robe the same color. They may color the rest of the picture as they wish.

As children work, play the cassette story. Encourage them to read the story independently at their own level. Even if children can't read every word, they can point to words they know and tell about the story.

❸ Practice Using a Bible

Using My Bible

Before class, print Bible book names (your choice) on index cards, one name on each card. Print enough for each child to have five cards. If you have more than thirteen children, you will have to repeat some book names.

Play a game to help children find Bible books. Ask children to stand in a circle with their Bibles. Place the index cards face down in the middle of the circle and spread them out. At your signal, each child grabs two or three cards. They look up the book names in the table of contents, find each book, and place the index cards at the first pages of the books in their Bibles.

Finding Bible Verses

Distribute the Gospel folders.

What are some special things we learned about the Gospel of John? (It is different from the other three Gospels. John calls himself "the disciple whom Jesus loved.") Explain that today's story about Lazarus is only found in the Gospel of John.

Before class, print John 11:1-44 and the following key words on a large piece of paper: *life, Christ, died, cave, cloth (KJV, napkin).*

Show **John 11:1-44** on a large piece of paper. Ask the children to find the reference in a Bible.

Ask the children to search for the key words in John 11. When they find each word, they should print the word and the reference for the word on their John 11:1-44 paper.

If you have time, the children can draw a picture on the page to remind them of the Bible story. Ask the children to take the pages out of their folders and follow your instructions.

Put together all the pages about the catch of fish and Jesus' team of twelve. How were the stories alike? How were they different?

Snacks
Serve rice cakes and peanut butter. The rice cake reminds us of the stone rolled from the tomb.

Materials
• *The Young Reader's Bible*
• Bibles
• Gospel folders
• photocopies of the cube (page 158)
• transparent tape and masking tape
• scissors
• large piece of paper
• marker
• index cards
• poster board

Options
• For younger children, work in pairs. Or have each child grab only one card.
• Refer to unit page 138 for ideas for teaching the unit key verse, Psalm 92:5.

Matching references
John 11:25; John 11:27; John 11:32; John 11:38; John 11:44

Put together all the pages about the man who couldn't walk that Jesus healed. What were some of the same words that each Gospel used?

Put together all the pages about Jesus calming the storm. What were some of the same words that each Gospel used?

Put together all the pages about Jesus feeding more than 5,000 people. How were the stories alike? How were they different?

Ask the children to put their folders back together with title pages for each Gospel in order and reference pages in order behind each title page.

Give children extra paper to add to their folders. Encourage the children to take their folders home. As they read Bible stories at home, they can print Bible references and words they know on the papers and put them in the correct place in the folder.

Close the folders. Read the key verse together.

Before class, divide poster board into nine sections. In each section, print one of the following Bible references: *John 11:1; John 11:3; John 11:6; John 11:17; John 11:27; John 11:32; John 11:38; John 11:43; John 11:44.* Lay the poster board on the floor and make a masking tape line behind which children will stand to toss their cubes. Cut out several cubes, fold and put them together.

Ask children to work in pairs. Children will take turns tossing a cube onto the poster board. Then they will follow the instructions on the top side of the cube for the verse reference on which the cube lands.

 ## 4 Share What We've Learned

Materials
• photocopies of page 157
• five stations

Gather everyone in a circle to talk about what they have been doing and learning. Use the aims for this lesson as an outline for the kinds of questions you ask.

What great thing did Jesus do in today's story? (He made Lazarus come back alive.) **Why was what Jesus did so great?** (Dead people always stay dead—unless God makes them come back alive.) **What other great things has Jesus done? Why can Jesus do great things?** (He is the Son of God.)

What new words did you learn today? What new thing about the Bible did you learn? Allow children to share and express joy in their developing skills and knowledge.

If you worked on unit posters, children can remove the strips of cloth from the Lazarus figure they drew. They can draw and color Bible times clothing on the figure.

Distribute the photocopies of page 157. Ask children to choose a way they will worship Jesus for the great things He does. They may fill in any one of the four sections on the paper.

Before class, prepare five stations in the room to represent five great things Jesus did—a blanket or empty mat for the man who couldn't walk, strips of cloth for Lazarus, a lunch bag or box for the 5,000 who were fed, a fishing net for the great catch of fish, an outside window where the weather can be viewed for the storm that was stopped.

When children have completed their personal worship, have a group worship time. Lead the children to each of the five stations prepared before class. At each station, have the children name the great thing Jesus did that is represented at the station. Tell Jesus He is great by saying a prayer or singing a song.

 Teaching at Home

Talk about burial practices. Visit a funeral home or a cemetery.

Reading tip
Review the purpose of quotation marks. Let children copy the words that Jesus said. Include quotation marks.

Peter and Andrew left everything
and followed Jesus.
So did James and John.

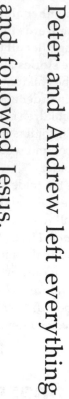

And later Jesus also called Philip,
Bartholomew, Matthew, Thomas,
another James, Thaddaeus,
Simon the Zealot, and Judas
to be with him
on his team of twelve.

Jesus thanked God for the food.

He broke the bread and fish

into pieces.

"Give the food to all the people,"

Jesus told the disciples.

Five thousand men,

plus women and children,

had enough to eat.

The leftovers filled twelve baskets.

"Jesus must come from God,"

the people said.

Then Jesus quietly went up

the mountainside to pray.

155

When Jesus came to Bethany,
Lazarus was dead.

"Lord," said Martha,
"if you had been here,
my brother would not have died."

"Your brother will live again,"
said Jesus.

"I am the resurrection and the life.
He who believes in me will live."

"I believe you are the Son of God,"
said Martha.

156

I Can Pray.

Circle what you will say to Jesus.
Or write your own words.

Dear Jesus,
I love You.
You do great things.
Thank You.
You are the special Son of God.

We Worship Jesus. He Does Great Things!

I Can Sing.

What song do you like to sing to Jesus?

Write the name here.

Sing the words softly to yourself.

We Worship Jesus. He Does Great Things!

I Can Tell.

Circle or write one great thing to tell about Jesus.

Jesus found fish for Peter and Andrew.

Jesus made a sick man well, inside and out.

Jesus made a terrible storm stop.

Jesus fed 5,000 people with one boy's lunch.

Jesus made His friend Lazarus come back alive.

We Worship Jesus. He Does Great Things!

I Can Draw.

What great thing will you worship Jesus for?
Draw a picture of the great thing here.

We Worship Jesus. He Does Great Things!

Gospels

Four Bible books tell about Jesus.

Sometimes the same story is told in more than one Gospel. Find this word in your Bible and read stories of Jesus.

Find the word _____.

Look in Matthew _____.

Look in Mark _____.

Look in Luke _____.

Look in John _____.

These books are called **Gospels.**

1. Cut out along solid lines. 2. Fold all dotted lines. 3. Slip grey squares inside cube. 4. Tape together.

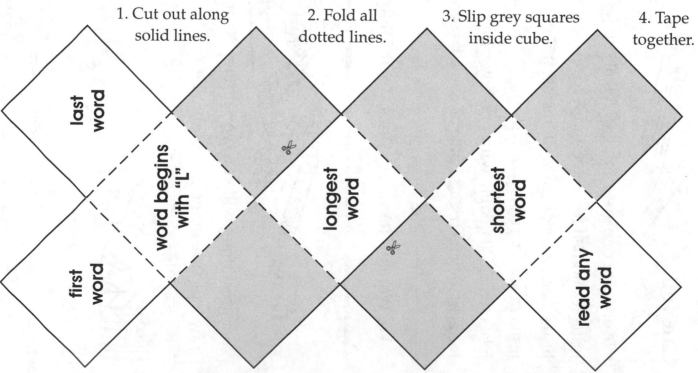

last word

word begins with "L"

first word

longest word

shortest word

read any word

Children find a verse, roll the cube, and name the word.

Here is a boy with 5 loaves and 2 fish.

Jesus held the bread and gave thanks.

Everyone had enough to eat.

They filled twelve baskets with leftovers.

Write the Bible reference.

Match the pictures.

Mix up the pictures.

Cut apart the pieces.

We Obey Jesus' Teachings– the Word of God

Key Verse

"Never tire of doing what is right."   2 Thessalonians 3:13, NIV

Unit Aims

By the end of the unit, learners will be able to
- tell five Bible stories about what Jesus teaches us to do.
- feel confident in finding verses in a Bible and reading *The Young Reader's Bible*.
- locate books, chapters and verses in their own Bibles.
- read (at their level) stories from *The Young Reader's Bible*.
- obey Jesus' teachings.

Unit Project

The Right Things to Do T-Shirt

Children will design and make a T-shirt reminding them of right things to do. Each session you will talk with children about a key word or phrase about a right thing to do. Children print the word or phrase on the shirt. Then they will decide how to picture the idea.

Words can be printed directly on the T-shirt with iron-on fabric crayons. Children can then draw a reminder of the right thing to do. Simple designs with few colors are best.

If you prefer, have children draw and color on paper. They can start over and over until they are satisfied with their design. You can iron their drawings onto their T-shirts. (In order to iron on words, however, letters must be reversed.) Recruit extra adult help for this project or gather the children's art so that you can work on them at home. Experiment to use the most effective heat setting and timing for your iron.

Unit Vocabulary

bandages
comfort
enemy
example
finished
foolish
heavenly
humble
important
innkeeper
Kingdom of Heaven
mercy
neighbor
preached
priest
question
reward
robbers
servant
soldier
Spirit of God
temple
travelers
wounds

Key Words
Lesson 35

Lessons 32, 33, 34
   page 168
Lesson 36
   page 177

Love Your Neighbor
Love Your Neighbor

	The Singing Bible (3 tapes)	Kids on the Rock (More Songs)	Follow the Leader (The Donut Man)	I'm a Helper (The Donut Man)	Good News (The Donut Man)
Lesson 32					
Lesson 33	Blessed Are . . .	Teach Me Your Ways	With All My Heart		Jesus Loves Me
Lesson 34	Who Do You Say I Am?				
Lesson 35			More and More Like Jesus	Good Samaritan	
Lesson 36	The Lord's Prayer (NIV)				
Key Verse		Love Your Neighbor			
Unit Theme		That's What I'm Gonna Do	We're Following Jesus	Love and Obey	Use Me
All Lessons	The Books We Love the Best The Bible Book Is True	God's Word Is for Me			

The Singing Bible (3 tapes), ©1993 by Lightwave Publishing, Inc. Manufactured and distributed by Word Publishing, Dallas, TX 75234
Kids on the Rock! More Songs, ©1994 Gospel Light, Ventura CA 93006
The Donut Man (3 tapes): *Follow the Leader*, ©1990; *I'm a Helper*, ©1991; *Good News*, ©1991; Integrity Music, Inc., P.O. Box 16813 Mobile, AL 36616

John
Get ready!
Change how
you live.
The kingdom
of heaven is
coming soon.

John
I need to be
baptized by
you. Why do
you come to *me?*

Jesus
It is important
to baptize me.
It is the right
thing to do.

boy
John, I am
sorry I have not
obeyed God.

girl
John, I am
sorry I have not
obeyed God.

cloud
You are my Son.
I love You. I am
very pleased
with You.

Key Verse Activities

Never tire of doing what is right.
2 Thessalonians 3:13, NIV

Materials
- a large safety pin and five beads per child (one necklace from a dollar store can provide enough beads for the class)

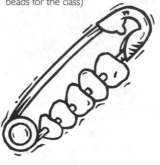

Friendship Pins

How is one of these beads different from another? (Its color.) **Is one better than any other?** (No.)

God wants us to love everyone and treat them well even if they look different from us. When Jesus says to love your neighbor as yourself, is He talking about the people who live on your street? (Yes, but He also means everyone else.) **How do you show that have not stopped doing what is right?** (Treat others as you want to be treated.)

You can earn a bead for a friendship pin today and every time you come to class for the next four lessons if you remember your memory verse. When you have collected all five beads on your pin, you can give it to someone to show love and friendship.

Seesaws

Divide the class into pairs and have them face one another. **We're going to practice our memory verse by doing "Seesaws." One person goes down as if on a seesaw, says the first word of the verse, and stands back up. The other person squats down and says the second word, and so on. Keep playing faster and faster.** Pair up with one of the children to demonstrate.

Materials
- plastic disposable tablecloth
- permanent markers
- small index cards
- a pen

Bend Over Backwards

Before class, draw twelve hearts on the tablecloth and print words of the memory verse in the hearts as shown. On each index card, draw two things: 1) a heart with a word from the memory verse on it and 2) a hand or foot with the word *right* or *left* on it. Make at least fourteen cards so the parts of the memory verse are used twice. Do not make any identical cards.

Do you know what it means to "bend over backwards" for people? It means you're willing to do anything to help them. Even when we are getting tired of always doing right, God wants us to do things that show love for people. Today we're going to *really* bend over backwards as we play a memory verse game. We'll take turns picking two cards and putting our hands or feet on the words of the memory verse as the cards instruct. The goal is to stay standing and not knock down anyone else.

Hearts shown:
Never / tire / of doing
what / is right / 2 Thes. 3:13, NIV
Never / tire / of doing
what / is right / 2 Thes. 3:13, NIV

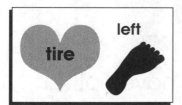

tire / left

John Baptizes Jesus

Tell why Jesus told John to baptize Him. (It was the right thing to do.)
Choose a way to obey Jesus.
Tell the messages of the Old and New Testament.

"Never tire of doing what is right."   2 Thessalonians 3:13, NIV

① Get Ready to Read

Materials
- *The Young Reader's Bible*
- plain white T-shirt for each child
- fabric crayons
- plain drawing paper
- large sheet of paper

See unit 7 pages for a complete explanation of this T-shirt project.

The Bible stories in this unit tell about things we do to obey Jesus. Jesus gave us an example by doing right things himself. The key word for today is the name *Jesus* because we know that Jesus always did the right thing.

Ask a child to find page 262 in a *Young Reader's Bible*. Explain that in today's story Jesus tells John to baptize Him. Briefly tell what happened by showing the pictures. **Why did Jesus tell John to baptize Him?** (It was the right thing to do.)

Ask the children to decide what they will draw on their T-shirts to remind them of Jesus' example of doing right. Two wavy blue lines can remind them of the river where Jesus was baptized.

Print the word *Jesus* on the large paper. The children can practice printing the name *Jesus* before they copy it on the shirt.

② Read the Bible Story

Materials
- *The Young Reader's Bible*, pages 262-267
- photocopies of the Bible story (pages 295-297)
- photocopies of pages 161 and 181
- *The Young Reader's Bible Audio Cassette* or a cassette on which you have recorded unit stories
- cassette player(s), earphones optional
- scissors
- craft sticks
- colored pencils
- tape
- white crayons
- watercolor paints
- paintbrushes
- a large sheet of paper

"The Right Thing to Do"

Plan to have your story time in a different area of the room than usual. If your children usually sit on the floor, plan to have them sit on seats or on carpet squares. If they usually sit on chairs, have them sit on the floor. Do not explain any of these changes to the children ahead of time.

When it is time for children to gather, go to the area of the room you have prepared for the story time. Wait for children to follow you there. Sit on the floor or chair and wait for children to follow your lead. Encourage them to join you if they are reluctant.

Did you notice anything different about our large group area? (a different spot, sitting in a different way) **How did you know to come to a different place and sit on the floor (on a chair)?** (because you, the teacher, showed them) Explain that the children followed your example, so they knew the right thing to do.

When you did what I did, you were following my example. Have you ever dressed or talked or acted like someone else? (Allow children to share times they have copied others whom they like. If they need help thinking of people, mention older brothers or sisters, friends at school, teachers, parents.)

Listen to hear one way people follow Jesus' example.

Listen

Read the story aloud expressively to the children. Ask children to follow along. **What did John do for Jesus?** (baptized Him) **Have you ever seen a baptism? What happened?** (Allow children to tell what they saw. If your children have never seen a baptism, spend a few minutes explaining what happens when someone is baptized.)

Why did Jesus want to be baptized? (It was the right thing to do.) **How can we follow Jesus' example?** (We can do right things too.)

Participate

Before class, make photocopies of reproducible pages 161 and 181. Cut out one each of the two John puppets, Jesus, and the cloud (181). Cut out enough of the boy and girl puppets (181) so that everyone will have a puppet. Cut out and tape the dialogue (161) onto the back of each puppet.

Distribute the puppets. You will need good readers to speak for the two John puppets, the Jesus puppet, and the voice of God in the cloud. Remaining children can use boy or girl puppets who are baptized by John. Ask children to color their puppets. When they are finished, they should tape their puppet to a craft stick or around two fingers.

Use the puppets to act out the story. You should read all non-speaking parts and cue children when to read. Boy and girl puppets can come to John and read their sentence together as a group.

If you have time, switch puppets and act out the story again.

Give each child a copy of the Bible story (pages 295-297). Give children white crayons and ask them to circle and completely color over the words that tell why Jesus said it was important to baptize Him. ("It is the right thing to do," page 296.) Then give children paintbrushes and watercolor paints and ask them to paint over the entire page. The crayoned words will not accept the paint color.

Read

Children can listen to the cassette story as they paint.

As you have time, allow children to experiment with coloring different sections of the pictures on pages 295 and 297 with the white crayons and then painting over the pages. Each child can reread the story at his own level.

❸ Practice Using a Bible

Using My Bible

Before class, print the following phrases on large sheets of paper. Make two identical sets of papers. *Worshiped God, Obeyed God, Worshiped Jesus, Obeyed Jesus, Told others about Jesus.* Attach the papers randomly to a wall near the floor.

Play a game to review what each part of the Bible tells about. Go to each paper and read it aloud. **As I read an instruction, you should go to one of these papers and do what I read.** Note: It is not necessary for children to keep their nose on one card as they put their elbow on another.

1. Put your nose on a card that tells what people did in the Old Testament.

2. Put your knee on a card that tells what people did in the New Testament.

3. Put your ear on another card that tells what people did in the New Testament.

4. Put your shoulder on a card that tells something people did in both the Old and New Testaments.

Options
- If you are working with only one child, make only the John and Jesus puppets. You play one part, and the child can play the other part.
- If you are working with very early readers, have half the class make John puppets and the other half make Jesus puppets. You read through the story for the group. Each time they hear or read the words John or Jesus, the children with the corresponding puppets can hold them up.

Snacks
Serve honey-roasted peanuts and water.

Materials
- *The Young Reader's Bible*
- Bible for each child
- piece of paper
- tape or Plasti-Tak
- large sheets of paper

5. Put your little finger on a card that tells something people did in the New Testament only.

6. Put your index finger on a card that tells what we will be learning about in this unit. (obeying God or obeying Jesus)

Allow everyone to laugh and enjoy this game. Next, have the children hold their Bibles and put a finger in the place between the Old and New Testament.

Hold the part of your Bible that is the Old Testament. What does the Old Testament tell about? (how people worshiped and obeyed God)

Hold the part of your Bible that is the New Testament. What does the New Testament tell about? (how people worshiped and obeyed God and Jesus; how people told others about Jesus)

Finding Bible Verses

Remind children that we know that the Bible has the words of God in it, because the Bible tells us so. We can be sure that the Bible tells us the right things to do. Print **Hebrews 4:12** on a large sheet of paper. Review the Reference Rhyme (page 32) to remind everyone how to find verses. Ask the children to find the verse in their Bibles. Then read it aloud together.

Print **2 Thessalonians 3:13** on the large paper. Explain that this is the key verse for the unit. Ask the children to find it in their Bibles. Read the verse aloud together. **What should we never get tired of doing?** (right things)

How do we know what is right? (The Bible tells us what is right.)

Explain that the Bible tells even more about the story than they read in the *Young Reader's Bible.* Give each pair a photocopy of the questions and Bible references you prepared before class (narrow column). Ask the groups to find and read the verses to answer the questions. The group can draw a picture of the Bible story, incorporating the new facts they learned. (They could draw John dressed as he is described, and they could draw soldiers and tax collectors in the crowd.) ·

Questions and References
Before class, print the following three instructions and Bible references on a piece of paper.

Photocopy the paper so that each pair of children can have one paper.

1. What was John to do for Jesus? Mark 1:2

2. How did John look? Matthew 3:4

3. Who were some of the people in the crowd? Luke 3:12, 14

4 Share What We've Learned

Gather everyone in a circle to talk about what they have been doing and learning. Use the aims for this lesson as an outline for the kinds of questions you ask. Children can use the puppets to answer the questions.

What thing did Jesus do as an example for us? (He was baptized by John.)
Why was Jesus baptized? (It was the right thing to do.)

How can we follow Jesus' example? (We can choose to do right things.)

What are some right things we can do? Print children's suggestions on the large paper. (some ideas: tell the truth, obey parents, share, read the Bible, pray, say only kind words, pick up my toys)

Play a game to help children identify some right things they can do to be like Jesus. Sit in a circle.

I will begin by saying my name and telling a way to obey Jesus that starts with the same sound as my name. For example, My name is Kyle, and I can say kind words. Then we will continue around the circle, letting each of you say your name and tell a way to obey Jesus.

Children can use suggestions from the list or make up their own. If a child has trouble coming up with a suggestion, brainstorm as a group a way to obey that begins with the same sound as his name. Plan to ask children to name ways they have obeyed Jesus to follow up this lesson.

Materials
• large sheet of paper
• puppets made earlier

Teaching at Home

During this unit, adjust the family job list so that it includes a section called "the right thing to do." Each family member can choose something he or she will do because God says it is right. Plan to reward those who do right things, even those not on the list.

Reading tip
Look for words that add *ed: baptized, pleased, sinned, preached, obeyed, opened, landed.* Notice that sometimes the final e is dropped, sometimes the final consonant is doubled and sometimes no change is made to the root word.

The Wise and Foolish Builders

Tell how we can do what Jesus taught.
Choose a way to obey Jesus.
Read Bible references and find Bible verses.

"Never tire of doing what is right."   2 Thessalonians 3:13, NIV

Materials
- *The Young Reader's Bible*
- T-shirts begun last session
- extra T-shirts for new children
- fabric crayons
- plain drawing paper
- a large sheet of paper

Note
See unit 7 pages for a complete explanation of this T-shirt project.

① Get Ready to Read

Ask a child to find page 284 in a *Young Reader's Bible*. Read or ask a good reader to read the page. **What does Jesus tell us to do to build a strong house?** (hear and obey)

The key word about right things for today's story is *obey* **because Jesus compared the person who obeys to a house built on a strong rock.**

Print the word *obey* on a large sheet of paper. The children can practice printing the word *obey* before they copy it onto the shirt.

Materials
- *The Young Reader's Bible*, pages 280-285
- photocopies of the Bible story (pages 298-300)
- *The Young Reader's Bible Audio Cassette* or a cassette on which you have recorded unit stories
- cassette player(s), earphones optional
- two similar pans, one filled with sand, one with a large, flat rock
- Lego blocks
- two water pitchers
- colored pencils
- smile-face stickers
- a large sheet of paper
- crayons or colored pencils

② Read the Bible Story

"Jesus the Teacher"

Before class, ask a man to dress in Bible times clothing and play the part of Jesus. He will be the teacher for today's story. The man should prepare to read or recite the words that Jesus says on pages 281-285 in the *Young Reader's Bible.* If weather permits, have the story time outside. Children can sit on the grass just as the crowd in today's story did.

What is something that makes you really happy? Tell about a time when you were very happy. (Allow children to tell about happy times.)

Explain that Jesus tells us how doing right things makes us happy. **Let's listen for right things we can do. You can help me make a list of right things after you hear the story.**

Listen

If you are having your story time outside, lead children outside. If your schedule permits, serve your snack outside as well. The volunteer who portrays Jesus should greet children before beginning to read or recite words from the story. Children should simply listen to Jesus' teachings, When he has finished, lead the children back inside. Give each child a copy of the Bible story (pages 298-300). Explain words that children may not understand—humble, comfort, mercy, peace.

What right things did Jesus tell us to do? (List children's answers on poster board or chalkboard—be humble, love mercy and peace, love enemies, forgive those who do wrong, don't worry about getting rich, live to please God, pray always, hear and obey me.) Talk about how people can do those things.

Who did Jesus say we are like if we do right things? (a wise man who built his house on a rock) **Who did Jesus say we are like if we do not do right things?** (a foolish man who built his house on sand)

Participate

Divide the children into two groups. Give each group a pan of sand or a pan with a rock. Supply Legos blocks for building a house on the sand or on the rock. They should build the strongest, best house that they can. When the groups have completed their houses, give each group a pitcher of water. Each group can take a turn pouring the water in the area around (not on) the house. Discuss what happens to the houses.

What happened to the sand when water was poured around it? (It moved around, washed away, caused the house to move.) **What happened to the rock when water was poured around it?** (It didn't move.)

Sing the song "The Wise Man Built His House Upon the Rock" with motions.

Read

Give children smile-face stickers and ask them to put a sticker by every right thing that Jesus teaches us to do. Children can use colored pencils to color the Bible story pages. They can listen to the cassette while they color.

③ Practice Using a Bible

Using My Bible

Help children practice using their Bibles without looking up books in the table of contents. Instead, call out instructions to find books. Children should close their Bibles after following each instruction.

Open your Bible to the first book. What is it? (Genesis) **Open your Bible to the middle. What book is it?** (Psalms) **Open your Bible to the last book. What is it?** (Revelation)

Call out the names randomly and have children close and reopen their Bibles to the proper book—**Psalms, Genesis, Revelation, Genesis, Psalms, Psalms, Genesis, Revelation, Revelation, Genesis**.

Now open your Bible to the first book in the New Testament. What is it? (Matthew)

This book may take children a little longer to find. Ask them to look carefully at the pages of their Bibles to see about where Matthew is—more than halfway through the Bible.

Call out names as before, but include Matthew in the list—**Genesis, Psalms, Matthew, Revelation, Matthew, Psalms, Revelation, Genesis.**

Finding Bible Verses

Print **Hebrews 4:12** on the chalkboard or poster board. Help the children to find the verse in their Bibles. Then read it aloud together. **Why is this verse important to us when we study the Bible?** (It helps us know that the Bible has the words of God.)

Explain to the children that the story in *The Young Reader's Bible* names only a few of the right things that Jesus taught on the hillside. Those teachings were called "The Sermon on the Mount."

Lyrics
"The wise man built his house upon the rock. (Repeat twice.) And the rains came tumbling down. The rains came down, and the floods came up. (Repeat twice.) But the house on the rock stood firm. The foolish man built his house upon the sand. (Repeat twice.) And the rains came tumbling down. The rains came down, and the floods came up. (Repeat twice.) And the house on the sand crashed down!" (lyrics: public domain)

Snacks
Serve raisins and juice. Pretend to be a crowd on a hillside listening to Jesus.

Materials
• *The Young Reader's Bible*
• Bible for each child
• index cards
• tape or Plasti-Tak
• large sheet of paper
• markers

Before class, print the following Bible references on index cards. The right thing described in each Bible verse is provided in parentheses for your reference only. *Matthew 5:34-37* (don't swear), *Matthew 5:42* (give to those who ask), *Matthew 5:44* (love and pray for enemies), *Matthew 6:2-4* (give to others in secret), *Matthew 6:6* (pray in secret), *Matthew 6:25* (don't worry about food and clothes), *Matthew 7:1, 2* (don't judge others), *Matthew 7:7* (ask God for what you need).

Divide into groups of two or three. Give each group one or two of the index cards with Bible references you prepared before class. Tell the children to look up the Bible verse, find the right thing that Jesus is teaching us to do and decide how to act it out.

When the groups are finished, ask them to act out the ways to do right. When each group is finished, print the right action they acted out on a large sheet of paper.

④ Share What We've Learned

Gather everyone in a circle to talk about what they have been doing and learning. Use the aims for this lesson as an outline for the kinds of questions you ask.

What right things did Jesus teach us to do in today's story? (Children can refer to the list you made.)

Ask the children to look at the list of things Jesus taught and decide a way they will obey Jesus this week. Have children sing a song to the tune "London Bridge." You and another leader make a bridge and lower your arms to "catch" a child after the song is sung each time. The child you catch will tell a way the class can obey Jesus this week. Continue until each child has been "caught."

Materials
• list of right things written earlier

Lyrics to sing to the tune of "London Bridge"
I will do the right thing, right thing, right thing.
I will do the right thing. I will obey Jesus.

Key words
Lesson 32
Lesson 33
Lesson 34

Teaching at Home

Help everyone in the family understand the Beatitudes by writing simplified versions on strips of paper. Plan to think about one Beatitude each week. Notice examples, both positive and negative, of the Beatitudes

Reading tip
Practice finding antonyms (opposites) such as *wise/foolish; rich/poor; humble/proud; enemies/friends;* and so on.

The Centurion's Faith

Tell how we can obey Jesus' teaching about faith.
Choose a way to obey Jesus.
Read Bible references and find Bible verses.

"Never tire of doing what is right."   2 Thessalonians 3:13, NIV

❶ Get Ready to Read

Ask a child to find pages 288 and 289 in a *Young Reader's Bible*. Read or ask a good reader to read the pages.

What did the soldier think Jesus needed to do to heal his servant? (just say the word) **The soldier believed Jesus could do what He said He would do. Jesus used a great word to describe the soldier's belief.**

Turn to page 290 and show the word *faith*. **The key words about "right things" for today's story are *have faith* because Jesus praised the soldier's belief in Him—his faith.**

Print the words *have faith* on the large paper. The children can practice printing the words *have faith* before copying them onto the shirt.

A medicine bottle can remind children that Jesus didn't need medicine to make the servant well. He only had to say the word and the servant was healed.

Materials
• *The Young Reader's Bible*
• T-shirts begun in session 32
• extra T-shirts for new children
• fabric crayons
• plain drawing paper
• large sheet of paper

Note
See unit 7 pages for a complete explanation of this T-shirt project.

❷ Read the Bible Story

"Just Say the Word"

Before class, gather items that help us feel better when we are sick, such as medicine bottles (empty), copy of a prescription, thermometer. Also, ask another adult to play the part of the messenger. The messenger will need to learn the short script printed in "Listen." Print a message on a slip of paper: *I am not good enough to have you in my house. Just say my servant is healed and he will be healed.*

Have you ever been to the doctor when you were sick? How did the doctor help you feel better? Show children the medicine and other items you brought. Discuss the ways doctors can help us feel better.

Listen

As you prepare for story time, have a messenger burst into the room.
Messenger: Have you seen Jesus?
Teacher: No. I'm sorry. Who are you? Why are you looking for Jesus?
Messenger: I am one of the leaders of the Jews in this town. We want to ask Jesus to heal a sick servant of one of the soldiers. This soldier has been very good to us, and his servant is dying. I need to hurry. Thank you for your help.
Teacher: Good-bye. I hope you find Jesus. We'll let you know when we see Him.

Materials
• *The Young Reader's Bible*, pages 286-291
• photocopies of the two-page Bible story (page 178)
• *The Young Reader's Bible Audio Cassette* or a cassette on which you have recorded unit stories
• cassette player(s), earphones optional
• a large sheet of paper
• items that help us feel better when we are sick
• helper to be messenger
• message paper
• colored pencils

Continue preparing for the story, then have the messenger burst into the room again, carrying the message paper you prepared before class.

Messenger: Sorry to bother you again. Have you seen Jesus yet?

Teacher: No we haven't. You still haven't found Him?

Messenger: Well, yes, I did. He is somewhere on His way to the soldier's house. He is going to heal the servant. But I need to give Him this message before He gets there.

(Messenger holds up piece of paper. Then pauses for a second, as if thinking.)

I'll tell you what. Would you mind reading this message. Then if you happen to see Jesus before I do, you can tell Him what it says.

Teacher: We'd be happy to help you any way we can.

(Take the piece of paper and read or ask a good reader to read the message aloud to the group. Then hand it back to the messenger as he quickly leaves.)

Wow! That man really believes Jesus can heal his servant. I wonder what Jesus will do. Let's read our story for today, and we'll find out what happens.

Read the story from pages 286-291 in a *Young Reader's Bible*.

What did Jesus say the Roman soldier had? (very great faith)

What is faith in God? (believing that God will do what He says)

How did the soldier show he had very great faith? (He believed Jesus could heal his servant just by speaking the word.)

Participate

Divide the class into four groups (soldiers, sick servants, Jewish leaders, Jesus). If the children do not divide evenly into four groups, put extra children into the Jewish leaders' group. Tell the children that you will read clues. If the clue describes their group, they should stand and do their motion. **Soldiers**—salute; **sick servants**—lay head on hands and look sick; **Jewish leaders**—kneel down as though begging Jesus to come; **Jesus**—smile and say "I'll do it."

If you have time when the game is complete, ask children to form groups including one soldier, one servant, Jesus, and one or two Jewish leaders. The groups can act out the story, playing the appropriate part.

Read

Give each child a copy of the two page Bible story (page 178). Children can use colored pencils to color the page. Children can draw Jesus and the Jewish leaders coming to the house. They can listen to the cassette story as they work.

 Practice Using a Bible

Using My Bible

Help children practice using their Bibles by working in pairs. Both children in the pair should have a Bible. Children will take turns opening the Bible to any book. Then the other child must find that book in the Bible. Children may choose whether or not to use the table of contents.

Each time a book is found, children should print the name on a piece of paper. Children may not repeat books. If you wish, provide small treats for pairs in various random categories—the pair who found the most books that start with the letter "J"; the pair who found the most books; the pair who found the most New Testament books; the pair who found the most Old Testament books; the pair who found the book with the longest name; the pair who found the book with the shortest name.

Clues
1. I had one hundred servants.
2. I took a message to Jesus from the soldier.
3. I was one out of one hundred.
4. I said I would come heal the servant.
5. I sent a message to Jesus.
6. I went with Jesus towards the soldier's house.
7. I was about to die.
8. I didn't think I was good enough to have Jesus in my house.
9. The soldier had been good to me and my friends.
10. Jesus said I had great faith.
11. Jesus made me completely well.
12. I said the servant would be healed, and he was.

Snacks
Serve fruit roll ups and water.

Materials
- *The Young Reader's Bible*
- Bibles
- photocopies of page 182
- props for skits

Finding Bible Verses

Ask the children to find Hebrews 4:12 in their Bibles. When all children have found the verse, read it aloud together.

How does this verse help us believe and have faith in God? (It tells us that the Bible contains the words of God, so we know we can believe and trust everything the Bible says.)

Before class gather props for the skits—a teddy bear, a blanket and pillow for a bed.

Divide children into four groups. Assign each group one skit from the page. Give each child in a group a copy of page 182 and the props the group will use. Ask the group to look up and read the four Bible verses at the top of the page and decide which one goes with their skit. Then ask them to decide how to act out the skit and choose one child to read the Bible verse that goes with the skit. Help groups to choose the correct verse and organize their skit.

When the groups are ready, ask them to present their skits and read their Bible verses to the large group. Discuss each skit and Bible verse after it is presented.

What did this verse teach us about faith? (We can imitate, or copy, other people to help us have faith. Just believing isn't enough faith; we have to act on what we believe. If we have faith, we can pray to God and He will always answer. If we have faith, we will never die!)

 ## Share What We've Learned

Before class, set up chairs in a circle. Be sure to have a chair for each child. Gather everyone in a circle to talk about what they have been doing and learning. Use the aims for this lesson as an outline for the kinds of questions you ask.

What right thing did Jesus teach us to do in today's story? (have faith) **What does it mean to have faith?** (believe and do what God says) **What are some ways to show faith?** (follow the example of other people who obey God; obey what God says; pray to God) **Who was an example of very great faith in our story today?** (the soldier)

Place the helmet you prepared before class on one of the chairs. Show children the soldier's helmet. Explain that we can show very great faith just as the soldier did.

Ask the children to think of a way they can show faith this week. Play a game of musical chairs, using a tape your children enjoy. When the music stops, the children should sit in a chair. The child who ends up in the chair with the helmet should put it on and tell a way to show faith this week. Encourage children to be specific. For example, instead of "pray," the children could decide to pray that God will help them be kind to a person no one likes at school. Instead of "obey," the children could decide to obey when their teacher says "no talking."

If you have time remaining, encourage children to reread the Bible story from pages 286-291 in the *Young Reader's Bible.*

Materials
- cover a child's safety helmet with aluminum foil
- cassette player and cassette of children's songs

Option

If you have more than twelve children, provide two circles and two helmets.

 Teaching at Home

Explore the vocabulary of officers and soldiers. The centurion was a commander over 100 men. Help children identify modern officer titles. Emphasize that we have faith in Jesus as our leader.

Reading tip

The words *heel* and *heal* that appear in this story are examples of homophones—words that sound alike but mean different things and are spelled differently. Start a list of these words as children find other examples.

The Good Samaritan

Tell why we obey Jesus' teaching, "Love your neighbor."
Choose a way to obey Jesus.
Find Bible books and read Bible references.

"Never tire of doing what is right."   2 Thessalonians 3:13, NIV

❶ Get Ready to Read

Materials
- *The Young Reader's Bible*
- T-shirts begun in session 32
- extra T-shirts for new children
- a large sheet of paper
- fabric crayons
- plain drawing paper

Note
See unit 7 pages for a complete explanation of this T-shirt project.

Ask a child to find pages 316 and 319 in a *Young Reader's Bible*. Read or ask a good reader to read each page. **Name those we are supposed to love.** (God, our neighbor.) **How was the Samaritan man a neighbor to the hurt man?** (He cleaned and bandaged the man's wounds.)

The key words about "right things" for this story are *love your neighbor* **because Jesus helped us understand who our neighbors are—everyone, even those we don't like.**

Print the words *love your neighbor* on a large sheet of paper. The children can practice printing the words *love your neighbor* before copying them onto the shirt.

Add a tiny bandage to remind children that the Samaritan man bandaged the hurt man's wounds.

❷ Read the Bible Story

Materials
- *The Young Reader's Bible*
- photocopies of the two-page Bible story excerpt (page 179)
- props to act out story
- plastic strip bandages

"A Neighbor Shows Kindness"

What is an enemy? (Let children discuss. An enemy is someone who doesn't like you or who fights against you, someone who is mean to you, and so on.) Talk about the opposite of an enemy (a friend). Contrasting the characteristics of a friend with the characteristics of an enemy will give children a more complete understanding of the word. **Do you have a friend? an enemy? Do you know someone who has an enemy? How do people treat their enemies?**

Pay close attention as children talk. Try to gather examples from their conversation of ways people show love to all neighbors. This is a difficult lesson—not because children can't understand and apply the Bible truth, "Love your neighbor," but because they do not understand first century society described in Jesus' story.

Jesus told a story about an enemy. Listen to find out who were enemies and how people treated enemies in the story. You can form two listening teams.

Listen

Read the story from pages 316-321 in a *Young Reader's Bible*.

Who do you think the Jews might have thought would be the enemy and the good guys in the story? (Tell about how Jews felt about Samaritans and priests and Levites.) **Who did the kind thing in the story?** (the enemy, the Samaritan) **Who do you think Jesus was telling us to love?** (We should show love to everyone, not just the people we know and like.)

Participate

Before class, gather props to help the children act out the story—Bible times costumes, strips of cloth for bandages, water and a cloth to clean the man's wounds, a blanket and pillow for a bed at the inn.

Help children decide how to use the props to act out the story. Choose children to be Jesus, the teacher of the law, the hurt man, robbers, the priest, the Levite, the Samaritan, and the innkeeper.

Have the children walk through the actions of the story as you read it aloud again. Then let the children act out the story entirely on their own. Prompt them as needed. If you have time, let children switch characters and act out the story again. If you have a small class, leave out the introductory part about Jesus and the teacher of the law.

If the children are very familiar with the story, read quotes from the story and ask the children to find each quote and tell who said it. Depending upon the ability of your children, you may wish to briefly discuss quotation marks and what they mean.

Read

Give each child a copy of the two-page Bible story (page 179). Children can use colored pencils to color the page. Ask children to turn their pages over and draw a picture of the hurt man. Provide bandages for them to put on the man's wounds. They can listen to the cassette while they work.

Snacks
Serve strawberry bar cookies and milk.

❸ Practice Using a Bible

Materials
• *The Young Reader's Bible*
• Bibles
• index cards
• photocopies of page 183
• scissors
• tape
• ribbon

Using My Bible

Hold the part of your Bible that is the Old Testament. What does the Old Testament tell about? (how people worshiped and obeyed God)

Hold the part of your Bible that is the New Testament. What does the New Testament tell about? (how people worshiped and obeyed God and Jesus, how people told others about Jesus)

Give each child an index card and a Bible. Divide the class into two groups. Each child will look at a table of contents, choose a Bible book, and print the Bible book name on the index card. Children in one group will choose Old Testament books. Children in the other group will choose New Testament books.

When children are done, collect and shuffle the cards. Draw cards one at a time and call out the Bible book name on the card. Groups will race to see who can find the book in the Bible first. If time is limited, it is not necessary to use all the cards.

Finding Bible Verses

Print *Hebrews 4:12* on a large sheet of paper. Review the Reference Rhyme (page 32) to remind everyone how to find verses. Ask the children to find the verse in their Bibles. Then read it aloud together.

Remind children that we know that the Bible has the words of God in it, because the Bible tells us so. We can be sure that the Bible tells us the right things to do.

Print *2 Thessalonians 3:13* on the large paper. Have children find this key verse in their Bibles. Read or recite the verse together. **What right thing did we learn to do in today's story?** (love our neighbor)

Tell children that the Bible tells us many great things about love. Give each child a copy of page 183. Children may work in pairs to look up the Bible verses on the hearts and fill in the blanks. When the children are finished, discuss the verses (Matthew 5:33, 34; Galatians 5:14; 1 John 3:18; 1 John 4:21).

Whom should we love according to these Bible verses? (Children can name family members, neighbors, friends, even people they don't like. Do not allow children to say unkind things in the process!) **What do these verses say that help us know how important it is to love others?** (We can't love God unless we love others. "Love your neighbor" is like saying the whole law.)

4 Share What We've Learned

Before class, print one of the following words on each adhesive bandage: *love, neighbor (use this word twice), teacher, robbers, priest, temple worker, hurt man, Samaritan, bandages, inn, money.* Put only the bandages with words on them back into the bandage box.

Play a game. Ask the children to sit in a circle. Pass around the bandage box. Ask one child or pairs of children to choose a bandage from the box and use the word on the bandage in a sentence that tells something about the story. Children get to keep the bandage after they say the sentence.

How did the Samaritan man in today's story show love? (He helped the hurt man.) **Who can you love? How can you show love?** (Let children share their ideas.)

Ask the children to think of a way they will show love to someone this week. Ask them to print or draw a picture of the way they will show love on the blank heart on page 183. Then give each child a length of ribbon to string through the hearts. Then children cut out the string of hearts, being careful not to cut across the top of the hearts. Add a length of ribbon and tape the bottom of the hearts together.

Ask the children to tell where they will hang their hearts to remind them to love others this week. Suggestions: Over the doorway to their room, on the mirror in the bathroom, on the headboard of their bed, on their bike handlebars, on their backpack.

Talk about what the children learned today. **What new thing did you learn from the Bible today? What new word could you read today? What new way to obey did you think of today?** Encourage them as they progress in both knowledge and skill.

Materials
• a box of large adhesive bandages

Teaching at Home

List actual neighbors that your family could help. Choose some ways to show love. Put heart stickers next to the names when helping actions have been done.

Reading tip

Help children focus on the story sequence. List the main actions on strips of poster board or pieces of paper. Let children illustrate each event. Then, mix up the pages and let the children put the events back in story order. They can check their ideas by rereading the story.

The Lord's Prayer

Tell why we obey what Jesus teaches about prayer.
Choose a time to pray.
Find Bible books and read Bible references.

"Never tire of doing what is right."   2 Thessalonians 3:13, NIV

① Get Ready to Read

Ask a child to find page 322 in a *Young Reader's Bible*. Read or ask a good reader to read the page. **What did Jesus' disciples ask Him to teach them?** (how to pray).
The key word about "right things" for today's story is *pray* because Jesus taught His disciples to pray. Print the word *pray* on the chalkboard. The children can practice printing the word *pray* before copying it on the shirt.

② Read the Bible Story

"Teach Us to Pray"
Name times you can remember hearing someone pray. What kinds of things did they say? (Let children discuss. If they need help remembering, ask about people in the church service, parents at home, teachers or friends in Sunday school.) **How do you think those people know what to pray about? How do you know what to pray?** (Let children discuss.)
One reason that we can know how to pray is because Jesus prayed a special prayer just to show us. This prayer is called "The Lord's Prayer." It is an example or a model prayer for us.

Listen
Read the story from pages 322-327 in a *Young Reader's Bible*. Emphasize the words of Jesus.
What great things did Jesus tell God in this prayer? (Your name will always be great and holy! The kingdom is yours with power and glory forever.) **What did Jesus ask God for in this prayer?** (Set up your heavenly kingdom here on earth. Give us our food for today. Forgive our sins. And help us forgive others who have done wrong to us. Lead us away from wanting to do wrong things. Free us from the evil one.) **What do you think the "heavenly kingdom" is?** (people like us who love and serve God) **Who is the evil one?** (Satan)

Participate
Before class, cut each piece of poster board in half. Stack seven of the pieces of poster board together to make the pages of a book. Punch three holes at even intervals along one side. Do not tie the book together at this time.

Materials
- *The Young Reader's Bible*
- T-shirts begun in session 32
- extra T-shirts for new children
- fabric crayons
- plain drawing paper

Note
See unit 7 pages for a complete explanation of this T-shirt project.

Materials
- *The Young Reader's Bible*, pages 322-327
- photocopies of the two-page Bible story excerpt (page 180)
- four large pieces of poster board
- construction paper
- yarn or string
- hole punch
- colored markers
- scissors
- glue

Print a copy of the prayer, putting each phrase or sentence on each poster board page:

The Lord's Prayer
Our Father in heaven, your name will always be great and holy.
Be our king! Set up your heavenly kingdom here on earth.
Give us our food for today.
Forgive our sins and help us forgive others who have done wrong to us.
Lead us away from wanting to do wrong things. Free us from the evil one.
Because the kingdom is yours, with power and glory forever. Amen.

Divide the class into groups of two or three. Depending upon the size of your class, give each group one or two pieces of the poster board. Ask each group to decide how they will picture the title or the part of the prayer that is printed on their poster board. Children can draw with markers or cut out poster board or construction paper shapes and glue them to their page.

When the groups are finished, place the pages in order and tie them together. Then read the book together as a large group.

Read

Give each child a copy of the two page Bible story (page 180). Children can use colored pencils to color the page. They can listen to the cassette as they work. Help children who have trouble reading the words of the prayer.

❸ Practice Using a Bible

Using My Bible

Before class, print different Bible book names on masking tape strips. Print the names of easy to find books, such as *Psalms* or *Genesis*, in blue. Print the names of hard to find books, such as *Amos* or *Jude*, in red. Tape an assortment of the strips to four large balls.

Be sure each child has a Bible. Divide children into four groups, and give each group a sheet of paper. Seat the groups at the four corners of the room. Show a masking taped ball. Explain that blue names are worth 1 point, red names are worth 2 points.

Throw a ball to each of the groups. At your signal, each group will look up the Bible book name listed on one of the masking tape strips. When each person in the group has found the book, the group may take the masking tape strip off the ball and attach it to the group's paper. Remove no more than one strip at a time from each ball.

When you give a signal, each group must throw their ball to the next group. (Allow ample time at first, gradually shortening each time.)

The balls should move clockwise around the room. Continue until time runs out or until all the masking tape strips are gone. The group with the most points wins the game.

Finding Bible Verses

Before class, print the following references on a large piece of paper: *1 Kings 18:36-38; 2 Kings 20:3; Psalm 139:14; Jonah 2:2; Matthew 26:39; Acts 9:40.*

Also gather props for skits—several sheets, a variety of Bible-times clothing, sticks, stones, a small autoharp or similar instrument if available, blankets and pillows, candlesticks with candles, a bowl with a damp cloth in it. Tell children

Snacks
Serve mini-muffins and juice.

Materials
• *The Young Reader's Bible*
• Bibles
• four large balls
• masking tape
• sheets of paper
• props for skits
• a large sheet of paper

that, although the Lord's Prayer is a very well-known prayer, there are many other prayers in the Bible.

Ask children to work in groups of three or four. Assign each group one of the Bible references from the list on paper. Each group should choose someone to print their reference on a piece of paper and then find the prayer in their Bibles.

They should read the prayer and decide how they could act it out. Let children choose from the props you brought to help them act out the prayer. When the groups are ready, have them act out the prayers for the class. After each prayer is acted out, have everyone practice finding the Bible references.

 ## Share What We've Learned

Materials
- a variety of treats, such as stickers or gum. (Treats must have paper wrappers to write on.)
- a bowl for the treats

What four ways to obey Jesus have we learned? (live to please God; have faith; love others; pray) **What are some ways you can live to please God? have faith? love others? pray?** (Pause after each question and allow children to respond.)

Encourage children to praise God because they can talk to Him every day. Pray praise prayers.

Encourage children to pray a silent prayer telling God they are sorry for wrong things they have done. Pray aloud, thanking God for forgiving us for the wrong things that we do. Invite children to pray for the needs of their friends and family. Thank God for meeting our needs.

Read the "Lord's Prayer" book together.

Ask the children to think of a time that they will pray each day this week. Set the bowl of treats in the middle of the circle. Ask the children to come to the bowl and choose a treat. The children should print their names on a treat and put it back in the bowl. (Empty the bowl of unclaimed treats before children put the treats with names back into the bowl.)

Next, allow children to take turns drawing a treat from the bowl. They will say the name on the treat, and the person named will tell when they plan to pray. Give the children their treats afterwards. Encourage children to keep the treat as a reminder to pray. After they have prayed every day for a week they can eat or use the treat. They will be able to remember to pray on their own. Continue until everyone has had a chance to tell when they will pray.

Talk about what the children learned today. **What new thing did you learn from the Bible today? What new word could you read today? What new way to obey did you think of today?** Encourage them as they progress in both knowledge and skill.

Key word
Lesson 36

Teaching at Home

The art in the story suggests scrolls. Investigate how the Bible books were written and preserved.

Reading tip
Practice letter writing skills.

Jesus turned to the people
following him.
"This Roman soldier
has very great faith,"
he said.
Then Jesus said
to the soldier's friends,
"Go back to the house.
What you have asked
will be done."
The soldier's friends
went back to the house.

They opened the door
and saw the soldier.
And next to him was his servant,
who was completely well!

178

A Neighbor Shows Kindness

A teacher of the Jewish law

came to Jesus with a question.

"God's law tells me to love God

with all my heart, my soul,

my strength, and my mind.

And to love my neighbor

as myself.

But who is my neighbor?"

Jesus told a story.

Then Jesus asked

the teacher of the law,

"Which of the three travelers

was a neighbor to the hurt man?"

"The one who helped him,"

said the teacher of the law.

Jesus said, "Go and do the same."

179

"When you pray," said Jesus, "pray like this."

Our Father in heaven,
your name will always be
great and holy.

Be our king!

Set up your heavenly kingdom
here on earth.

Give us our food
for today.

Forgive our sins.

And help us forgive others
who have done wrong
to us.

John

John

Jesus

Bible Verses Help Us

Amy: Kara, we had a fire at my house. My clothes and toys burned up.

Kara: I'm sorry, Amy. That must be awful!

Amy: I got new shoes, but I miss my teddy bear.

Kara: My teddy bear can help you not be lonely. I'll give him to you.

Amy: Oh, thank you! I'll take good care of him.

Suzanne: Daddy, why do you look so sad?

Daddy: Grandma has been very sick. She died today, Suzanne.

Suzanne: Will I ever see her again?

Daddy: I'm sure we will see her in Heaven. Jesus promised.

Suzanne: I'm glad I'll get to talk to Grandma again!

Jason: Mom, Mom! I heard thunder. I'm scared!

Mom: I used to be afraid, too, Jason.

Jason: What did you do?

Mom: Well, my mom told me that God promised to take care of me—all the time.

Jason: Even during a thunderstorm?

Mom: Always!

Matthew (*kneeling or sitting*): Dear God, please help me at my new school. I'm afraid I won't have any friends. Please help me find a good friend. Help me get a teacher I like. Thank You for listening, God. I'm glad I can talk to You because of Jesus.

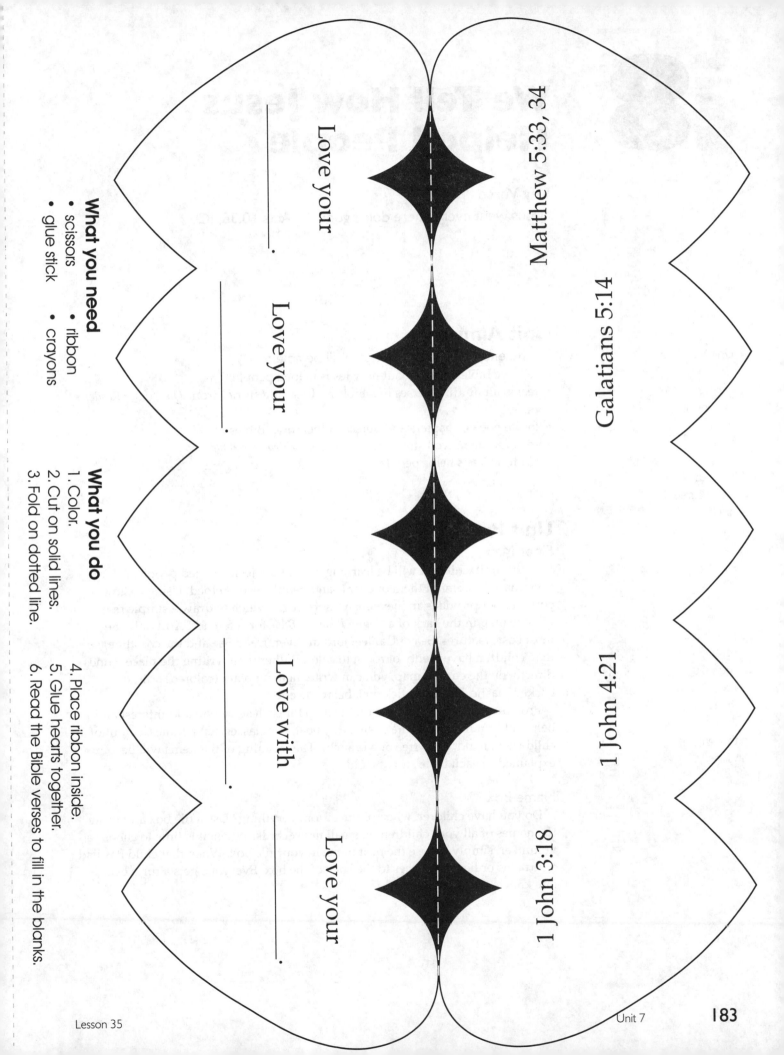

Matthew 5:33, 34

Galatians 5:14

1 John 4:21

1 John 3:18

Love your
_____ .

Love your
_____ .

Love with
_____ .

Love your
_____ .

What you need
- scissors
- ribbon
- glue stick
- crayons

What you do
1. Color.
2. Cut on solid lines.
3. Fold on dotted line.
4. Place ribbon inside.
5. Glue hearts together.
6. Read the Bible verses to fill in the blanks.

unit 8

We Tell How Jesus Helped People

Key Verse
"Jesus went everywhere doing good."   Acts 10:38, ICB

Unit Vocabulary
afraid
believe
blessing
blind
bowed
carry
climbed
disappeared
doubt
ghost
healed
leprosy
liar
quickly
shore
skin disease
sores
squished
tax collector
themselves
thief
thought
village

Unit Aims

By the end of the unit, learners will be able to
- tell five Bible stories about how Jesus helped people.
- feel joy in finding verses in a Bible and reading stories from *The Young Reader's Bible*.
- locate books, chapters and verses in their own Bibles.
- read (at their level) stories from *The Young Reader's Bible*.
- tell how Jesus helps people.

Unit Projects

Floor Map

In this unit, children will be learning about how Jesus helped people. A large floor map can remind them of events and people Jesus helped. Using a shower curtain liner provides an inexpensive surface on which to draw a simple map. Use the map in the back of a *Young Reader's Bible* for reference. Add only the most basic features (Sea of Galilee, Jordan River, Dead Sea and the coastline) so that children have plenty of room to color. Rather than writing the place names directly on the curtain map, you can write them on plain (colored) adhesive-backed plastic. Peel and stick on labels as needed.

Providing fun items to place on the map for each story will add interest and help children remember the events (toy boat, sunglasses, ten pennies, cutout of a child-sized hand, a toy tree or a branch). The meaning of the items will be explained as each Bible story is told.

Name Box

Do you have children who volunteer for everything? Use a file box and write the names of all your children on small index cards. When it is time to choose a volunteer, simply choose the next name in your file box. When that child has had a turn, his or her name goes to the back of the box. Everyone gets a turn; everyone knows that it is fair.

	The Singing Bible (3 tapes)	Kids on the Rock (More Songs)	Follow the Leader (The Donut Man)	I'm a Helper (The Donut Man)	Good News (The Donut Man)
Lesson 37	Who Do You Say I Am?				
Lesson 38	Who Do You Say I Am?				
Lesson 39	Who Do You Say I Am?				
Lesson 40		Jesus Loves Me			Jesus Loves the Little Children
Lesson 41			Zaccheus		
Key Verse					
Unit Theme		Jesus Came to Town			
All Lessons	The Books We Love the Best The Bible Book Is True	God's Word Is for Me			

The Singing Bible (3 tapes), ©1993 by Lightwave Publishing, Inc. Manufactured and distributed by Word Publishing, Dallas, TX 75234
Kids on the Rock! More Songs, ©1994 Gospel Light, Ventura CA 93006
The Donut Man (3 tapes): *Follow the Leader*, ©1990; *I'm a Helper*, ©1991; *Good News*, ©1991; Integrity Music, Inc., P.O. Box 16813 Mobile, AL 36616

Key Verse Activities

Materials

- brightly colored paper cut into 6-inch squares
- scissors
- paper punch
- unsharpened pencils
- nail
- hammer
- brad fasteners
- two spangles* per pinwheel
- adhesive stars or other colorful stickers

*Spangles are 20 mm flat circles sold with sequins in craft departments or stores.

Pinwheel Pencils

Before class, hammer a nail through the eraser of each pencil to make a large hole. Remove the nail carefully. Draw lines from corner to corner across each paper square, forming an X. Cut slits from the corners to within ½ inch of the center. Punch a hole in each spangle with the hole punch.

Make a sample pinwheel. Put a brad through the hole of a spangle. Then bend the corners of the paper square toward the center of the paper and push the brad through the center. Turn the brad around a few times so the pinwheel moves freely on it. Put another spangle on the end of brad and push the end of the brad through the hole in the eraser. Leave some space between the pinwheel and the eraser so the pinwheel spins easily, and then bend back the ends of the brad.

This is a memory verse pinwheel. When you have memorized Acts 10:38, I will give you a paper square to decorate with stars. Stars like these remind of things that we have done well. Remember, "Jesus went everywhere doing good."

Later we'll make the square into a pinwheel. If you can remember the memory verse at the beginning of class for the next four lessons, we'll fold down a flap each time and it will become a pinwheel that you can take home. Print "I know Acts 10:38." on the flaps as shown.

Materials

- chalk and chalkboard
- Scrabble tiles
- a stopwatch or a watch with a secondhand

Spell It Out

Print the memory verse on the chalkboard. **What does our memory verse say?** (Read it together.)

Let's list on the chalkboard five good things Jesus did. Now think of something good you can do for others today. Raise your hand and tell me what you will do. I'll write on the chalkboard one good thing each of us plans to do today.

Divide the class into two teams. **Let's see which team can find the letters that spell our memory verse and put them in order fastest. (You don't need to spell out the reference.) I'll time one team and then the other team can try to beat the first team's time.**

Memory Verse Tag

We're going to play a fun game of Memory Verse Tag. First we'll practice saying Acts 10:38 until we can say it easily. Then we'll let someone be "It." As "It" chases a person and tries to tag him or her, the person must say the memory verse and sit down before being tagged. If the person gets tagged first, he or she becomes "It."

Jesus Gives Peter a Helping Hand

37

Tell how Jesus helped Peter.
Praise Jesus because He helps people.
Find and sort Old Testament and New Testament books.

"Jesus went everywhere doing good."   Acts 10:38, ICB

❶ Get Ready to Read

See unit page 184 for a complete explanation of this activity. As children arrive in class, invite them to help you color a simple map you drew on a shower curtain of places Jesus went. Title the map "Places Jesus Helped." Label the water *lake* and *Galilee*. Label *John 6:16* beside it. Children can choose to color the lake Galilee, decorate the title words and/or the Bible reference, or set the boat afloat! When the map additions are complete, praise the children for their creativity.

What are we making? (map, land, water) **What is special about this map?** (It's about places Jesus lived.) **Who will read the name of the water?** (a lake, Galilee) **There's a story in the Bible about this lake called Galilee. It's in the book of** (Point to Bible reference and allow children to respond: John, Bible).

❷ Read the Bible Story

"Peter Takes a Walk"

Gather children in the story center. Ask children to tell about trips they have taken in a boat or tell about movies or TV shows about boats.

Display the pictures in a *Young Reader's Bible*, pages 304 and 305. Discuss the differences between the two scenes. **How would you feel if you were in the boat (page 305)? What would you do?**

Display the map children colored earlier. Ask children to read the title on the map (Places Jesus Helped), the name of the lake (Galilee), and the Bible reference (John 6:16) for today's Bible story. Place the toy boat in position on the lake. **Listen to find out what happened to Peter when he went in a boat.**

Provide a bowl and spoon to mix food coloring into whipped topping to color it blue. Give each child a piece of paper and a large spoonful of blue whipped topping. Tell them to finger paint Lake Galilee in the middle of the paper. Older children can label the name, Lake Galilee.

Let the whipped topping dry as the children listen to the story.

Listen

Read "Peter Takes a Walk" with animation and suspense.

Materials
- cardboard box with lid
- white shower curtain liner
- large plastic storage bag
- toy boat (plastic banana split dish works well)
- markers
- labels for map: lake, Galilee, John 6:16

Options
- If you have a large class, provide several shower curtains to draw on.
- You may also expand this activity by making clothespin Bible characters to tell the Bible story that is related to the part of the map being colored. Your map will then become a place for children to act out and review all of the unit Bible stories. The clothespin Bible characters can be stored with the story symbols in a plastic bag.

Materials
- *The Young Reader's Bible,* pages 304-309
- photocopies of the two-page Bible story (page 202)
- *The Young Reader's Bible Audio Cassette* or a cassette on which you have recorded unit stories
- cassette player(s), earphones optional
- a large sheet of paper
- map used earlier
- toy boat
- drawing paper
- frozen whipped topping (thawed)
- blue food coloring
- bowl and spoon
- construction paper
- crayons or markers
- several baby blankets

Why were the disciples having trouble rowing? (the storm) **How did Jesus get to the boat?** (walking on water) **What did Peter want to do?** (walk on the water to Jesus)

Why do you think he wanted to meet Jesus on the water? Why did Jesus have to help Peter? (Peter looked away and was afraid.)

Read the key verse for the unit, "Jesus went everywhere doing good," Acts 10:38, NIV. **What good work did Jesus do in this story?** (rescued Peter) **What does this tell us about Jesus?** (He is the Son of God. Only God could walk on water or help someone else walk on water.) **Where was Jesus when He did good work?** (lake of Galilee)

Divide children into three groups. Distribute paper, crayons or markers to each child. Choose at least one good reader for each group.

Group 1 will listen as the reader reads pages 304 and 305. They will then plan, draw, and color a picture about that part of the story.

Group 2 will listen and draw for pages 306 and 307.

Group 3 will listen and draw for pages 308 and 309.

When the pictures are completed, ask **Group 1** to display their pictures as pages 304 and 305 are read. Continue until all pictures have been displayed and the story has been read. **Which page shows Jesus helping Peter?** (308)

Participate

Ask children to use their imaginations. Pretend to be with Jesus on the lake called Galilee. Distribute small blankets to the group. Arrange children in groups of twos or threes sitting on the blankets—each blanket is a boat. One child in each boat will be Peter.

Choose a child to be Jesus. Ask the children to follow the actions in the story as you read. Be sure to pause after each action to give children time to participate.

Read

Give each child a copy of the Bible story excerpt (page 202). Children can color the pages. They can listen to the cassette as they color. Children can draw a circle around the art that shows Jesus helping Peter.

③ Practice Using a Bible

Using My Bible

Display your Bible and read the front cover to the class. Turn the Bible around and read the back cover. Turn back to the front and ask children what you are holding. (My Bible!) As you turn it over, ask the children to tell what the Bible is. (God's Word)

Explain that the Bible is divided into two parts: Old Testament (display) and the New Testament (display). Ask children to put their hands in their laps when they think they can tell you the two parts of the Bible. Choose a child to tell the answer. Repeat this question enthusiastically until each child has given the correct answer.

Explain that today's story is in the New Testament. New Testament stories tell about God and His Son Jesus. Repeat the question procedure just used until each child can tell what New Testament stories are about.

Give each child a copy of page 205 and provide red and blue pencils or crayons. Talk about how to draw loops around words and pictures that match. Children can draw lines between words that match. **Which picture has no match?** (Zaccheus)

Examples
• "Jesus went up into the hills to pray"—child leaves group, kneels and prays.
• Disciples try to row against fierce wind—children hold on to the sides of their blankets as if gripping the sides of the boat.
• Peter steps off of the blanket into the sea.

Snacks
Serve floats—ice cream in soda.

Materials
• Bible for each child
• brown paper Bible cover titled "My Bible" on the front and "God's Word" on the back
• photocopies of page 205
• pencils
• red and blue crayons

Finding Bible Verses

Help children find Acts 10:38 using the Reference Rhyme (page 32). Read the verse together. "Jesus went everywhere doing good," Acts 10:38, NIV. **What good thing did Jesus do in today's story? What other good things has Jesus done?**

Before class, print the following Bible references on a large sheet of paper: *Matthew 14:33; Mark 10:16; Luke 19:5.* Have children find each Bible verse and match one reference to each picture pair on "Bible Two of a Kind" page 205 used earlier.

Take another look at the map you made as children arrived today. **Where did Jesus walk on water? Who else walked on water? Where can we read about this event?** (John 6:16) Add *John 6:16* to the list on the paper.

We can read these four Bible references. Let's read them together. Who can tell us another name for these four books—Matthew, Mark, Luke, and John? (Gospel books) **What is written in the Gospels?** (things Jesus said and did)

Challenge children to find the Bible reference, John 6:16. Read it together.

 # **Share What We've Learned**

Before class, use construction paper to make four signs—two signs reading *Old Testament* and two reading *New Testament.* Tape string or rope in two straight lines to the floor. The lines should be several feet apart. On either side of the lines tape the Old Testament and New Testament signs.

Divide the class into two groups. Instruct each team to stand along a line. If the class is too large, divide into four groups and let the groups take turns jumping.

Read aloud together the New Testament and Old Testament signs. Explain that when you call out a Bible book, they are to decide if the book belongs in the Old Testament or the New Testament and jump to that side of the rope.

Call "John." After everyone has jumped, tell the children that John is in the New Testament. Instruct all children to move to the New Testament side if they are not already there.

The teams will then reassemble along the line. Call out "John" again giving everyone a chance to jump correctly. Call out Genesis; then Acts. If time or interest permits, call out books from previous lessons.

Gather everyone in a circle to talk about what they have been doing and learning. Use the aims for this lesson as an outline for the kinds of questions you ask.

Using a Name Box (see unit page), choose children to tell something they know about the Bible.

Teach children the lyrics to sing to the tune of "The B-I-B-L-E."

Sing the song again. When you sing the words "Old Testament," those who remember a book or Bible person from the Old Testament may call out the name.

Sing and call out names as long as time or interest permits. Name ways God helped the Bible people the children named. Continue with the words "New Testament," repeating this procedure.

Remind children that God helps us today. Tell how God has helped you, how He helps others in your congregation, or how He helps the missionaries your church supports. Let children tell how God helps them. Pray and thank God for His help.

End the story time by asking for volunteers to read from the *Young Reader's Bible* or to reread their pictures made for the story.

Pictures/References
Jesus and Peter in the boat, Matthew 14:33
Jesus and the children, Mark 10:16
Zaccheus looking for Jesus, Luke 19:5

Note
A project for making Gospel folders was included in unit 6. If children did not make that project, they may not know the term Gospels referring to the first four books of the New Testament.

Materials
• two 8-to-10-foot lengths of string or rope
• construction paper
• tape

Song Lyrics
The B-I-B-L-E, it is God's Word to me,
The Old Testament, the New Testament, the B-I-B-L-E!

 Teaching at Home

Have fun discovering which items sink and which float. Make a chart to record information.

Reading tip
Find the word sink in this story. Some words may sound and be spelled exactly like a word that has an entirely different meaning. Ask children to think of another kind of sink. Be on the lookout for these kinds of words.

Jesus Gives Sight for Sore Eyes

Tell how Jesus helped a blind man.
Praise Jesus because He helps people.
Read Bible references and find Bible verses.

"Jesus went everywhere doing good."   Acts 10:38, ICB

① Get Ready to Read

Materials
- map materials from previous lesson
- pair of child's sunglasses
- markers
- large plastic food storage bag

Option
You may wish to use this activity to involve children who arrive early. They may continue coloring or make use of the symbols to retell Bible stories from previous lessons.

Before class, outline the words *Jerusalem* and *Pool of Siloam* on the appropriate places on the map. (Refer to the New Testament map in the back of a *Young Reader's Bible*.) Outline the shape of a pool beside the words *Pool of Siloam* and print the Bible reference *John 9* underneath the pool shape.

As children arrive, invite them to help you color a new place Jesus went. Children may wish to fill in and decorate the outlined words or fill the pool with blue marker. When coloring has been completed set the symbol for this session (sunglasses) on the pool. Last session's symbol (boat) should also be included.

What is special about this map? (It's about places Jesus went.)

Who can say the name of the pool? (Siloam) **A story in the Bible happened at this pool.** Point to the Bible reference and allow children to complete this statement: **The story is told in the Bible book named** (John) **in chapter number** (9).

② Read the Bible Story

Materials
- *The Young Reader's Bible,* pages 310-315
- photocopies of the Bible story (pages 301-303)
- *The Young Reader's Bible Audio Cassette* or a cassette on which you have recorded unit stories
- cassette player(s), earphones optional
- a large sheet of paper
- map made earlier
- blue construction paper
- blindfolds
- photocopies of page 206
- brown finger paint

"Now I See"

Before class, print the words *Pool of Siloam* on each sheet of blue construction paper.

Gather children in the story center. **Read the title on the map** (Places Jesus Helped). **Match the symbols** (boat, sunglasses) **with the correct Bible references.**

Display the first page of the Bible story in a *Young Reader's Bible.*

What might be wrong with the man in the story? (something wrong with his eyes, blind) **Have you had trouble with your eyes? Has anyone you know had trouble with their eyes? Have you ever talked with a person who was blind?**

Talk about how the sunglasses (on the map) remind us of someone who cannot see.

Listen closely to find out what happens to the person who is blind.

Listen

Read "Now I See" with great expression.

Who did Jesus help in this story? (blind man) **How?** (The blind man can see.)

Was the story different from what you thought it might be? Were any parts of the story the same?

Participate

Group children in pairs. Give each pair props to act out the story as you read it again. One child in each pair will play the part of Jesus and the other will be the blind man.

Distribute one blindfold and one piece of blue construction paper (Pool of Siloam) to each pair. The child playing the part of the blind man can be loosely blindfolded at this time. The Pool of Siloam should be placed on the floor behind Jesus.

Pantomime suggestions:
1. Jesus places mud on the blind man's eyes.
2. The blind man is helped to the Pool of Siloam.
3. The blind man washes his face (takes off his blindfold).
4. The blind man looks happy and thanks Jesus because he can see.

Read slowly allowing children time to pantomime as the story unfolds. If time permits, children may switch roles and volunteer readers may narrate the story. Good readers can take turns reading while others pantomime.

Give each child a copy of page 206. Read the instructions together. When children finish, let them show their drawings and tell why they think the man would have wanted to see that item.

Read

Give each child a copy of the Bible story (pages 301-303). They can color the story pages as they listen to the cassette story. Children can add thick brown finger paint to the blind man's eyes. When dry insert these pages in the book cover children will make later in the lesson.

Snacks
Serve chocolate pudding. If milk or chocolate allergies are a problem, blue gelatin squares can remind children of the pool where the blind man washed.

❸ Practice Using a Bible

Using My Bible

Display your Bible and read the front cover to the class (My Bible). Turn the Bible around and read the back cover (God's Word). Turn back to the front and ask, **What am I holding?** (My Bible) As you turn it over, ask, **What is the Bible?** (God's Word)

Display the poster board. Ask the children to put their hands in their laps when they know how many parts the Bible has. Choose a child to answer (2).

Ask a child to choose a picture from the assortment. Decide together whether the story pictured is found in the Old Testament or the New Testament.

Allow the child to tape the item on the correct side of the poster board. Follow this procedure with the remaining pictures, symbols and words. Point out that Old Testament stories tell about worshiping and obeying God. New Testament stories tell about worshiping and obeying God and His Son, Jesus.

Involve the entire group in a timed Bible search. Encourage everyone to help someone else find the book of John before the timer runs out. Repeat this challenge until the entire class is successful in locating John. If time permits, repeat the search with other Bible books.

Children can make their own Bible book covers. Children can wear their paint shirts and work at covered tables. Have each child fold a sheet of construction paper in half to make a book. Print each child's name on the cover inside. Open

Materials
- Bible for each child
- brown paper Bible-cover used last session
- poster board divided by the titles "New Testament" and "Old Testament"
- assortment of picture cutouts (Bible stories, Bible symbols, Bible names or books—an assortment that represents both Old Testament and New Testament stories)
- Plasti-tak or tape
- photocopies of Bible story (pages 301-303)
- light colors of construction paper
- assorted colors of poster paint
- paint shirts, table covering
- clean-up supplies
- pencils

the paper. Re-crease the paper so that it will fold easily either way. Put a few drops of poster paint of various colors on one side of the outside of the cover. Fold the paper shut to transfer paint to the other side making a design. Open and allow the design to dry completely while you continue the lesson.

Talk about the colors we see and enjoy.

Before class is over, help the child print the words *My Bible* on the front page and *God's Word* on the back of the cover. Add the pages of the Bible story (301-303) that the children colored earlier.

Finding Bible Verses

Ask children to find a verse in the Bible that tells about Jesus helping. They will find Acts 10:38 by answering the questions as they follow these directions.

If I want to find a verses about Jesus, would I look in the Old Testament or the New Testament? (usually the New) **I want to find a book called Acts. It tells about Jesus' church.** (Print *Acts* on a large paper.) **Shall I look in the Old Testament or the New Testament?** (New)

Show the class the table of contents page. Find Acts on the New Testament list. **What is the page number for the book of Acts in my Bible?** Choose someone to read the number. Some children will still turn one page at a time. Help children to turn past Psalms, to the New Testament, to a page near the correct one. Find Acts in your Bible.

Now, I want to find chapter 10. Should I look at big numbers or little numbers? Show chapter 10. **I need to find verse 38. Should I look for big numbers or little numbers?** Display verse 38 to the class. Go over the process again using the Reference Rhyme (page 32).

Thank you for helping me find this very important verse. Can anyone read this verse? If no one responds, read the verse for the class.

Help children locate the Bible reference for today's story. Ask them to read the Bible reference from the map. Copy the reference, John 9:11. Children may then locate the name *John* in their table of contents. Explain that after they have turned to the page and found the book of John they will need to search for the large number 9. When they have located chapter nine, ask them to look for the small number 11.

4 Share What We've Learned

Gather children in a circle. Have them tell you about the things they have been learning. Focus the conversation with questions related to the lesson aims. Encourage their efforts and their skill. Encourage them to help one another.

Pray, thanking God that Jesus went everywhere doing good. Ask God to help each one do good to others.

Before class, choose ten Old Testament and ten New Testament Bible book names. Copy each name on a small index card. Tape lengths of rope and the Old Testament and New Testament signs to the floor as described in lesson 37.

Divide class into two teams. Divide cards at random evenly into lunch sacks. Hand each team a lunch sack. Explain that at the word "go" each team will try to place the Bible book names on the correct side of the rope. Give each team two minutes. Work together using a table of contents to check their work. Correct misplaced books.

Sing "The B-I-B-L-E" learned in lesson 37 of this unit. Teams may then switch bags and repeat the game.

Materials
- two lengths of rope or string and the Old and New Testament signs used in lesson 37
- twenty small index cards
- two brown lunch bags
- tape

Note
Remember to complete the Bible book covers.

Teaching at Home

Investigate helps available to people who cannot see.

Reading tip
Place an item in a feely bag. Let children tell you what they feel. Print their description on a large sheet of paper. Help them decide what the object might be from the description they wrote. (If you do this in two groups, one group can guess the object from feel, and the other must guess the object from the description the other wrote.)

Thank You, Jesus

Tell how a leper learned about Jesus' love and concern.
Praise Jesus because He helps people
Read Bible references and find Bible verses.

"Jesus went everywhere doing good."   Acts 10:38, ICB

① Get Ready to Read

Before class, add the names *Samaria* and *Galilee* to the map. Print the Bible reference *Luke 17:11* in a spot between the two cities. (We are not given a specific city for today's Bible story—it happened somewhere between the two cities.)

As children arrive, invite them to color this section of the map. When children have finished coloring, tape the dime (or penny) on a spot between Samaria and Galilee. (A dime represents ten who were healed; a penny represents the one who said thank you.) Allow children to place symbols from previous lessons on the map.

What are we coloring on this shower curtain map? (places Jesus went) **Who will read the places Jesus went in today's story?** (Samaria, Galilee) **Who will read the Bible book for today's story?** (Luke)

What book can we look in to find the story of Jesus walking on the water? (John) **of Jesus healing the blind man?** (John)

Materials
- dime or penny
- markers
- map materials from previous lessons

② Read the Bible Story

"One Thankful Man"

Before class, put ten treats in each plastic bag.

Give one snack bag to each child. If any child says, "Thank you," take special notice. Have the children count the pieces in the bag. Suggest that each child eat one piece. Count the pieces that are left. Save the rest of the snack for later in the lesson.

Gather children in the story center. **Read the title on the map** (Places Jesus Helped), **the names near today's story village** (Samaria, Galilee) **and the Bible reference** (Luke 17). Notice the penny and the dime. Applaud children for their work.

Display the picture in a *Young Reader's Bible* (page 341). Ask children to count the people (other than Jesus). **Why might ten people be coming to see Jesus? Let's listen to find out.**

Listen

Gather children in the story center. Ask the children to listen closely as you read the story to find out if their ideas were right! Read "One Thankful Man" with great expression.

Why did ten men come to see Jesus? (They were sick.)

Materials
- *The Young Reader's Bible,* pages 340-345
- photocopies of the Bible story (pages 304-306)
- *The Young Reader's Bible Audio Cassette* or a cassette on which you have recorded unit stories
- cassette player(s), earphones optional
- a large sheet of paper
- cornstarch
- measuring cup, bowl, spoon
- water
- old sheet or shower curtain
- large jump rope or ball (that bounces)
- small clear plastic bags
- pretzels, crackers, or candy pieces

Who did Jesus help? (10 sick men)

What did the men do after they were helped? (Nine went away and one returned to say, "Thank you.")

Who can name others Jesus helped? (Peter to walk on water, blind man to see, me)

Where can we read about Jesus helping? (New Testament, John, Luke)

Who can tell a Bible verse about Jesus helping? (Acts 10:38—unit key verse)

Participate

Before class, prepare PUD by mixing ½ box of cornstarch with ¾ cup of water in a medium-sized bowl until mixture is smooth—the consistency of cake batter.

Choose volunteers: one child to be Jesus and (up to ten) to be lepers. Have a sheet or shower curtain on the floor for these volunteers to stand or sit on. With your fingers, spread some of the PUD mixture on arms, legs, and faces (even ears). Allow a few minutes drying time before rereading or retelling the story. Act out the story. At the appropriate time, wash off the children and send one child back to tell Jesus "Thank-you."

Clean up the area and then read the following story rhyme. After reading the rhyme, ask for volunteers to jump rope as you read it again. Depending on the length of your jump rope, this can be done using a team (two turning, one jumping) or individual jumpers.

Select new jumpers for each verse of the rhyme.

1. *Ten sick men saw the Savior*
   walking down the road one day.
   Ten sick men cried out, "Please help us!"
   Take our sickness all away!

2. *Jesus gave them some instructions,*
   "See the Priest." He told the men.
   Down the road they all did hurry—
   1, 2, 3, 4, 5, 6, 7, 8, 9, 10!

3. *Jesus healed ten men that day—*
   made their skin brand-new.
   But only one man stopped to tell Him,
   "Jesus, thank You! Thank You!"

4. *The moral of this story's clear,*
   and it is always true.
   For all of Jesus' special gifts,
   remember to say, "Thank You!"

Read

Give each child a copy of the Bible story (pages 304-306). Children can read or listen to the cassette story as they color the Bible story pages and enjoy the rest of the snack.

❸ Practice Using a Bible

Using My Bible

Practice dividing the Bible into Old and New Testaments. Practice finding Genesis, Psalms, and Matthew.

Before class, fill in Task Cards #1-4. Use the Bible reference *Acts 10: 38*. Photocopy the filled-in cards. Save Task Card #4 for use in *Finding Bible Verses*.

Give one or more Task Cards (#1-3) to the children according to their abilities. When most children have finished, talk about how they completed their cards. Praise their developing skill at using a Bible.

Finding Bible Verses

Before class, print *Luke 17:11* on the sheets of light-colored construction paper. Then print *Luke 17:11* on a large sheet of paper. Using a new color, trace around

Note
PUD is very messy, but it cleans up easily and children love the feel of it. When dry, it really does look like a skin disease.

Note
If jumping rope is not feasible for either your facility or your children, try allowing groups to bounce balls in rhythm or lead hand-clapping in pairs (playground style).

Snacks
Choose a snack bag idea.

Materials
• Bibles
• white or light-colored construction paper
• colored pencils, markers, or crayons
• a large sheet of paper
• photocopies of Task Cards #1-4 (page 110)

the reference on the large paper. Repeat several times using a different color. Distribute construction paper to children and invite them to make their own design of "rainbow writing" using colored pencils, markers or crayons to trace around the letters and numerals.

Show the class the table of contents in your Bible. Ask children to listen as you begin to read the books of the New Testament. Tell them to listen for the book name *Luke*. When they hear the Bible book name *Luke* they should put their hands in their laps.

Read the table of contents beginning with Matthew. When children have identified that they heard Luke, turn the Bible around and show them where Luke is located in the Bible.

Close your Bible and ask volunteers to find the name *Luke* in your Bible's table of contents. Ask volunteers to read the page number and locate Luke in your Bible. Encourage everyone to follow the same process in their own Bibles. Recall the Reference Rhyme (page 32)

When children have located the book of Luke, ask them to find the big number 17 (chapter 17). Repeat this procedure finding the small number 16 (verse 16). Read the verse aloud. **What did the man do?** (bowed at Jesus' feet) **What did the man say?** (Thank You.)

Look again at the picture on page 341. Recall the earlier discussion.

Give each child a copy of Task Card #4. Ask volunteers to complete the card and find Acts 10:38. Encourage others to help them remember the procedure for finding the verse. Read the unit key verse, Acts 10:38, "Jesus went everywhere doing good."

What good thing did Jesus do in this Bible story? (healed ten men)

 ## Share What We've Learned

Recall the jump rope activity learned earlier. Children can participate both by jumping rope and chanting the jump rope rhyme. Help the children name ways that Jesus helps us today. Using simple words, list them on a large sheet of paper.

Work together to print new words for the jump rope rhyme to tell others how Jesus helps us today. Recite and jump rope to the new verses.

Give each child ten strips of construction paper. Have children copy words or draw ways that Jesus helps their families. Glue or tape the papers to make a construction-paper chain. Children can wear their paper chains or you can make one very long paper chain to decorate your room.

Pray, thanking God for Jesus. Thank God for helping us every day.

Materials
• large sheet of paper
• construction paper strips (ten per child)
• pencils
• transparent tape or glue

Option
If you have extra time, play the Old Testament/New Testament game learned in lesson 37. Call out book names and let children use the table of contents to find the book before choosing where to stand.

 Teaching at Home

Find out more about leprosy.

Reading tips
• Emphasize the number words *one-ten*. Child can match the word with the numeral. You can also match the ordinal forms, *first-tenth*.
• Count syllables (rest chin on hand while saying word) for these words from the story: *Samaria, Galilee, leprosy, suddenly, disappeared, disciple, Samaritan.*

40

Never Too Busy

Tell how Jesus treated the children.
Praise Jesus because He helps people.
Read Bible references and find Bible verses.

"Jesus went everywhere doing good."   Acts 10:38, ICB

1 Get Ready to Read

Materials
- map materials from previous sessions
- cutout of a child-size hand
- markers or labels

Before class, print two labels for the map: *Jordan River, Mark 10:13.*
Draw an outline of the Jordan River. (See a *Young Reader's Bible* map, page 441.) As children arrive, invite them to help you color a map of places Jesus went. Color and label the Jordan River and Mark 10:13.

Ask a child to place the hand cutout beside the Jordan River. Allow children to predict what the hand cutout will represent.

Who can read the title of our map? (Places Jesus Helped) Read the new labels.
Who can tell something about today's new story? (in the book of Mark, happened near the Jordan River, about Jesus helping)

Name other places where Jesus helped. (pool of Siloam, Lake of Galilee, town between Samaria and Galilee)

2 Read the Bible Story

Materials
- *The Young Reader's Bible,* pages 346-351
- photocopies of the two-page Bible story (page 203)
- *The Young Reader's Bible Audio Cassette* or a cassette on which you have recorded unit stories
- cassette player(s), earphones optional
- map materials used earlier
- a large sheet of paper
- poster board or heavy construction paper
- clothesline
- clip clothespins
- small pretzels

"Let the Children Come"

Before class, use the poster board or heavy construction paper to prepare ten story cards. Make two sets of cards, three per set. Mount pictures (page 203) or simple sketches on the cards. Leave four cards blank.

You will need these story cards, two of each type:
1. people with children trying to pass the disciples to see Jesus
2. Jesus welcoming the children
3. The printed Bible reference: *Mark 10:16*

Gather in the story center. Talk about the map. **Read the title on the map** (Places Jesus Helped). **Name the river** (Jordan). **Read the Bible reference** (Mark 10:13). **The people in the pictures on the story cards were near the Jordan River.**

Show two picture story cards. Ask children to predict what each picture is about.

What do you think Jesus will be doing in our story today? (helping)
Name other people Jesus helped. (Peter, lepers, blind man)
Listen to find out who Jesus helped when He was near the Jordan River.

Listen

Read "Let the Children Come" with great expression. After the story, have the children help you use two story cards to retell the main action of the story. **Who did Jesus help in this story?** (children, parents)

Participate

Before class, string a clothesline along one wall. Make certain children can reach the clothesline to attach story cards with clothespins. Talk about other things that happened in the story that are not on the cards you made before class. Have children choose another part of the story to illustrate. Let children show their pictures. Choose two pictures to add to one set of three story cards made earlier and two to add to the other set of three cards.

Divide children into two groups. Distribute one set of five story cards and ten clothespins to each group. Explain to the children that their job is to "hang up" the five cards to tell the story as you read it aloud for them a second time. When the story is finished and the groups have completed their story lines, ask each group to tell the Bible story and point to each card as it is recalled.

For further review, mix all cards in a small container or bag. Choose volunteers to select a card and tell what each is about. Children who choose a reference card may either point out the different parts of the reference or find the verse in their own Bibles.

Read

Give each child a copy of the Bible story excerpt (page 203). Encourage children to read the Bible story pages at their own level. Children can color the Bible story page. Give each child ten small pretzels. See who remembers to say, "Thank you." Offer prayer, thanking God for food and for help.

Option
Make a rebus of the story words, *"Let the children come to me. Don't stop them,"* said Jesus. Give children paper, pencils, and stickers. They can copy the word and use stickers in place of *children* and *Jesus*. Add a stop sign shape around the word *stop*.

Snacks
Ten pretzels passed out to each child during *Read*.

Option
Make hand-shaped cookies using cookie cutters from a craft store and a basic sugar cookie recipe. Let each child bake two hand cookies to remind them that when we follow Jesus, we want to help others with our hands (what we do).

③ Practice Using a Bible

Materials
- Bibles
- photocopies of page 207
- photocopies of Task Card #4 (page 110)
- Bible reference visuals
- small paper sacks
- construction paper
- tape or glue
- pencils

Using My Bible

Before class, prepare a set of Bible reference visuals:
1. a large blue paper circle titled **book**
2. a large red paper circle titled **chapter**
3. a large yellow circle titled **verse**

Choose several Bible references and print them on small circles using the **book, chapter, verse** color coding. (Include the colon on the red circle after the chapter number, both on the large circle and the smaller circles used for references.)

Place one Bible reference (three small circles) in each paper sack. Attach large circles to poster board or flannel board.

Group the children in pairs. Give each pair a sack, a piece of construction paper and glue or tape. Display the three large circles. Explain that each pair will glue or tape their Bible reference in correct order using the pattern shown with the Bible reference visuals.

Give each child a copy of page 207. Read the title together, "Which Books Don't Belong?" Read the books parts: Old Testament and New Testament. Read every book name.

Challenge the children to find each book in a Bible table of contents to discover which testament it belongs in. Have them cross out the books that are listed under the wrong testament. If you have confident readers who are also competent writers, they can copy the names onto the correct column.

Finding Bible Verses

While children are working on page 207, check to make certain they have arranged their reference circles correctly. When they finish page 207, they can find the references in their Bibles.

As each team uses the Bible reference to locate the verse in a Bible, have them practice reading it together. When all pairs have finished, have the teams read their verse aloud.

Ask, **How do Bible references help us?** (find verses in a Bible) Print Mark 10:13 on the board. **Which part of the reference tells us the Bible book?** (the first part, the word, Mark) **Which number is the chapter number?** (follows the word, 10) **Which is the verse number?** (follows the colon, 13)

Before class, fill in Task Card #4 with the Bible reference *Mark 10:13.* Make copies of the filled-in Task Card for each child.

Use Task Card #4 as a timer challenge. Turn the timer over and do what it says before the sand runs out.

- *Find the book, **Mark**.*
- *Find the book, **Mark**, chapter **10**, verse **13**.*
- *Close your Bible.*
- *Find **Mark 10:13** again.*

"Jesus went everywhere doing good" is a verse from the Bible. **Who can remember where to find it?** Have a child who remembers the book name, print it on the board. Repeat this procedure with chapter and verse numbers. Ask children to read the completed reference aloud as a group (Acts 10:38). Children can add Acts to the list of New Testament books.

❹ Share What We've Learned

Invite the children to play Bible story charades with you. As one child acts out a Bible story, the others will try to guess not only the story but also the name of the Bible book that it's found in. The child who guesses correctly both the story and the book will take the next turn at acting.

Whisper the following stories:
- Jesus helps Peter (walk on the water).
- Jesus makes the blind man see.
- Jesus heals ten sick men.
- Jesus blesses the children.

Gather everyone in a circle to talk about what they have been doing and learning. Use the aims for this lesson as an outline for the kinds of questions you ask.

Close the session by singing "Jesus Loves Me," reminding the group about the love Jesus shows to children.

Option
Provide pictures of children from magazines or catalogs. Have children add these modern-day children to the copy of the Bible story (page 203). If you prefer, take pictures of the children and have them glue their pictures to the scene next week.

Teaching at Home

Make cookies to take to neighbors, soup for a homeless shelter, or work together in some way to follow Jesus' example of helping others.

Reading tip
This is a good lesson to focus on the number words.

A Very Taxing Lesson

Tell how Jesus helped Zaccheus.
Praise Jesus because He helps people.
Read Bible references and find Bible verses.

"Jesus went everywhere doing good."   Acts 10:38, ICB

① Get Ready to Read

Before class, add the name *Jericho*, and the Bible reference *Luke 19* to the map.
Follow the procedure for marking the map used in previous lessons. Jericho is near the place where the Dead Sea and the Jordan River meet. (See the map in a *Young Reader's Bible*, page 441.)

When the map is completed, put the branch or tree beside Jericho. Ask volunteers to place the story symbols from previous lessons on appropriate places on the map. Ask children to tell about each symbol as they place it on the map.

Ask children to close their eyes as you incorrectly place story symbols on the map. Work together to correct the map.

Materials
- map materials from previous lessons
- tree branch or toy tree
- markers

② Read the Bible Story

"Big News for a Little Man"
Read the title on the map (Places Jesus Helped). **Read the name of the town** (Jericho) and the Bible reference for today's story (Luke 19).

Who can tell about people Jesus helped? Ask volunteers to tell about each person as they show the corresponding symbol and Bible reference.

Who is the tallest person you know? Name some good things about being tall. How is it helpful to be tall when you're watching a parade? What problems might short people have when trying to see a parade? How can you see a parade when tall people are all around you?

Show the picture on page 352 of a *Young Reader's Bible*. **Why might the short man be peering through the crowd?** Show the picture on page 353.

Have everyone stand very close together so they can feel squished—just like Zaccheus. **What did the short man do when he felt squished and could not see? How did the short man solve his problem? Who is talking with him?** (Jesus)

Listen closely as I read the story to find out what Jesus told the little man.

Listen
Read "Big News for a Little Man" with great expression.

What problem did Zaccheus have that was much worse than not being able to see a parade? (He had cheated people.)

Materials
- *The Young Reader's Bible*, pages 352-357
- photocopies of the two-page Bible story (page 204)
- *The Young Reader's Bible Audio Cassette* or a cassette on which you have recorded unit stories
- cassette player(s), earphones optional
- map made earlier
- yellow crayons
- white or light-blue colored construction paper
- green and brown one-inch tissue paper squares
- glue sticks or white glue
- pencils
- chenille wire stems

What did Zaccheus decide to do? (share with the poor; give back even more than he had taken)

How did Jesus help Zaccheus? (Jesus went to Zaccheus's house—even though everyone knew Zaccheus had been a liar and a thief.)

Jesus was pleased that Zaccheus wanted to change. Jesus had helped Zaccheus right in his hometown of Jericho.

Recall the unit key verse, "Jesus went everywhere doing good," Acts 10:38, NIV. **What good did Jesus do for Zaccheus?** (helped him change from doing wrong to doing right)

Participate

Divide the class into three groups.

Group 1 will shake their heads and say, "Uh-oh!" every time the name *Zaccheus* is read.

Group 2 will wave their hands and shout, "Hallelujah!" every time the name *Jesus* is read.

Group 3 will listen for the word *house* and make building motions with their hands.

Read the story again pausing at each of the key words to give children plenty of time to respond with their assigned action.

Give each child a copy of the Bible story excerpt (page 204) and a yellow crayon. Have them find and circle the words to complete statements about the story pages. For example, **This is how Zaccheus probably felt when Jesus talked to him** (happy); **This is where Jesus went to visit Zaccheus** (house); and so on.

Give each child a sheet of construction paper. Have each child draw a large tree with branches. Fill in the green leafy areas with green tissue paper squares that are first "squished" onto the eraser end of a pencil. Place the tissue squares close together on the tree branches for leaves. Fill in tree trunk and branches with either flat or "squished" brown tissue paper.

Make a chenille-wire figure of Zaccheus.

Read

Children can read or listen to the cassette story as they color a Bible story page.

❸ Practice Using a Bible

Using My Bible

Copy *Luke 19:1* on a large sheet of paper. Display the Bible reference "chapter," "book," and "verse" visuals for the class to read. Ask volunteers to match the circles to the correct part of the Bible reference written on the board. Help children locate the verse in their own Bibles.

Show how much of chapter 19 actually tells the story of Zaccheus. Print the entire reference for the story of Zaccheus: *Luke 19:1-10*.

(Note: The account of Zaccheus is found only in Luke.)

Print the following words near the top of the large paper: *Zaccheus, Jesus, tax, tree.* If you wish, include other words from the Bible story that appear in the Bible versions the children are using.

When a child locates one of the listed words, help everyone find it in a Bible. Read the verse aloud and decide together how to print the reference for that verse. Print the reference under the word. Children may find several references for each word.

Chenille Figure

For a six-inch figure, use a twelve-inch chenille wire cut in half. You can cut about six wires at a time using a paper cutter. Bend one piece of the wire in half around the thumb. Twist for the head and arms. Bend a second piece of wire in half and slide it through the circle of the head and twist under the head making a neck. Twist once or twice more to make the body. Separate the wires for the legs.

Snacks

Offer a variety of fruit that grows on trees: slices of apples, oranges, pears.

Materials

• Bible reference visuals from lesson 40
• Bibles
• a large sheet of paper
• markers

Practice reading each word and the list of Bible references under that word. Next allow children to read a reference and choose someone to tell which word the reference is listed under. That person may then erase the reference. Continue until all references have been read. If some children did not get to erase a reference, ask them to read one of the words. They can then erase that word. The activity is completed when all words have been erased.

Finding Bible Verses

Practice locating Bible verses.

Find a verse that tells about a blind man healed. (John 9:11)

What verse tells about Jesus' visit with a short man? (Luke 19:1-10)

Find a verse that tells about a man walking on water. (John 6:19)

Ask each child to demonstrate how they find the book (or reference if possible).

Nonreaders may participate by telling the teacher how to find the reference. The teacher will look up the reference as directed by the child.

End this section with group practice.

Open to an Old Testament book.

Open to a New Testament book.

Find Psalms. Find Revelation. Find Genesis. Find Matthew.

Find our key verse (Acts 10:38).

Find a Gospel book.

 ## Share What We've Learned

Materials
• Old Testament/New Testament jumping game (from lesson 37)

Gather children in a circle. Have them tell you about the things they have been learning. Focus the conversation with questions related to both the unit and the lesson aims. Encourage their efforts and their skill. Encourage them to help one another.

Choose volunteers to read from a *Young Reader's Bible* or to narrate stories from this unit. Use the symbols from the map to recall the event.

Repeat the Old Testament/New Testament jumping game found in lesson 37 of this unit. When playing the Old Testament/New Testament jumping game, ask children to jump to either side of the rope. Ask each child to then name a Bible book or Bible person that belongs in the testament on which they are standing.

Sing these lyrics to the tune of the "The B-I-B-L-E."

The B-I-B-L-E, it is God's Word to me,

The Old Testament, the New Testament, the B-I-B-L-E!

 Teaching at Home

Emphasize problem solving. Zaccheus solved the problem of not being able to see Jesus. But Zaccheus had a bigger problem. Only Jesus can solve the problem of sin. Encourage children to be resourceful problem solvers, but to turn to God for help when only He can meet the need.

Reading tip

This is a good story to practice sequencing of events. Print the events of the story on cards. Let the child put them in story order.

Peter stepped out of the boat
and began to walk to Jesus
on the water.

But the wind and waves
pushed and pulled at him.

Peter was afraid,
and he began to sink.

"Lord, save me!" he cried.
Jesus reached out to Peter
and helped him back into the boat.

"Why did you begin to doubt?"
said Jesus.

Jesus got into the boat, too.
And the wind stopped!

Jesus' disciples worshiped him
in the boat.

Jesus heard his disciples.

He reached out his arms

and called to the children.

"Let the children come to me,"

he said. "Don't stop them."

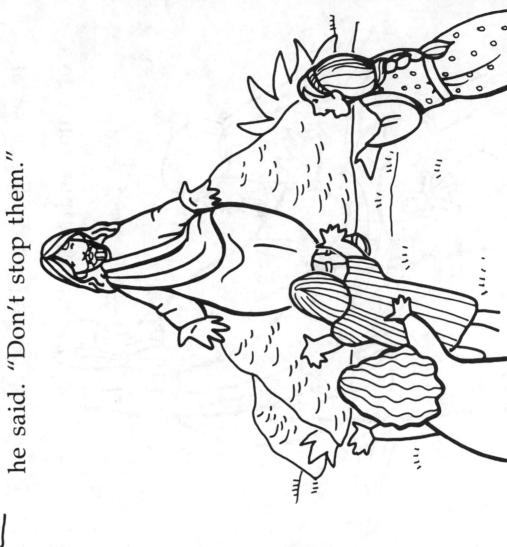

But Jesus' disciples tried to stop

the mothers and the fathers.

"Get back!" they said.

"Can't you see that Jesus is busy?

He does not have time

for children!"

Zaccheus was happy.

He welcomed Jesus to his house.

People in the crowd were saying,

"Zaccheus is a bad man!

Jesus has gone to the house

of a liar and a thief!"

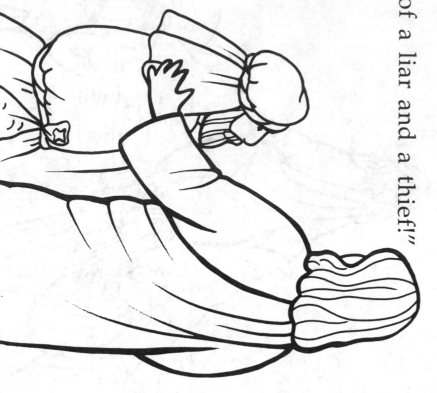

"What the people say is true,"

Zaccheus told Jesus.

"I have cheated people.

But I am sorry."

"I know," said Jesus.

"That is why I came."

Bible Two
of a Kind

1. Find two pictures that match. Circle them in red.

2. Find two other pictures that match. Circle them in blue.

3. Draw a line between words that match.

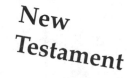

New
Testament

Acts

Jesus

New
Testament

Jesus

Acts

Genesis

Bible

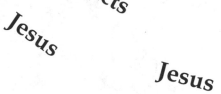

Bible

Genesis

Old
Testament

Old
Testament

Look at That!

Jesus healed a blind man. The man had never seen shapes or colors or somebody smiling.

Nobody! Never! Nothing at all.

What would this man like to see? Draw a picture to show your idea.

Which Books Don't Belong?

Old Testament

Malachi

John

Habakkuk

Hebrews

Jeremiah

New Testament

Romans

Matthew

Jonah

1 Peter

Ruth

Find each Bible book name in a Bible table of contents. Is the book in the Old or the New Testament?

Cross out the book names that are in the wrong list.

Unit 9

We Tell What Jesus Can Do Because He Is the Son of God

Key Verse
"Go and make followers. . . . Teach them to obey."
Matthew 28:19, 20, ICB

Unit Vocabulary

colt
donkey
garden
gardener
gathers
gentle
grabbed
hymn
palm branches
poured
prophets
sadness
served
spread
suffering
sweet-smelling spices
together
tomb
risen
Upper Room

Unit Aims

By the end of the unit, learners will be able to
- tell five Bible stories about what Jesus, the Son of God, can do.
- feel joyful in finding verses in a Bible and reading *The Young Reader's Bible*.
- locate books, chapters and verses in their own Bibles.
- read (at their level) stories from *The Young Reader's Bible*.
- tell what Jesus can do.

Unit Project

Gospel Trees

Find a well-branched tree limb and anchor it with sand or gravel in a 3-pound coffee can or institutional-sized can. If a branch tree is not usable in your classroom, plan a bulletin board or a poster collage. Before each lesson, cut shapes (palm branch, cup and bread, hearts, long strips, cloud) for each child in your class. Use heavy weight construction paper, poster board or art paper to produce sturdy tree decorations. Use light colors so children can read the reference easily and color creatively. Children trace and cut a shape and print a Bible reference. Then they trace over the letters and numerals of the Bible reference making "rainbow writing." Children find and read the Bible verses and illustrate them on the other side of the cutout shape. Prepare extra shapes each week so children can catch up when they miss a session.

As children add to the Gospel Trees, they can tell important events about the end of Jesus' time on earth (triumphal entry, death, burial, resurrection, and ascension). As the children add visuals to the Gospel Tree, they will be adding reminders of the gospel, the good news Jesus brought.

If most of your readers are less advanced, have everyone copy, decorate, and find the same verse. Confident readers can be challenged with the optional verses listed in each lesson.

Children can decorate the shapes with stickers, cutouts from used Sunday school literature, markers, crayons, stencils and so on.

	The Singing Bible (3 tapes)	Kids on the Rock (More Songs)	Follow the Leader (The Donut Man)	I'm a Helper (The Donut Man)	Good News (The Donut Man)
Lesson 42				Stand Up and Sing	
Lesson 43					
Lesson 44					Good News
Lesson 45	Easter Song	Jesus Christ Is Risen Today			Good News
Lesson 46	Just Like Lightning				Good News
Key Verse					
Unit Theme		Praise the Lord; That's What I'm Gonna Do			
All Lessons	The Books We Love the Best The Bible Book Is True	God's Word Is for Me			

The Singing Bible (3 tapes), ©1993 by Lightwave Publishing, Inc. Manufactured and distributed by Word Publishing, Dallas, TX 75234
Kids on the Rock! More Songs, ©1994 Gospel Light, Ventura CA 93006
The Donut Man (3 tapes): *Follow the Leader*, ©1990; *I'm a Helper*, ©1991; *Good News*, ©1991; Integrity Music, Inc., P.O. Box 16813 Mobile, AL 36616

Key Verse Activities

Materials
- picture of Jesus' tomb (*The Young Reader's Bible,* pages 380, 384, 388)
- peeled boiled eggs and their crushed eggshells (colored or white)
- blue dessert-sized paper plates
- green crayons and markers
- glue
- large paper clips
- masking tape

Easter Eggs-amples

Boil eggs. If you let them sit in the hot water until it cools naturally, the yolks will have a slightly green tint (instead of yellow). Write the memory verse around the edge of each plate. Use a green marker to trace around the inner circle of the plate and draw the outline of continents.

How can eggs remind us of Jesus' resurrection? (They look like a tomb and something alive comes out of them.) **Chicks come out of farm eggs alive and Jesus came out of His tomb alive.** Show the picture from a *Young Reader's Bible.*

Chicks won't come out of these eggs, but let's look at what's inside. Pull out a yolk. **Yolks are shaped like our world, aren't they? Jesus said He wants us to go into all the world and tell everyone about Him.**

These plates are round like the earth, too. Let's color in the land areas green. Next, help the children make a cross shape out of glue. They can stick on pieces of crushed eggshell.

Tape a paper clip to the back of the plate so you can hang up your picture at home. The cross on this plate reminds us to tell the world to follow Jesus.

Materials
- globe or atlas
- removable tape or removable square note papers
- a pen

Cross the Globe Game

Before class, draw a cross on small pieces of removable tape or on square note pad papers.

The Bible says that Jesus told His followers to go into all the world and tell the good news about Him, teaching people to obey Him. He wants everyone in every country to know Him.

Let's find the names of some countries on this map (or globe). I'll name a country and give you some time to find that country and put a cross on it. You can help one another.

As each cross is put in place, repeat the memory verse, inserting the name of the country. For example, "Go and make followers in Mexico. Teach them to obey."

Materials
- paper
- pen
- jelly beans

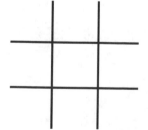

Jelly Bean Tic-Tac-Toe

Before class, draw a simple grid on each piece of paper as shown.

Divide the class into pairs. **We're going to play Jelly Bean Tic-Tac-Toe. I'll give each of you five jelly beans that are all the same color. Your opponent will have a different color.**

To see who goes first, one of you puts a jelly bean in his hand behind his back. If the other player guesses the hand correctly, she goes first. If she guesses incorrectly, you go first.

To play, you take a turn reciting the memory verse and then put a jelly bean on a square. Then it's your partner's turn to recite the memory verse and put a jelly bean in a square. The first player to get three jelly beans in a row wins.

42

Hail to the King!

Tell how people praised Jesus, the Son of God.
Praise Jesus because He is the Son of God.
Read Bible references and find Bible verses.

"Go and make followers. . . . Teach them to obey."
  Matthew 28:19, 20, ICB

1 Get Ready to Read

Before class, cut two palm branches for each child from green construction paper. Leave a large uncut center section so that children can copy the Bible reference *Luke 19:30* on the branches. Punch a hole near the top edge of each palm branch.

As children arrive invite them to choose a palm branch to decorate. Explain that after copying the reference with pencil, they may trace over it with colored glue or glitter crayons. They can also decorate the palm branch. Explain that they will be using these palm branches later today.

Assist children in attaching yarn to the palm branches. Help children hang them on the tree. Be sure children's names are on the palm branches before hanging them on the tree.

2 Read the Bible Story

"Praise to the King of Kings!"

Gather children in the story center. Display the article or item about a celebrity or hero. Tell children about the person represented by the item. Invite children to name someone famous. **How would you feel if this person visited our church today? What kinds of things might we do to get ready for their visit?**

Today, we will read about an important visit from an important person.

Listen to find out who came to visit and what the people did. (Children who are familiar with Bible stories might guess the story because of the palm branches. Praise their Bible knowledge. Include them in the reading of the story by allowing them to tell what will happen next in a few key places in the story.)

Listen

Read "Praise to the King of Kings" with great expression.

How was the story different from what you thought it might be?

What would you do to get ready if you knew Jesus was coming to visit our town?

Why might we decide that Jesus is the Son of God after hearing this story? (He knew about the donkey; people called Him blessed.)

Materials
- tree branch to represent a tree
- construction paper palm branches
- colored glue or glitter crayons

See the unit page for a complete explanation and materials list for this "Gospel Tree" project.

Option
If you have students who are ready to find more challenging Bible references, allow them to print one of these references on the palm branch.
Zechariah 9:9
Psalm 118:26
Mark 11:2
Luke 19:30
John 12:15

Materials
- *The Young Reader's Bible*, pages 358-363
- photocopies of the two-page Bible story (page 226)
- photocopies of page 229
- *The Young Reader's Bible Audio Cassette* or a cassette on which you have recorded unit stories
- cassette player(s), earphones optional
- a large sheet of paper
- rolled-up blanket for each child
- paper palm branches
- rope (for leading imaginary donkey)
- balloon for each child
- string for each balloon
- pencils or markers
- newspaper article or item to remind us of a celebrity
- scraps of construction paper, greenery, and fabric
- glue

Participate

Before class, roll up baby blankets or small sections of material for children to roll out as they reenact the Bible story.

In our story, the people called Jesus "blessed." What words can we use to tell Jesus how special He is?

Talk about praise words. List ideas on a large sheet of paper as you talk together. **What do people say to thank or praise one another? What do people say to you to praise you or thank you? What might we say to God?**

Give each child a balloon. Let children blow up their balloons. Some might need help. Tie a string on each balloon. After discussing praise words, print each child's name and praise ideas on a balloon.

Hand each child a blanket. Distribute plain paper palm branches.

Today, we will pretend to be part of the crowd welcoming Jesus to Jerusalem. Have the class line up on both sides of the room. Prepare the scene and ask the children to use their imaginations to see Jesus and the donkey. Choose a child to lead the donkey. (Slowly walk down the center, holding a rope over the shoulder as though leading a donkey.)

As the child leading the donkey walks along, the class (the crowd) will roll out blankets or lay down the palm branches to walk on.

After the sentence "Blessed is the one who comes from the family of David!" is read, invite the children to add their own praise words (listed earlier). They can wave palm branches and balloons.

Set the balloons aside.

Give everyone a copy of page 229 and encourage children to print or draw ideas to complete each statement:

Jesus, You help me . . .

Thank You, Jesus, for . . .

Jesus, I think You're really . . .

Jesus, one of the greatest things about You is . . .

Children can color the page.

Read

Give each child a copy of the Bible story excerpt (page 226). Children can decorate the story by adding scraps of construction paper, greenery, and fabric. Encourage children to copy praise words at the end of the story. They can listen to the cassette as they work.

❸ Practice Using a Bible

Using My Bible

Before class, draw a line down the middle of a large sheet of paper. Label the left column *Old Testament* and the right column *New Testament*.

Divide the class into groups of two or three. In each group, include a child who is familiar with using a Bible. Each group is to locate the first page of any Bible book by using the table of contents.

When all groups have located a book, take turns telling the name of the book and showing the Bible open to the first page of that book. Decide if the book is in the Old Testament or the New Testament. Print the book name on the paper under Old or New Testament. Repeat the Bible book name together.

If you have time, allow every group to find the first page of that book. Notice the fact that the page numbers change from Bible version to Bible version.

Snacks
Serve Royal pudding cups.

Materials
• *The Young Reader's Bible*
• Bible for each child
• palm branches made earlier
• sand timer (found in some board games) for use with Task Card #4
• photocopies of Task Cards #1-4 (page 110)
• a large sheet of paper

Next, challenge each group to find chapter five and then verse five of the book they named. Be prepared for some surprises because not every book has five chapters. If there are not five chapters, look to see how many chapters are in that book.

Finding Bible Verses

Ask children to display the palm branches they decorated earlier, read the accompanying Bible reference, and then read the verse from a Bible. Nonreaders may display their palm branches and ask the teacher or a volunteer to read the Bible reference and verse.

Children will work on the four task cards. (See page 110 of this book.) If children are more advanced, you may not need to offer Task Cards #1 or #2.

Fill out Task Cards as follows.

Card #1 *Matthew*

Card #3 *Matthew*

Card #4 *Matthew*   *Matthew 28:19, 20*   *Matthew*

Read the shortened version of this unit key verse (ICB). "Go and make followers. . . . Teach them to obey." Have the children repeat each phrase after you. **Some of the people who had worshiped and praised Jesus when He came into Jerusalem became followers.**

4 Share What We've Learned

Before class, cover two chip cans with paper and print *Old Testament* on one of the chip cans and *New Testament* on the other chip can. Make two sets of Bible-book cards, sized to fit inside the chip cans. Each card should have the name of an Old Testament or New Testament book written on it.

Divide class into two groups. Hand each group a set of Old Testament/New Testament cards. Play a game to celebrate their expanding knowledge.

Each team starts with 20 points.

You will have five minutes to place the Old Testament/New Testament cards in the correct cans. (Adjust the time according to the ability level of the children.)

Two points will be taken away for each incorrectly placed card. One point will be taken away for every card not placed in either can. The team with the most points at the end of the game wins.

Gather everyone in a circle to talk about what they have been doing and learning. Use the aims for this lesson as an outline for the kinds of questions you ask.

End the session by singing songs that praise Jesus. Have children pray praise prayers, including some of the ideas they wrote or drew on page 229.

Option

Provide art materials for children to illustrate their verse on the other side of the palm branch.

Option

See the unit page for ideas for teaching the unit key verses, Matthew 28:19, 20.

Materials
- four potato chip cylinder cans covered with paper
- two sets of Bible-book cards
- large sheet of paper
- markers

Note

Although this game will take extra preparation, it can be used often as a learning center for early arrivals or for practice at the end of a session.

 Teaching at Home

Begin preparing for events of the final week leading up to the resurrection. Mark this year's calendar with the events from the triumphal entry to Pentecost.

Reading tip

Notice the verb changes: *bring* and *brought*. Help the children discover the reason for the differences. Give simple sentence examples. "Today you bring. Yesterday you brought." List other similar examples. "Today I catch. Yesterday I caught."

The Last Meal With Jesus

Explain that the Lord's Supper helps us remember that Jesus is the Son of God.
Remember Jesus and praise Him because He is the Son of God.
Read Bible references and find Bible verses.

"Go and make followers. . . . Teach them to obey."
  Matthew 28:19, 20, ICB

1 Get Ready to Read

Materials
- construction paper or Fun Foam (See Finding Bible Verses.)
- tree branch used last session
See the unit page for a complete explanation and materials list for this "Gospel Tree" project.

Option
If you have children who are ready to find more challenging Bible references, allow them to copy one of these onto the shape. They will be used later in the lesson.
Luke 22:19
Deuteronomy 8:11
1 Corinthians 11:24

Materials
- *The Young Reader's Bible*, pages 364-369
- photocopies of the two-page Bible story (page 227)
- *The Young Reader's Bible Audio Cassette* or a cassette on which you have recorded unit stories
- cassette player(s), earphones optional
- towel
- water bottle (container of water)
- loaf of bread
- juice bottle (or word juice) cut from carton
- cup
- hymn book
- birthday card (new or used)
- six large paper bags
- tan and purple construction paper
- glue

Before class, cut cup and bread shapes from construction paper. (See the art on pages 367 and 368 of the *Young Reader's Bible*.) Copy the Bible reference **Mark 14:22** onto the shapes.

Give each child a shape. Have a child read the Bible reference and verse aloud to the group. Children can trace and decorate the Bible reference.

When children have finished decorating their shapes, help them punch a hole at the top and thread a piece of yarn for hanging. Label each shape with the child's name and hang it on the Bible tree.

2 Read the Bible Story

"Remember Me"

Display the birthday card. Encourage children to talk about birthday cards. **Why do people send birthday cards? How do you feel when you get a birthday card? How often do you get birthday cards?**

It makes us feel good when someone remembers our birthday. Jesus asks His followers to remember Him, too. As you hear the story, listen to find out how Jesus wants us to remember Him.

Listen

Read "Remember Me" with great expression.

How did Jesus say the disciples could remember Him? (Drink the cup; eat the bread.)

Participate

Before class, place the following six items in grocery bags, one item per bag: towel, water bottle, loaf of bread, juice bottle, cup, hymn book.

Seat children in six groups. Give each group a grocery bag containing one item. Explain that each bag includes an item from the Bible story. Choose someone from each group to carry and open the bag.

After each group has examined the item in its bag, talk with them about how each item relates to the Bible story. The other groups will listen as each item is discussed.

Next, have the groups arrange themselves in proper story order. Ask the groups to retell the story, paper bag by paper bag. Or, ask a volunteer from each group to read their section of the story. Nonreaders may display the item from the bag while an adult reads.

Read

Give each child a copy of the Bible story excerpt (page 227). Read about the bread and the cup. Provide scraps of tan and purple construction paper for children to paste onto the bread and the cup. Children can draw and decorate circles around the bread and the cup. They can listen to the cassette while they work.

❸ Practice Using a Bible

Using My Bible

List the following three Bible book names (names only) on a large sheet of paper. Read each book name as you print it. Have children repeat the name after you.

Luke
Deuteronomy
1 Corinthians

Help children locate the tables of contents in their Bibles. Ask children to cover the Old Testament books with one hand. Check hand positions. Uncover. Then ask them to cover the New Testament books with the other hand. Check and then have them uncover.

Read the three Bible book names, one at a time. Decide whether the book is found in the Old Testament or New Testament. Then have each child locate the book name in the table of contents.

Give each child a copy of page 230. Let them help each other do the word search. Nonreaders can circle each word as the reader finds it. Have children look again at the Bible story excerpt (page 227). Find and underline the words "This is my body."

Emphasize that the stories in the *Young Reader's Bible* are the same stories that we can read in our Bibles. Talk about the differences. (The words are larger. The words are easier to read. There are pictures to help us understand the words.)

Help children find the words "remember me" on each story page. (They are the last words on each page.)

Finding Bible Verses

Add the chapter and verse numbers to the three Bible books you printed earlier. Read the Bible references together. Use the Reference Rhyme (page 32) to recall how to find each Bible verse. Find Luke 22:19; Deuteronomy 8:11; 1 Corinthians 11:24 and read each verse aloud.

Luke 22:19 ("This bread is my body that I am giving for you. Do this to remember me.")

Deuteronomy 8:11 ("Be careful not to forget the Lord your God.")

1 Corinthians 11:24 ("This is my body; it is for you. Do this to remember me.")

Use filled-in copies of Task Cards #1-8 (pages 110, 111) to provide practice reading, writing, and locating the three verses used today. Choose Bible references that will allow your children to experience success.

Option
Children love to find hidden things. Use pictures of the six items and hide them around the room. When all pictures have been found, ask children to place them in order.

Snacks
If you want to use crackers and juice, make certain the children know that just eating these foods as a snack is not the same as remembering Jesus in the Lord's Supper.

Materials
• Bibles
• shapes decorated earlier
• undecorated shapes
• a large sheet of paper
• photocopies of page 230
• photocopies of Task Cards #1-8 (pages 110-111)
• copies of page 227 used earlier

Option
Craft stores sell Fun Foam—an easy-to-cut craft foam available in many colors. Purchase tan foam for bread and purple foam for the cup. Prepare a cardboard pattern of a flat oval loaf of bread and a pattern of a cup with a stem similar to the one pictured on page 230. Children can trace the patterns onto the foam, or you can trace them onto the foam before class. (Unlike felt, Fun Foam can be easily cut by children.) Glue a piece of magnet onto the back of the foam. Children take these home as reminders: Remember Jesus.

4 Share What We've Learned

Gather everyone in a circle to talk about what they have been doing and learning. Use the aims for this lesson as an outline for the kinds of questions you ask. Play the "Remember Game."

Seat everyone in a circle. Limit the circle size by the age and Bible knowledge of your group. Some circles can be limited to three or four children so that everyone can experience success. Provide an adult leader in each group to help children word their ideas in a simple way.

Ask the children to tell the class something they remember about Jesus. The second child will repeat the first child's idea and then add another idea. The third child will repeat the first two (the order the ideas are stated is not important) and add another idea.

Repeat the process a second time in the form of a litany. After each idea, everyone says, **Jesus is the Son of God**.

Sing these new words to the tune of "God is So Good."
We remember You.
We remember You.
We remember You.
You're the Son of God.

Pray together. Offer statements of praise and let the children respond, **Jesus is the Son of God**, as they did during the earlier activity.

Note

Because the object of this game is to remember things about Jesus, help children recall the ideas—especially as the list gets longer. We want them to be successful in remembering about Jesus.

Some ideas to remember include:
Jesus is the Son of God.
Jesus rode on a donkey.
Jesus healed a blind man.
Jesus washed the disciples' feet.
Jesus was born in Bethlehem.
Jesus loves me.
Jesus' mother was Mary.

 Teaching at Home

Expand children's understanding of this special supper of remembrance. Make unleavened bread. Make grape juice. Tell the Passover story.

Reading tip

This story provides an excellent opportunity to practice sequencing of events. Write story events on poster board sentence strips. Let children arrange them in the story order.

Jesus Dies

44

Tell what Jesus did for us because He is the Son of God.
Thank Jesus because He died for us.
Read Bible references and find Bible verses.

"Go and make followers. . . . Teach them to obey."
   Matthew 28:19, 20, ICB

❶ Get Ready to Read

Before class, copy one of the following Bible references onto each construction paper cross: *Matthew 27:29; John 19:17; Luke 23:33; Mark 15:37; Mark 15:46.*
   Repeat the Bible references so that you will have a cross for each child. Have children draw a heart around the Bible reference. Punch a hole in each cross and string yarn through the hole. Label each cross with the child's name. Set it aside until later in the lesson.

❷ Read the Bible Story

"King of a Different Kingdom"

Gather children in the story center. Ask children to tell about times when people have made fun of them. Begin by giving an example from your own life. Encourage children to talk about how they felt when people made fun of them.
   Help children get ready to listen to this sad, difficult story. If the examples they have given have been funny, be prepared to offer some more serious examples and emphasize the hurt that often results when we make fun of others.
   Today we will hear about a very sad event. Listen to find out what some people said to make fun of Jesus.

Listen

As you begin to read, help children understand why calling someone "the king" would be sad. Read the Matthew 27:29 Bible reference aloud. Show the children where Matthew 27:29 is found in a Bible.
   Read the verse to the children. **"The soldiers used thorny branches to make a crown. They put this crown of thorns on Jesus' head. They put a stick in his right hand. Then the soldiers bowed before Jesus and made fun of him. They said, 'Hail, King of the Jews!'"** (ICB).
   Let the children explain how each action made fun of Jesus.
   Continue reading the rest of the story.
   What hard things did Jesus do because He is the Son of God? (He forgave the people who put Him on the cross. He called God His Father.) **Who understood that Jesus is the Son of God?** (soldiers at the cross) **What happened after**

Materials
• construction paper cross for each child
• tree branch used last session
See the unit page for a complete explanation and materials list for this "Gospel Tree" project.

Option
If you prefer to use only one verse, copy Matthew 27:29 onto each cross shape.

Materials
• *The Young Reader's Bible*, pages 376-381
• photocopies of the Bible story (pages 307-309)
• *The Young Reader's Bible Audio Cassette* or a cassette on which you have recorded unit stories
• cassette player(s), earphones (optional)
• Styrofoam or construction paper cross
• one red construction-paper heart for each child
• thumbtacks or pushpins
• crayons or markers

Note
Save the Styrofoam cross to use in lesson 45. See page 222.

Option
Allow children to smudge the red hearts using washable stamp pad ink.

Snacks
Serve cups of dry cereal and cold water.

Materials
- *The Young Reader's Bible*
- Bibles
- photocopies of Task Cards (page 110)
- sand timer (found in some board games) for use with Task Card #4
- a large sheet of paper
- one black construction paper cross for each child
- one cup buttermilk
- one half-box of colored chalk
- glue
- pie pan
- paper towels

Jesus died? (A temple curtain was torn in two pieces.) **How did a rich man named Joseph show that He knew Jesus was special?** (He took care of Jesus' dead body, wrapping it in linen cloths and putting it into a new tomb.)

Participate

Before class, cut a cross shape from Styrofoam. (If Styrofoam is not available, cut a cross from construction paper and attach to a bulletin board easily reached by the children.) Also, cut hearts from red construction paper. (These will be pinned to the cross.)

Give a red heart to each child. **These hearts remind us of feelings like love. But the hearts also can remind us of how we feel when people hurt us and make fun of us. When we do wrong things other people feel hurt. God is sad. Wrong things we do are called** *sin.*

These hearts will help us learn how God planned to help us when we do wrong (sin). Explain that everyone has a red heart because every person sins.

Explain the following concepts in a way that is appropriate for the children you teach. **Because Jesus is God's Son, Jesus never ever sinned. When Jesus died on the cross, His Father God knew that His Son Jesus was perfect. But God let Jesus take all of our sins with Him to the cross.**

Invite children one by one to attach their hearts to the cross using a thumbtack or pushpin.

All of these red hearts remind us that Jesus took our sins with Him to the cross. When God sees us, He does not see our sin, our red hearts. He sees His children who really love Him and want to obey Him. God knew that Jesus never sinned. Jesus is with God in Heaven.

Pray, **Thank You, Jesus, for dying on the cross for our sins. Amen.**

Give each child a copy of the Bible story (pages 307-309). Help children find the words that Jesus spoke. Underline or highlight those words. ("Father, forgive them. They do not know what they are doing." "Today you will be with me in my heavenly kingdom." "Father, I give myself to you!")

Read

Children can color and read their copy of the Bible story at their own level as they listen to the cassette.

❸ Practice Using a Bible

Using My Bible

On a large sheet of paper, list the Bible references that were printed on the crosses earlier: *Matthew 27:29; John 19:17; Luke 23:33; Mark 15:37; Mark 15:46.*

Find each book name in the table of contents. When children have found the book name, ask them to read the page number of the first page. They can show the first page of the book they have found.

Help children realize that these books are the first four books of the New Testament. Recall that these four books about Jesus' life and ministry are called the Gospels. Print *Gospel* above the list. Recopy the list, putting the books in Bible order.

Finding Bible Verses

At least one day before class, prepare the buttermilk chalk and the mosaic crosses. Place colored chalk in a pie pan with buttermilk to cover the chalk. Soak for about one hour until the liquid is absorbed. Rinse off the chalk and place the pieces on paper towels to dry. Cut out black construction paper crosses. Use glue to make mosaic (stained glass) pieces on each one (6-8). Dry until glue is set. (Place crosses on foil in rows and drizzle glue on them all at one time.)

Work together to complete four Task Cards. The Task Cards (page 110) for this lesson should be filled out as follows:

Card #1
Romans
Card #3
Romans
Card #4
Romans   *Romans 3:23*   *Romans*

God knows what is right because He is God. God's Word, the Bible, helps us know how to do what is right. The Bible says that at one time or another, each of us has sinned.

Read Romans 3:23. **Jesus died on the cross so we could have a way to make our hearts clean. Because Jesus gave His life which was not sinful, He has God's power to forgive and clean our sinful hearts.**

In class, each child colors in each section with a different color of chalk. As it dries, the chalk will change to soft, muted colors. Talk about how dark and bleak it was when Jesus died on the cross, and how bright and beutiful it is for us now because He is alive with God in Heaven.

Share What We've Learned

Gather everyone in a circle to talk about what they have been doing and learning. Use the aims for this lesson as an outline for the kinds of questions you ask.

Give the children the construction paper crosses made earlier. Review the Bible story by finding and reading the Bible verses in the order listed (story sequence order: Matthew 27:29; John 19:17; Luke 23:33; Mark 15:37; Mark 15:46). If children have the Bible references written on their crosses, they can stand as you read their verse.

Children can illustrate a verse on the other side of the cross. (Refer to unit page for ideas.) When crosses have been completed assist children in hanging them on the Bible verse tree.

Before class, print the following Bible verse and reference on a large construction paper cross. *"Father, forgive them. They don't know what they are doing,"* **Luke 23:34**. Cut the cross into as many pieces as you have children. (Cut no more than eight pieces from any one cross. If you are working with more children, make several crosses.)

Form a circle of eight or fewer. Hand each child a piece of a large cross. Ask children to work together to form the cross in the center of the circle. When the cross has been completed, read the verse together. **"Father, forgive them. They don't know what they are doing."**

Who was Jesus speaking to? (His Father, God) **Who was Jesus speaking about?** (people who had sinned and put Him on the cross; everyone who sins) **What had they done?** (made fun of Him; put Him on a cross until He died) **Did they know who Jesus was?** (They did not know what they had done until after He died.)

Pray, **Father forgive us when we do wrong things. Thank You for sending Jesus to die for our sins. In Jesus' name, amen.**

Materials
• Bible for each child
• large construction paper cross
• scissors
• crosses made in *Get Ready to Read*
• markers or colored pencils

Option
Children can act out their verses.

 Teaching at Home

Many videos and books can greatly expand a child's understanding of the crucifixion. Preview videos, making sure they are age appropriate.

Reading tip
Since the word *third* is used in the story, explore the meanings of *first*, *second* and *third*. The first time Jesus went to His disciples, they were asleep. The second time, they slept still. The third time, the soldiers came.

Jesus Is Alive!

Tell the good news that Jesus, the Son of God, is alive.
Celebrate the happy ending for Jesus and for us.
Read Bible references and find Bible verses.

"Go and make followers. . . .Teach them to obey."
Matthew 28:19, 20, ICB

Materials
- tree branch used last session
- eight-inch narrow paper strips (adding machine paper strips)
- long strip of cloth (from an old sheet) or toilet paper

See the unit page for a complete explanation and materials list for this "Gospel Tree" project.

① Get Ready to Read

Before class, print each of the four Bible verses on a strip of paper or photo-copy strips from page 225 and tape onto adding machine paper. If you prefer to use only one verse, copy Mark 16:4 onto each strip of paper. Pin the verse papers on a long strip of cloth in the order the events occurred in the Bible.

Wind the cloth strip around a child volunteer. As you unwind the cloth reveal-ing each Bible verse, read the sentences.

Give each child a strip of paper. Children can choose one Bible reference to write on the strip of paper. Proceed as in previous sessions of this unit by direct-ing children to "decorate" their Bible reference. Save the reference strips for use after the Bible story. Then put them on the unit Gospel tree branch.

Materials
- *The Young Reader's Bible*, pages 382-387
- photocopies of the Bible story (pages 310-312)
- *The Young Reader's Bible Audio Cassette* or a cassette on which you have recorded unit stories
- cassette player(s), earphones optional
- Bible reference strips made earlier
- assortment of spices (cinnamon, nutmeg, cloves, ginger, etc.)
- cheesecloth
- twist tie
- regular size refrigerator biscuits, two (or four) for each child
- large marshmallows, one (or two) for each child
- 1/2 cup cinnamon and sugar mixture
- pie pan
- cookie sheets
- napkins
- Christian instrumental cassette
- crayons or markers
- strips of paper
- glue sticks

② Read the Bible Story

"Could It Be True?"

Encourage children to talk about happy endings. Tell about happy endings in movies and stories.

Explain that today you will be reading a story with a very special happy end-ing. The story is special because it is true. The ending is special because it is true. **Listen to find out how the happy ending helps each one of us.**

Listen

Ask the children to listen closely as you read "Could It Be True?"

Who can tell about the happy ending? (Jesus lived again; He rose from the dead.) **Why is this happy story for us? What good news could you tell now that you've heard this story?** (Jesus is still living in Heaven with God; He can forgive our sins; we can live with Him forever in Heaven.)

Participate

Before class, combine spices on a cheesecloth square. (Or place in a tea ball and loosely wrap.) Secure spices in cheesecloth with a twist tie.

Tell the class that the spice ball smells something like the spices that the women brought for Jesus' body. Let everyone smell the spice ball.

Explain a game. Players stand in a circle and pass the spice ball from one to another while the music is playing. When the music stops, the child holding the spices is asked a question. The child can answer or choose someone to answer.

What can Jesus do because He is the Son of God? (resurrect, forgive, heal, etc.)

What day of the week did the women go to Jesus' tomb? (the first day of the week, Sunday)

Name a woman who went to Jesus' tomb. (Mary Magdalene)

What did the women bring to Jesus' tomb? (sweet-smelling spices)

When the women came to the tomb, what did they find? (The tomb was empty.)

Who did Mary tell that the tomb was empty? (Peter and John)

Somebody came to the other two women and told them not to be afraid. Who were they? (two angels)

What else did the angels tell the women? (Jesus had risen!)

Two men came running to Jesus' tomb. Who were they? (Peter and John)

What did John believe about Jesus when he saw the empty tomb? (Jesus is alive!)

Choose four children—one for every Bible reference decorated earlier. Have the children stand in front of the class. Read or have each reference read. Read the Bible verse that goes with each reference. Work together to put the children in Bible story order according to the Bible reference they are holding.

Let the children smell the cinnamon and sugar mixture. Talk about spices. Make sure each child has washed hands. Give each one two biscuits and a marshmallow. Show them how to completely wrap the biscuits around a marshmallow, carefully sealing all the edges. Let the children roll each biscuit in the cinnamon sugar mixture to coat and place on a foil lined cookie sheet to bake (10 minutes at 425 degrees). Let them cool on the cookie sheet. Find an edge and poke a small hole for the opening of the empty tomb. (Marshmallow will melt during baking leaving a hollow space inside.)

Read

Give each child a copy of the Bible story (pages 310-312). Children can color and read at their own level. Children can add strips of paper to represent the strips of cloth on the last page of the story. They can underline or circle the names of people who went to Jesus' tomb (Mary Magdalene, other women, two angels, Peter, John). As they work, they can listen to the cassette story.

③ Practice Using a Bible

Using My Bible

Fill out Task Cards #2-6 so children can choose to work on one or more.

Card #3	*Isaiah*		
Card #4	*Isaiah*	*Isaiah 1:18*	*1:18*
Card #5	*Isaiah 1:18*		
Card #6	*Isaiah 1:18*	*sins*	

Finding Bible Verses

Print *Isaiah 1:18* and *Matthew 28:19, 20* on a large sheet of paper. Ask children to locate the table of contents in a Bible.

Which book will we find in the Old Testament? (Isaiah) **in the New Testament?** (Matthew) Let several children name the pages the books begin on.

Options
• A video depicting the resurrection events would be meaningful.
• Allow each child to make two buns—one to eat for a snack and one to take home and retell the story.

Snacks
Serve surprise buns, gingersnap cookies, or heart-shaped cookies and milk.

Materials
• *The Young Reader's Bible*
• Bibles
• photocopies of filled-in Task Cards #2-6 (pages 110, 111)
• a large sheet of paper
• paper
• sand timer (found in some board games) for use with Task Card #4

Materials
- Styrofoam cross (from last lesson)
- white paper hearts

Notice that the page numbers vary. Not all Bibles are the same.

Use the Reference Rhyme (page 32) to help children locate each Bible verse. **What will we look for first?** (Isaiah or Matthew) **Which number will be the big number?** (1 or 28) **How many verses are we looking for?** (1-verse 18 or 2-verses 19 and 20) Ask children to find each Bible verse. Keep a slip of paper in the Bible at the Isaiah 1:18 reference. Read Matthew 28:19, 20 to the class. **What good news did we read about today?** (Jesus is alive.) **What do followers do?** (Go and tell good news.)

④ Share What We've Learned

Gather everyone in a circle to talk about what they have been doing and learning. Use the aims for this lesson as an outline for the kinds of questions you ask.

Before class, replace the red hearts with white hearts on the cross prepared last session. Keep the cross hidden until after the Bible story is read.

Recall the children's conversations about doing wrong things. **What things did we remember doing wrong? Last session we learned that the Bible tells us that everyone has sinned or done wrong things.**

Remind the children that they put heart cutouts on a cross. **What color were the hearts that we put on the cross?** (They were red.) **The red hearts reminded us that we do wrong things. Placing them on the cross reminds us that Jesus died on the cross so that the wrong things we do can be forgiven.**

Explain the concept of atonement in a way that is helpful to the children in your class. They can understand that Jesus never did wrong. They can learn that Jesus obeyed God by dying on a cross. They know that people do wrong. They can learn that sins can be forgiven because God loves us and Jesus died for us. Reread lesson 44, or your notes from that lesson, so that you present the concept in the same simple terms that you used last week.

Display the cross. Read Isaiah 1:18 (found earlier) to the class.

The Lord says, "Come, we will talk these things over. Your sins are red like deep red cloth. But they can be as white as snow. Your sins are bright red. But you can be white like wool," (ICB).

Talk about this very important happy ending. When we do wrong, we can be forgiven. The red hearts remind us of the things we do wrong. The white hearts remind us that, because of Jesus, God does not see our sins (our red hearts). He sees we are forgiven: our white hearts.

Sing and praise God for Jesus because only Jesus can die and be made alive again. Thank God for forgiving us. Only Jesus makes our hearts clean and new!

Teaching at Home

Continue working on the calendar begun with lesson 42. Decorate resurrection Sunday. Make it a family celebration day!

Reading tip
Practice reading questions and exclamations with expression. Children can practice writing question marks and exclamation marks.

Jesus Goes to Heaven

Tell how Jesus' followers go and make more followers.
Tell others Jesus loves them.
Read Bible references and find Bible verses.

"Go and make followers. . . . Teach them to obey."
  Matthew 28:19, 20, ICB

❶ Get Ready to Read

Before class, copy one of the following Bible references onto construction cloud shapes: *Matthew 28:19; Luke 24:50, 51; Acts 1:9; Acts 1:10, 11; Luke 24:52, 53.* Give each child a cloud.

Distribute cloud shapes. Children can decorate their verses and place them on the tree as has been done in previous lessons.

❷ Read the Bible Story

"Parting Promises"
Display the car keys.
What do you think of when you see a car key? (Allow children to respond.) Give your ideas. **Car keys make us think of going somewhere, of leaving. Listen as I read the story to find out who is leaving and where they are going.**

Listen
Read "Parting Promises" with great expression.
Why do you think this story is called "Parting Promises"? Who left? (Jesus made some promises when He left.)
Who did Jesus make promises to? (the disciples)
Where did Jesus go? (Heaven)
Jesus not only made promises to His disciples, He asked them to do something for Him. What does Matthew 28:19, 20 say? (Read or repeat aloud.)

Participate
Before class, print the following words on small index cards: *forty, Galilee, power, nations, baptize, Holy Spirit, teach, Mount of Olives, heaven, cloud, white, sky, Jerusalem, temple, praising.* Mark the words in your *Young Reader's Bible* so you can pause as you reread.

Give each child an index card on which a word is written. Make sure each child can repeat the word written on the card. Explain that you will be reading the story a second time. Each time you read a word written on an index card, pause. The child holding the card will hold it up and repeat the word aloud.

Materials
• construction paper clouds
• tree branch used in lessons 42-45
See the unit page for a complete explanation and materials list for this "Gospel Tree" project.

Option
If you prefer to use only one verse, copy Matthew 28:19 onto each cloud shape.

Materials
• *The Young Reader's Bible*, pages 394-399
• photocopies of the two-page Bible story (page 228)
• *The Young Reader's Bible Audio Cassette* or a cassette on which you have recorded unit stories
• cassette player(s), earphones optional
• cardboard pattern for door hanger shape
• tagboard or construction paper
• markers
• scissors
• glue
• gold or silver glitter
• small index cards
• set of car keys

Continue reading the story in this manner.

Reread the story. Let children call out their words where they fit.

Have each child trace the door hanger pattern onto tag board or white construction paper. Cut out the door hanger. Print on the door hanger "Follow Jesus" or "Tell Others." Older children can write or trace the letters with glue. Younger children can outline the words with glue. Sprinkle wet glue with glitter. Let it dry.

Read

Give each child a copy of the Bible story excerpt (page 228). Allow children to read at their own level and color the pictures as they listen to the story cassette.

 # Practice Using a Bible

Using My Bible

Have each child hold a Bible in his or her lap. Separate the Old Testament from the New Testament. Find the first book of the New Testament (Matthew). Find the unit key verse, Matthew 28:19, 20. Read or recite the shortened form of the verse together. If your children have different Bible versions, choose one or two to read the verse.

Read together the verse written on the Bible story excerpt (page 228) or on pages 394, 395 of the *Young Reader's Bible*.

Ask each child to choose one of the shapes from the tree they decorated during this unit. The child can read the Bible reference. He can tell about Jesus by describing his drawing.

Have children look up, read, and tell about several Bible verses.

Finding Bible Verses

Invite children to work on at least one of the four task cards. The task cards for this lesson should be filled out as follows:

Card #1   *John*
Card #3   *John*
Card #4   *John*   *John 3:16*   *John*

Share What We've Learned

Gather everyone in a circle to talk about what they have been doing and learning. Use the aims for both the unit and this lesson as an outline for the kinds of questions you ask.

Assist children in assembling individual trees. Have the children remove their five Bible reference shapes from the classroom Bible reference tree. Children should attach or glue the references to their own branch or tree. Encourage them to use the trees to tell the stories they remember about Jesus. Encourage children to remember to share their Bible verses and stories by displaying their Bible reference trees at home. Emphasize that each story read from the *Young Reader's Bible* can be found in their own Bibles.

Jesus could do all of those things because He is the Son of God. Jesus had a very important job to do, and He did it. Now, Jesus lives in Heaven. Because

---

Option

Pairs of children can work together. One child reads the story; the other reads the word cards.

Snacks

Serve cloud pudding (pudding with mini-marshmallows).

Materials

• *The Young Reader's Bible*
• Bibles
• Bible reference tree filled with Bible reference shapes made in lessons 42-46
• photocopies of filled-in Task Cards (page 110)
• sand timer (found in some board games) for use with Task Card #4

Option

Nonreaders may choose a partner to read their Bible verse or simply tell about the story depicted on the shape.

Materials

• photocopies of page 231
• markers or crayons
• individual tree branch (or poster board tree) for each child
• pieces of ribbon or string

Jesus lived, died, and rose again, we can go to Heaven, too. God loves us that much!

Give each child a copy of the certificate (page 231).

Read the verse, including your own name when you come to the blank line. Choose several readers to take turns reading the verse, one at a time. They should include their own names when they come to the blank line. The rest of the group can follow along. Then, have one person read and have everyone else say their names in unison.

Jesus asked us to tell people that He loves them. Think of a person that you would like to tell about Jesus loving them. Instruct children to print that person's name in the blank.

Have each child read the Bible verse again—this time inserting the name they have written. (Readers can read for nonreaders, letting the children say the name they printed.) Encourage children to give the paper to the person whose name they have printed. They can roll it up like a scroll and tape or tie it with a ribbon or string.

Option
Instead of individual Bible reference trees, children make a poster or booklet using the shapes they have made in this unit.

 Teaching at Home

Recall promises kept and promises broken. Emphasize that God always keeps His promises.

Reading tip
Find beginning consonant blends: *stayed, Spirit, bless, cloud, dressed, stood, stayed, praising.*

Bible verse strips to use in *Get Ready to Read.* See page 220.

Mark 16: 4 "Then the women looked and saw that the stone was already moved. The stone was very large, but it was moved away from the entrance," (ICB).

Luke 24:3 "They went in, but they did not find the body of the Lord Jesus," (ICB).

Matthew 28:8 "The women left the tomb quickly. They were afraid, but they were also very happy. They ran to tell Jesus' followers what had happened," (ICB).

John 20:18 "Mary Magdalene went and said to the followers, 'I saw the Lord!' And she told them what Jesus had said to her," (ICB).

Jesus rode toward Jerusalem.
Some of the people
in the crowd
went ahead of Jesus.
Some of the people followed.
Everyone shouted,
"Blessed is the one
who comes in the name
of the Lord!
Blessed is the one
who comes from the family
of David!"

Jesus entered Jerusalem
like a gentle king.

During the meal, Jesus took bread.

He said a prayer of thanks.

He broke the bread

and gave it to his disciples.

"This is my body," Jesus said.

"My body will be broken for you.

Then I want you to break bread

together and

remember me."

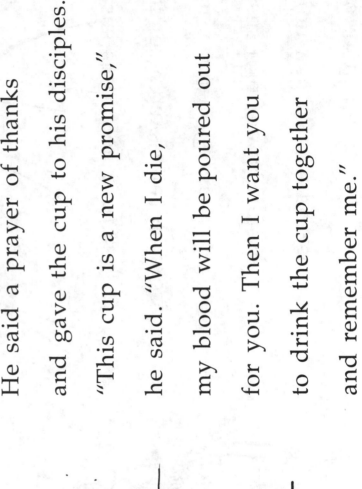

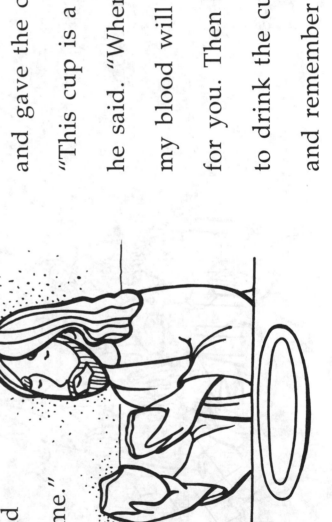

Jesus took a cup.

He said a prayer of thanks

and gave the cup to his disciples.

"This cup is a new promise,"

he said. "When I die,

my blood will be poured out

for you. Then I want you

to drink the cup together

and remember me."

227

Parting Promises

Jesus stayed on earth
for forty days after he arose.
On a hill in Galilee,
Jesus told the disciples,
"You will receive power.
Go to all the nations.

Make disciples everywhere.
Baptize them in the name
of the Father, Son, and Holy Spirit.
Teach them to obey
everything I have taught you.
I will be with you always."

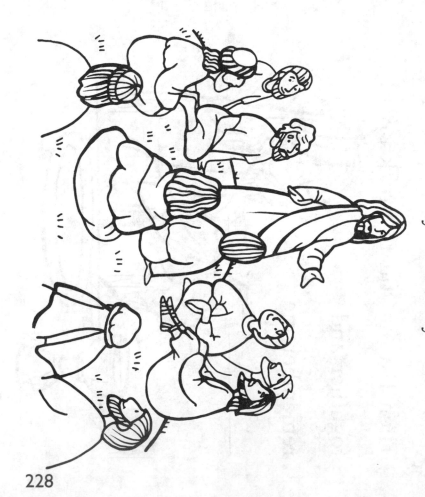

228

Hosanna!

If Jesus walked down your street today, what would you do or say to praise Him?

Jesus, You help me

Thank You, Jesus, for

Jesus, I think You're really

Jesus, one of the greatest things about You is

Remember This!

Jesus said:

"THIS BREAD IS MY BODY THAT
I AM GIVING FOR YOU."

New Century Version

Find and circle Jesus' words.

```
I  Y  R  M  S  G
B  O  D  Y  R  I
Z  U  L  I  S  V
T  H  A  T  Y  I
B  Q  B  T  H  N
F  O  R  H  H  G
T  I  E  I  A  A
A  R  A  S  M  T
Y  D  D  L  B  V
```

John 3:16

For God loved _____
so much that He gave His only Son.
God gave His Son so that whoever
believes in Him may not be lost,
but have eternal life.

New Century Version

Unit 10

We Tell How Jesus' Church Helps People

Key Verse
"Serve the Lord with gladness."   Psalm 100:2, KJV

Unit Vocabulary
added
arrest
blend
courtyard
earthquake
escape
flashed
gasped
grandmother
guard
happened
hurting
judges
languages
money
saved
stare
stock chains
stronger
suddenly
three thousand
traveled
wound

Unit Aims

By the end of the unit, learners will be able to
• tell five Bible stories about how Jesus' church helps people.
• feel joyful in finding verses in a Bible and reading *The Young Reader's Bible*.
• locate books, chapters and verses in their own Bibles.
• read (at their level) stories from *The Young Reader's Bible*.
• tell how Jesus' church helps people.

Unit Project

We-Will-Serve-the-Lord Puzzles

Challenging children to think in terms of service in the future tense as well as the present is important and exciting. Begin to plant ideas of ways children can honor God and serve others.

Make a banner to title the project *We Will Serve the Lord with Gladness.* Begin by tracing each child's outline onto butcher paper creating "full-size" puzzles. Let each child personalize only the head shape by writing his name and drawing, or cutting and pasting pictures from magazines to represent favorite activities, hobbies, foods, Bible hero, color, pets, etc. Provide lots of art supplies so children can represent their service ideas with various media.

Before the second session, cut the head from each child's shape. Cut the remaining part of each shape into five similarly-sized puzzle pieces. Label the back of each piece with the child's name. During each of the four remaining sessions, each child will use one puzzle piece to show a way in which he can serve the Lord with gladness! Focus on these ideas about serving: those who are sick, have handicaps, are widowed; friends and family who don't know Jesus; our church family; our missionary families. Plan ahead so that you can prepare a special missions emphasis with session 5.

Encourage creativity by discussing the session's focus with the children: What can be done? Who needs help? What can I do? List some serving ideas—this will serve as a handy reference and help for children who need extra think time.

When complete, each child can tell you what ideas their puzzle piece shows and then attach the piece to the puzzle on display.

"Full-size" puzzles may not be practical for a large class. This may also be true of a small classroom with little or no wall space. Small puzzles or service notebooks with personalized cover pages could be adapted to this project.

	The Singing Bible (3 tapes)	Kids on the Rock (More Songs)	Follow the Leader (The Donut Man)	I'm a Helper (The Donut Man)	Good News (The Donut Man)
Lesson 47					
Lesson 48			Walking and Leaping		
Lesson 49	The New Man Paul		I Will Arise		
Lesson 50	Acts		We Are the Light of the World		
Lesson 51					Earthquake
Key Verse					
Unit Theme		Good News		Be A Helper	Kids Telling Kids; The Bicycle Song
All Lessons	The Books We Love the Best The Bible Book Is True	God's Word Is for Me			

The Singing Bible (3 tapes), ©1993 by Lightwave Publishing, Inc. Manufactured and distributed by Word Publishing, Dallas, TX 75234
Kids on the Rock! More Songs, ©1994 Gospel Light, Ventura CA 93006
The Donut Man (3 tapes): *Follow the Leader*, ©1990; *I'm a Helper*, ©1991; *Good News*, ©1991; Integrity Music, Inc., P.O. Box 16813 Mobile, AL 36616

Key Verse Activities

Serve the Lord with gladness.
Psalm 100:2, KJV

Materials
- balloons
- sturdy paper plates (decorative if possible)
- paint stir sticks
- duct tape

Balloon Tennis

Let each child make a tennis racquet by taping a paint stir stick to the back of a sturdy paper plate. Divide the group into pairs. **We're going to play balloon tennis to help us learn our memory verse. One player says a word of the verse and "serves" the balloon into the air. The other player says the next word and hits the balloon back to the first player, and so on. Be sure to include the Bible reference.**

Materials
- round balloons
- markers
- chalk

Whining Balloons

We're a little like balloons. We can serve the Lord cheerfully and feel so full of the Holy Spirit that we could almost pop, or we can whine (make the balloon squeal until its air is gone) **and feel limp.** Demonstrate.

I have a balloon for each of you. Draw a smiling face on one side and a frowning face on the other. Let's list on the chalkboard some things we do every day, including things God has asked us to do. I will tell you a thought that a person could have about it. If it is complaining, lift up your balloon and show the frowning side. Choose someone to let air out to make the whining sound. **If it is serving with gladness, lift up your balloon and show the smiling side of your balloon.**

Materials
- balloons
- markers
- butcher paper
- masking tape

Balloon Search Race

Before class, make a banner for each child. Print the memory verse on them. See the sketch. Hang the banners around the room low enough for the children to reach them. Hang six pieces of masking tape loosely from the bottom of each banner. Blow up six balloons for each student and print one word of the memory verse and reference on each. Mix up the balloons and pile them in a corner of the room.

We're going to have a fun race. When I say "go," you'll run to the pile of balloons, grab one, run to your banner, and tape the balloon by its stem underneath the word it matches on the banner. (Demonstrate.) **To stay in the race, you must never have more than six balloons. The winner is the first person who has all six balloons hanging on his banner in the right order.**

Peter Tells a New Message

47

Tell what Peter told the people to do.
Give thanks because Jesus' church helps people.
Find Genesis, Psalms, and Matthew.

"Serve the Lord with gladness."   Psalm 100:2, KJV

① Get Ready to Read

As children arrive, ask them to lie down on a length of butcher paper. Trace their body outlines with a crayon. After their outline has been drawn, direct them to print their names on the face portion of the outline.

Encourage children to use the creative art materials you provide. When they have finished writing (drawing) their names, suggest that children further personalize their pictures by drawing or gluing pictures of some of their favorite things onto the face area only. When the faces are finished, assist children in cutting this portion from the rest of the picture and attaching it to the unit project wall.

Before the next lesson, cut the remaining portion of each child's outline into four similarly-sized pieces. These four parts should resemble puzzle pieces. Print each child's name on the back of his four puzzle pieces. One of the pieces will be used in each of the remaining sessions in this unit.

Materials
- butcher paper (to trace outlines of each child)
- pencils, crayons, markers
- old magazines
- glue
- tape
See the unit page for an explanation of this project and materials needed.

② Read the Bible Story

"The Very First Church"

Gather children in the story center. Display game or appliance directions.

I am trying to figure out how to (play this game/work this appliance) **but I just can't understand the directions! I need a volunteer to look at these directions and explain to the class why I am having such a hard time understanding them!**

Allow volunteer to examine foreign instructions and report to the class. Tell the class what language the instructions are written in.

I can't read these instructions because I can't read (language)! **It's a good thing somebody wrote these instructions in English too! I** *can* **read English!**

Today's story will tell us about a time when God did something really special with languages. Let's listen to find out what special event using many languages God planned. Listen for the name of the special event.

Listen

Read "The Very First Church" with suspense and enthusiasm.
What was the name of the special event? (Pentecost)

Materials
- *The Young Reader's Bible,* pages 400-405
- photocopies of the Bible story (pages 313-315)
- *The Young Reader's Bible Audio Cassette* or a cassette on which you have recorded unit stories
- cassette player(s), earphones optional
- a large sheet of paper
- example of written foreign language (game or appliance instructions)
- orange or red construction paper
- four pieces of construction paper with numeral on each (3-0-0-0)
- plain white paper
- variety of colors of wide markers
- cotton balls
- oil
- black construction paper to make frames
- stapler
- ribbon or yarn for hanging
- paper punch
- pencils

Why were so many people gathered in Jerusalem? (to celebrate the Jewish holiday, Pentecost)

Today, many churches celebrate Pentecost as the birthday of the church!

Participate

Before class, cut several "tongues of fire" from orange and/or red construction paper. Print the following numerals on pieces of construction paper, one on each piece: 3-0-0-0.

Today we will retell the story using these tongues of fire and these number cards. Ask for or choose a volunteer to read the part of Peter. Choose disciples and hand them the construction paper tongues of fire. Select four children to hold the number cards displaying the number 3,000 at the appropriate time in the story. Some children can make a wind sound at the appropriate time. Some can repeat aloud the phrase, "What shall we do?"

Reread "The Very First Church," acting as the narrator while the rest of the class participates in their assigned sections.

Who could speak in foreign languages? (the disciples) **How were they able to speak in other languages?** (They were filled with the Holy Spirit.) **Why was it important that the disciples could speak in other languages?** (so all those people could hear about Jesus)

What did Peter tell the people about Jesus? (He was killed, but God made Him alive again. He is in Heaven.) **What did Peter tell the people to do?** (trust in the Lord, repent, be baptized for the forgiveness of sins)

Print the following words on a large sheet of paper: *Pentecost, disciple, languages, prophet, repent, baptized.*

Read the word list together. Give each child a copy of the Bible story (pages 313-315). Ask children to find and underline in the story the words on the list.

As children locate each word, talk about what it means and use it in a sentence. Think of a way to decorate the word to help remember its meaning (birthday candles for Pentecost, stick figures for disciples, lips for languages, and so on).

Give each child a sheet of plain white paper. Have them draw with markers a church, a Bible, or something to remind them of the beginning of the church. (Crayons will not work.) Dab a cotton ball in oil and rub over the entire picture.

Wipe off any excess oil so that the picture is dry. Cut out two black construction paper frames to fit around the outside of the picture. Staple the frame and trim any excess from the edges. Punch a hole at the top and tie with ribbon or yarn to hang in the widow. With light behind the window, it will look translucent.

Read

Children can reread the story at their own levels, color the Bible story pages, and listen to the cassette story.

❸ Practice Using a Bible

Using My Bible

Before class, print the following Bible references on a large sheet of paper: *Hebrews 4:12; Psalm 119:105; Psalm 119:103; Mark 4:14.* List the following four words underneath the Bible references list: *lamp, sword, seeds, honey.*

Review basic Bible skills. **Open the Bible to divide the Old from the New Testament. Open to Psalms. Open to Genesis. Open to Matthew.**

Read Peter's words from a *Young Reader's Bible*, page 403. "Listen! What the prophet Joel wrote about is happening today." Help children find the little book, Joel, in the Old Testament.

Ask children to read the Bible references listed on the large paper. Read each reference aloud together. Decide whether each reference is from the Old or New Testament. Refer to a table of contents if necessary.

Finding Bible Verses

Give each child drawing paper, markers or crayons.

Choose one Bible reference from the sheet to find. Copy the Bible reference onto your drawing paper. Find and read the Bible verse. Draw a picture of the word (*lamp, sword, seeds* or *honey*) **that you found in that Bible verse.**

After children have finished, they can take turns showing their pictures and reading the Bible references.

The words we read from the Bible are not like words we read in any other book. These words are from God. The Bible is God's Word to us.

Before class, print the words of the unit key verse (Psalm 100:2) on white paper. Make one copy for every child. Cut each paper into puzzle pieces and place in an envelope.

Print Psalm 100:2 on the large paper. Give each child an envelope containing puzzle pieces. Instruct children to find Psalm 100:2 in their Bibles.

Explain that when they have found the Bible reference, they may open their envelopes and put the puzzle together. When all children have completed their puzzle, read the verse in several versions. Then read the key verse aloud together, "Serve the Lord with gladness," Psalm 100:2. Explain that different versions of the Bible might use different words; however, the idea of the verse is the same.

4 Share What We Learned

Before class, cut two sets of simple felt shapes that resemble a church building. Children can attach these pieces to flannel board. Pieces should include a building shape, a door, two windows, a steeple, etc.

Play a game similar to "hangman" with some of the following words: *Jerusalem, Holy Spirit, languages, forgiveness, three thousand, Pentecost, prophet, repent, baptized, disciples.*

Divide the class into two teams. Indicate how many letters the unknown word has by making blank spaces for each letter on the large paper.

Each team may guess one letter. The first team to correctly guess the word may begin to build their church using a felt piece. (Teams may only guess a word when it is their turn.) The first team to complete their church building wins.

When the game is finished, gather everyone in a circle to talk about what they have been doing and learning. Use the aims for this lesson as an outline for the kinds of questions you ask.

Sing special lyrics to the tune of "Jesus Loves the Little Children."

Sing the song a second time encouraging children to come up with ideas of ways to serve on Sunday. "Sunday we will (sing, pray, worship, etc.)."

Close the session by asking children to complete the following sentence prayer: **Dear God, help me serve You this week. This is what I will do. I will _____. In Jesus' name, amen.**

Encourage the children to do what they planned to do.

Materials
- several colors of felt pieces
- large sheet of paper
- markers
- flannel board

Option
This game can be played using familiar Bible book names in place of the story vocabulary words.

Teaching at Home

The library can provide foreign language tapes. Learn to say simple words in various languages. Perhaps you have a neighbor who can teach you some words.

Reading tip
Emphasize the importance of reading carefully. Notice that the disciples hear a sound *like* a strong wind. They saw what looked *like* tongues of fire. Help children realize that no one's hair was burning and the house was in no danger of blowing away. These things *looked* and *sounded like* the descriptions.

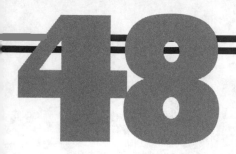

Peter and John Give Help From God

Tell how Peter and John helped the lame man.
Give thanks because Jesus' church helps people.
Read Bible references and find Bible verses.

"Serve the Lord with gladness."   Psalm 100:2, KJV

❶ Get Ready to Read

Repeat the key verse for this unit aloud together, "Serve the Lord with gladness," Psalm 100:2.

Guide the children to think of ways to serve the Lord. Begin by asking them to name someone who is sick; someone who needs a friend; someone who has a handicap and may need special help. Then think of ways to show God's love by helping. Emphasize that when we help others we are serving the Lord.

List children's ideas on the paper. Provide art supplies so children can decorate one of their body-shape puzzle pieces. Explain that they are to choose a way they can help (serve) and display it on this week's puzzle piece. (Puzzle pieces will be displayed at the end of the session.)

❷ Read the Bible Story

"Jumping for Joy"

Before class, print one of the following letters on each of the six index cards: B-E-G-G-A-R.

Give index cards to children and ask them to stand in random order in a line in front of the class. Work together to rearrange the children to make a word. Give hints at several intervals: the first letter is the same sound as the first letter of Bible. The last letter is the same sound as the first letter of Revelation. The middle of the word has a double consonant.

Read the word when it is in correct order. Make certain the children know the meaning of the word *beggar*. **What do beggars need? Why?**

Listen to find out what happened to a beggar in today's story.

Listen

Read "Jumping for Joy" with excitement and enthusiasm.

Why was the man in our story a beggar? (couldn't walk, couldn't work) **What did Peter and John give him that was better than money?** (He was healed; he could walk.)

Materials
- one puzzle piece from child's outline (See Lesson 47.)
- tape to attach puzzle pieces to wall
- large sheet of paper
- marker
- art supplies to decorate puzzle pieces

See the unit page for an explanation of project and materials needed.

Some "serve" ideas
calling on the phone, visiting, sending cards, inviting to play at house, sharing special books or toys, reading books aloud, singing, jokes, artwork

Materials
- *The Young Reader's Bible*, pages 406-411
- photocopies of the Bible story (pages 316-318)
- *The Young Reader's Bible Audio Cassette* or a cassette on which you have recorded unit stories
- cassette player(s), earphones optional
- poster board
- six small index cards
- musical arrangement for "Walking and Leaping"
- pencils
- paper
- scissors
- glue

Participate

Before class, photocopy pictures from pages 316-318 to fit in as you copy the lyrics in rebus form onto poster board. Children can label each picture with a word, or you can have them remove the pictures to reveal the words as they learn the song, "Walking and Leaping." Explain any unfamiliar words such as *alms*.

As children sing the italicized/boldfaced words, direct them to do the *walking* and *leaping* motions as the song indicates. Children may lift and wave their hands about to represent *praising*. Give each child a copy of the Bible story (pages 316-318).

Let's underline all the words we can find that tell about where the lame man met Peter and John. (temple, temple gate, gate, temple courtyard) Nonreaders can point to pictures of places where Peter, John, and the lame man met.

Why was the temple an important place to Peter and John? (Peter and John went to worship God at the temple.)

Why do you think the lame man chose the temple area to beg? (Many people passed by.)

How much money did Peter and John give the beggar? (none) **Why not?** (They gave him something better!)

How did Peter and John help the beggar? (They said, "In the name of Jesus, rise and walk!") **How did Peter say the man had been healed?** (by the power of Jesus)

How did Peter and John help someone and honor God at the temple? (healed the lame man who glorified God)

How did the lame man act when he was healed? (He walked, jumped and praised God.)

Children can trace the shape of the healed man leaping (page 317). They can cut out and color the man's shape. Then show them how to use two strips of paper to make a paper-fold spring. Glue the man to the spring and the spring to the paper. The figure will jiggle as the paper is handled.

Read

Children can continue reading on their own level and coloring the Bible story (pages 316-318). They can listen to the cassette story as they color or follow along.

❸ Practice Using a Bible

Using My Bible

Practice handling Bibles: separate Old and New Testaments, name and find the first book of each testament, find Psalms by opening to the center of the Bible.

Print "Psalm 100:2" on a large sheet of paper. Say the verse aloud together: **"Serve the Lord with gladness."**

Before class, "color" macaroni. Fill used margarine tubs with rubbing alcohol. Tint the alcohol with several drops of food coloring. (Use as many colors as you wish but only one color per dish.) Place macaroni in the alcohol mixture for ten minutes. Remove to dry. Use the colored macaroni for "writing" the Bible reference, Psalm 100:2.

Distribute paper, colored macaroni and glue. Show the children how they can use macaroni to form the letters and numbers of the Bible reference, Psalm 100:2. Children should glue the macaroni only after you have checked the arrangement of their completed design.

Option
Musical arrangements for this song can be found in many children's songbooks. (The author of the lyrics is unknown.)

Walking and Leaping
Peter and John went to pray.
They met a lame man on the way.
He put out his palm and asked for some alms,
and this is what Peter did say:
"Silver and gold have I none, but such as I have, give I thee.
In the name of Jesus Christ, of Nazareth, rise up and walk!"
He went *walking* and *leaping* and *praising* God,
walking and *leaping* and *praising* God.
In the name of Jesus Christ, of Nazareth, rise up and walk!

public domain

Snacks
Serve carrots sticks and dip.

Materials
- Bible for each child
- macaroni
- rubbing alcohol
- food coloring
- empty margarine tubs
- poster board or card-stock paper
- white glue
- a large sheet of paper
- marker
- five small index cards

Finding Bible Verses

Before class, print the following Bible references on a large sheet of paper: *Psalm 100:2; Acts 3:6; Hebrews 4:12; Genesis 1:1; John 3:16.* Print the five references on index cards as well.

Divide the class into as many as five groups. Give an index card to each group. Explain that the groups will work together to find the Bible verse for the reference printed on their index card. One person from the group will then read it aloud to the rest of the class. Talk about what we learn about God from each of the Bible verses. Emphasize the fact that the Bible is the Word of God.

 # Share What We've Learned

Materials
- puzzle pieces made earlier
- two dinner-size paper plates for each child
- medium-size paper fastener (brad) for each child
- scissors
- markers or crayons
- rulers
- *Just Like Everybody Else* (Standard #3661)

Before class, cut the rim from one paper plate (leaving the flat center section) for each child. Use the ruler and a pencil or marker to mark four or six pie-shaped wedges.

Display the list of ideas for helping others made earlier. Recall how Peter and John helped the beggar.

Pantomime, or have another adult pantomime, a helping action. Let the children guess the action. Invite children to choose an action pantomime. Allow the rest of the group to guess the action. Children can pantomime the action they displayed on their puzzle pieces.

Allow children to take turns telling about the ideas they have displayed on their puzzle pieces. As each action is correctly guessed, assist the child in attaching the puzzle piece to the unit project wall.

It is good to help friends, but it is good to help others as well. People who are part of Jesus' church help others. We help others and we are happy about helping. We "serve the Lord with gladness."

Give each child the paper plate center section you prepared before class. Have children draw a picture or write a way to serve the Lord with gladness in each wedge shape. With a paper fastener, attach the center section to a full-size paper plate. Draw a triangle for an arrow near the outside edge of the full-size plate. Take turns spinning the plate and acting out the picture or words for others to guess.

When all children have had an opportunity to share their helping ideas, ask children to gather in a circle. Read the book, *Just Like Everybody Else.* The story describes a zoo outing in which Derek and Granddaddy encounter people with disabilities. It includes suggestions for answering kids' questions about disabilities.

Talk about what they have been doing and learning. Use the aims for this lesson as an outline for the kinds of questions you ask. Encourage their developing knowledge and skill.

Close the session by singing the following lyrics to the tune of *"London Bridge"*:
I will be a friend to you,
friend to you, friend to you,
I will be a friend to you,
just like Jesus wants me to!
Ask children to suggest other words based on "helping" ideas.
Lyric suggestions:
I will walk to school with you . . .
I will help you read a book . . .
I can call you on the phone . . .
I can share my toys with you . . .
I can help you do your work . . .

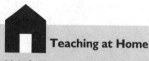

Teaching at Home

Help family members become more aware of appropriate ways to help people with disabilities.

Reading tip

There are lots of action verbs in this story. Find and read them. Notice any endings. Talk about how the words change when endings are added. *(pray, prayed; carry, carried; beg, begged)*

Saul Becomes a Believer

Tell how Saul became part of Jesus' church.
Give thanks because Jesus' church helps people and tells good news.
Read Bible references and find Bible verses.

"Serve the Lord with gladness."   Psalm 100:2, KJV

1 Get Ready to Read

Last week we spent some time thinking of ways to be helpful to people who might be sick, handicapped or lonely. We discovered ways that Jesus' church helps people.

This week we want to think of important ways to help friends or family who don't know who Jesus is or what He has done for us. Ask children to suggest ways in which they can serve by telling about Jesus. List these on the large sheet of paper. Repeat the unit key verse together. **"Serve the Lord with gladness," Psalm 100:2.**

Distribute another puzzle piece. Provide art materials. Allow children to draw, write, or glue on ideas about ways they can help someone find out about Jesus.

Materials
• large sheet of paper
• second puzzle piece from child's outline
• art supplies to decorate puzzle pieces
See the unit page for an explanation of project and materials needed.

2 Read the Bible Story

"Saul Sees the Light"
Gather children in the story center. **I'm going to read you our Bible story today, but I'm not going to tell you the title! I will tell you that I'm going to need this! (Display flashlight.) Listen and watch to hear and see why.**

Listen
Before class, print the title, "Saul Sees the Light," on a large sheet of paper.
Read "Saul Sees the Light" with suspense and animation. Turn on the flashlight as you read ". . . a light from heaven flashed . . ." Shine it briefly on the title you printed.
Who will tell me the title of today's Bible story? ("Saul Sees the Light")
If after a few moments no one guesses, tell the children the title.
Why was this story called "Saul Sees the Light"? (A bright light blinded Saul; Saul found out who Jesus is.) Explain that the phrase "see the light" also means "gets a new understanding or a new idea."
What did Saul do after Ananias touched him and he could see again? (was baptized, began preaching about Jesus)
Before class, print "Saul sees the light" heavily with white crayon on the white

Materials
• *The Young Reader's Bible,* pages 412-417
• photocopies of the two-page Bible story (page 250)
• photocopies of page 253
• *The Young Reader's Bible Audio Cassette* or a cassette on which you have recorded unit stories
• cassette player(s), earphones optional
• a large sheet of paper
• flashlight
• blindfold
• scissors
• construction paper
• white construction paper
• white crayons, marker
• blue poster paint (diluted)
• brushes
• glue
• paint shirts
• cleanup supplies

paper. In class, let the children use the diluted blue poster paint and a wide brush to paint wide horizontal strokes across the paper to reveal the message. Talk about how Saul was blinded but then he could see.

Participate

Before class, set up a simple maze. Use furniture to create a maze. For example, use a small table to go over or under, two or more chairs to go between or around. You can place children as barriers, too. Choose four volunteers to play the roles of Saul, his friends, and Ananias.

The teacher will flash the flashlight above Saul's head to "blind him." His eyes will then be covered with a blindfold. The friends then lead Saul through the maze. At the end of the maze Ananias will remove the blindfold. Saul can see again! Now Saul must say, **"Jesus is truly God's Son."**

Give each child a copy of page 250. Find and underline the words that Saul "preached." Act out the story with new volunteers.

Give each child a copy of page 253, scissors, construction paper and glue. Children will cut apart the blocks and glue them in order on the construction paper. Volunteers can read from the *Young Reader's Bible* the section of the story that corresponds with each block.

When the blocks are in proper order, a Bible reference can be read along the bottom of each block. Ask a volunteer to find the Bible verse and read it aloud for the rest of the class.

Our key verse is Psalm 100:2. Let's say it together. "Serve the Lord with gladness."

Did anyone in our Bible story do what this verse says? (Ananias, Saul)
How did Ananias serve? (He told Saul about Jesus.)
How did Saul serve? (He preached about Jesus; he was baptized.)

Pray together. Thank God for sending Jesus. Ask God to help each one serve with gladness.

Read

Children can read from a *Young Reader's Bible* at their own level. They can color the Bible story excerpt (page 250) while others listen to the Bible story cassette.

Materials
• Bibles
• index cards
• a large sheet of paper
• pencils, red and blue markers

❸ Practice Using a Bible

Using My Bible

Before class, print these Bible references on paper. Include the numbers.

1. Matthew 1:1   *4. Numbers 1:5-15*
2. 1 Kings 4:1   *5. Song of Solomon or Song of Songs 1:1*
3. Jonah 1:1   *6. Revelation 22:21*

Remind everyone that the Bible is a very special book. It is the Word of God.

Read the references aloud together. **Today, we are going to be Bible detectives. To begin with, I will give you a clue about a Bible book. You will decide which book on this list the clue is about. Whoever correctly names the Bible book may circle it. But be careful. Only circle Old Testament books in red. Only circle New Testament books in blue.**

Read the clues in random order.

I'm a disciple and first in the New Testament.   Matthew
Something smells very fishy in my book.   Jonah
This book sounds like math class.   Numbers

This book makes me think about castles.	1 Kings
When I am *last* in line, I'll think of this book.	Revelation
We need headphones for this book!	Song of Solomon
	or Song of Songs

Talk about other Bible book names. Perhaps the children can think of some clues of their own!

Finding Bible Verses

Distribute index cards and pencils to the class. Children will choose a Bible reference from the list on the paper and copy it onto an index card. (This can be done in pairs.) Using the Reference Rhyme (page 32) to find the book, chapter, and verse, help children find the Bible verses. Tell the children that they are to read the verse carefully, looking for clues.

When children have successfully located all the verses, ask for the following information from each verse by giving these clues:

1. In Matthew 1:1, read the two-word name of the son of David. (***Jesus Christ***)
2. Read 1 Kings 4:1 and tell the first two letters in the name of the country over which King Solomon ruled. (***is***—Israel)
3. Simple word used before *Lord*; rhymes with Jon*ah* 1:1. (***the***)
4. Skim and find this three-letter word. Extra clue: not a daughter but a (***son***).
5. What is the middle word of the three-word Bible book name? (***of***)
6. Father of the Lord Jesus named in Revelation 22:21. (***God***)

As answers are found, print them in order on the paper.

Ask class to read aloud the message written on the board:
Jesus Christ is the Son of God!

Note
These words can be identified using most translations of the Bible. *The New International Version* and the *New Century Version* work especially well.

④ Share What We've Learned

Gather everyone in a circle to talk about what they have been doing and learning. Use the aims for this lesson as an outline for the kinds of questions you ask.

Ask them to look at the block picture they made that tells the story of Saul. After the children have had a chance to review the story, explain that they will each retell a part of today's Bible story, "Saul Sees the Light." The first child begins telling the story.

When the bell sounds (or sand timer indicates time is up) the child sitting next in the circle will continue from where the last child finished. Use the story blocks to help children remember the sequence.

Children can tell one sentence, or you can let each one talk for one minute. Adjust your plan according to how your children respond to the verbal challenge.

For a second telling, give a child a flashlight. Have the child retell a part of the story and then shine a flashlight on another speaker. The next child holds the flashlight and continues the story. No one should participate a second time until everyone has participated once.

Let children tell about their puzzle pieces. After sharing their puzzle art ideas, children may attach them to the appropriate place on the wall.

Read again the message the clues revealed: ***Jesus Christ is the Son of God!***

Tell the children that they were very good detectives this week. Now they can decide who they will tell the message they discovered. Have each child name someone to tell the message that ***Jesus Christ is the Son of God!***

Sing songs that tell about Jesus.

Materials
- tape recording of bell tone at one-minute intervals (option: sand timer)
- block picture made earlier in lesson
- puzzle pieces made earlier

Teaching at Home

Include the family in making clues about various Bible stories.

Reading tip
Lots of questions to find in this story. Let children read and write questions.

Timothy and Paul Tell About Jesus

Describe how Paul and Timothy helped others.
Give thanks because Jesus' church helps people learn about Jesus.
Read Bible references and find Bible verses.

"Serve the Lord with gladness."   Psalm 100:2, KJV

Materials
- third puzzle piece from child's outline
- art supplies to decorate puzzle pieces
- large sheet of paper

See the unit page for an explanation of project and materials needed.

① Get Ready to Read

Our class has been doing a wonderful job thinking of ways to serve! We have talked about serving people who are sick and lonely. We named ways to help. We also thought of ways to serve people who don't know about Jesus. We named people to tell. This week we want to think about serving our church. One of the ways I like to serve my church is by teaching children about the Bible.

Print, *Teach children about the Bible.*

Let's hear some of your ideas! Encourage children to list ways in which they may be able to serve (help) now and ways they see themselves serving in the future. List ideas on the large sheet of paper.

Distribute the third puzzle pieces and art materials to the children. Allow them to draw, glue pictures or write about ways they can serve their church.

Materials
- *The Young Reader's Bible,* pages 418-423
- photocopies of the two-page Bible story (page 251)
- *The Young Reader's Bible Audio Cassette* or a cassette on which you have recorded unit stories
- cassette player(s), earphones optional
- a large sheet of paper
- construction paper city signs
- suitcase
- crayons or markers

② Read the Bible Story

"Timothy Joins the Journey"

Before class, prepare road signs. On construction or other heavy paper, print the following names: *Antioch, Derbe, Galatia, Lystra.*

On the back of each sign print one of the following Bible references: *Matthew 19:14; Psalm 119:105; Proverbs 3:5, 6; Acts 16:31.*

Place road signs inside a suitcase. Gather children in the story center. Display suitcase.

What questions would you ask someone who was carrying this? (Where are you going? What is inside?)

Packing a suitcase is one of the things we do to get ready for a trip. Today we'll hear about a man who did a lot of traveling! Let's listen to find out who went traveling and why they went.

You can assign two listening groups. One will listen for who traveled; the other will listen for why they traveled.

Listen

Read with suspense and animation "Timothy Joins the Journey."

Why did Paul and Silas make so many trips? (visit churches, visit new believers, preach about Jesus) **Has anyone ever visited our church?** (evangelists, missionaries, and "Timothies," once members of the congregation now serving God elsewhere) **What was the name of the man Paul and Silas invited to come with them?** (Timothy)

Participate

Place suitcase on your lap or at your feet. **Let's take a trip with Paul and Timothy! Where shall we go?** Open suitcase, take out signs, and read them aloud.

Read them again, this time inviting children to read with you. Attach the signs to various locations around the classroom.

Choose volunteers to play the parts of **Paul, Silas,** and **Timothy.** Divide the rest of the class into four groups to act as local church members in each place. **Silas** will be stationed at Derbe. **Timothy** will stand at Lystra. Read the story "Timothy Joins the Journey" again as **Paul** begins his trip.

Destination #1 —Antioch

After reading ". . . preaching about Jesus . . . ," **Paul** will go to Antioch and preach (tell about Jesus). **Paul** may then invite the congregation to choose a song to sing to Jesus.

Destination #2 —Derbe

Paul will go here and preach (tell about Jesus). **Paul** may invite the congregation to sing a song for Jesus or recite the key verse. Here **Paul** invites **Silas** to walk with him in Galatia.

Destination #3 —Galatia

Repeat the same process of preaching and singing or remembering Bible verses.

Destination #4 —Lystra

Paul and **Silas** walk to Lystra, meet **Timothy** and invite him to join their trip. Each one will preach (tell about Jesus) and repeat the unit key verse (Psalm 100:2).

Read

Give each child a copy of the Bible story excerpt (page 251). Children may color story pages as they read. Nonreaders may tell what is happening in the story pictures. They can listen to the cassette as they color and read along with the first and last story pages.

③ Practice Using a Bible

Using My Bible

Before class prepare trip tickets. Using colored paper, print tickets with the name of one destination per color per ticket: *Antioch, Derbe, Galatia, Lystra.* Make one ticket for each child. Divide tickets evenly among the four destinations so that groups will be similar in size.

Begin this activity by asking children to find the table of contents in their Bibles. **We are going to have a contest. I will begin printing a Bible book name one letter at a time on this large sheet of paper. You are to decide if the book belongs in the Old Testament or the New Testament. When you think you know the answer, raise your hand. If you correctly name the Testament, you will get a trip ticket to a Bible city.**

Cheer and be enthusiastic as you give the child the ticket. Say the city name as

Option
Substitute another child to be Paul at each destination.

Snacks
Serve popcorn and juice.

Materials
• Bibles
• large sheet of paper
• markers, pencils
• four colors of paper
• city signs used earlier
• ticket container

Note
Fill in all the letters of every Bible book.

Option

When the children correctly identify a Bible book, let them choose a
Bible book name to print, letter by
letter, for the class to guess.

you give the ticket. When children receive a ticket, they should help someone
else earn a ticket. Continue until each child has received a trip ticket. Cheer and
be enthusiastic. The children will join you.

Finding Bible Verses

Distribute pencils to the class. **Now we are all ready to take a trip. In order to
leave on our trip we must have a ticket, a Bible and a pencil.**

Children should read their tickets to discover their destinations. They can look at
the word on the ticket and compare it to the signs you put around the classroom.

Once they have arrived at their destination, direct them to find and copy the
Bible reference found on the back of the city sign. Children should then find their
Bible verse using the book, chapter and verse method. (Recall the Reference
Rhyme, page 32.) All children visiting that city will read the Bible verse together
to the rest of the class. Once again, encourage enthusiasm and cheering.

Nonreaders may be able to read a few Bible words with help. In order to come
home (rejoin the large group), each city group must recite Psalm 100:2.

④ Share What We've Learned

Materials

• photocopies of page 254
• pencils
• charade slips
• serving ideas listed earlier
• two foil pie pans
• stapler
• dried beans
• music stickers

Option

Invite several church helpers to
visit the class and tell how they
serve Jesus.

Look Ahead

Before the next lesson, gather
material concerning missionaries or
missions. Newsletters, pictures,
and maps will be helpful. Unusual
items that represent an area or
mission (currency, Bibles, stamps,
unusual clothing items) would add
interest.

Before class, print the following ideas on slips of paper: *giving offering;
singing; cleaning up hymn books; listening/worshiping quietly; calling friends to
invite them to church; praying.*

Place pantomime slips in basket or other container.

Recall children's ideas for helping (serving) our church. Share with the children that we can be like Paul, Silas and Timothy when we do things that help our
church family.

Explain pantomimes. Do a sample pantomime. Then ask volunteers to choose
pantomime slips from basket. Assist them in reading the written action if necessary. Each child will then act out action for the rest of the class. Join in the guessing so that each child is quickly successful.

When the class has correctly guessed the serving idea, add it to the list on the
large sheet of paper (if it is a new idea).

Give each child a copy of page 254 . **One way we serve in Jesus' church is by
telling others about Him. Today we will fill in a "Letter to a Friend." Read the
letter together, saying the words to fill in the blanks.**

Some children might need help spelling a friend's name.

Have the children fill in the blanks in the letter using the word bank at the bottom of the page. Fill in the page together if children need more help.

Gather everyone in a circle to talk about what they have been doing and learning. Have the children tell about their puzzle art made earlier. Use the aims for
this lesson as an outline for the kinds of questions you ask.

Give each child two foil pie pans and several dried beans. Put a few dried
beans inside before you staple the rims of two pans together. Add stickers.

To close the lesson, read the list of service ideas written earlier on the large
sheet of paper. Ask children to think of others who do these jobs for the church.
Cheer and shake the tambourines as you name each person.

Encourage children to pray for these people. Invite them to complete a sentence prayer such as: "Thank You, God, for (person's name) because (he or she)
(name job/service, etc.)."

**Let's remember to pray for these church workers every day. Praying for
people who serve is another way to serve Jesus!**

Teaching at Home

Look together at a modern map of
the area of Paul's travels. Locate
picutres of modern Turkey,
Greece, and Italy.

Reading tip
Look for words with endings, both
plurals (believers, others, churches)
and *ing words (preaching, growing,
traveling).*

51

Paul and Silas Tell About Jesus

Tell how Paul and Silas helped others.
Give thanks because Jesus' church helps people and tells good news.
Read Bible references and find Bible verses.

"Serve the Lord with gladness."   Psalm 100:2, KJV

❶ Get Ready to Read

Materials
• last piece of puzzle from child's traced outlines
• missions display (see explanation in activity)
• art supplies to decorate puzzle pieces
See the unit page for an explanation of project and materials needed.

Before class, prepare a missions display. A poster could include maps (showing location), newsletters, and photos. Other interesting related items (crafts, foreign language Bible, stamps from that country) can be displayed.

Begin by clarifying the word *missionaries*. **Missionaries go and tell others about Jesus. The missionaries serve Jesus.** Repeat the unit key verse, Psalm 100:2.

Use the display to begin a discussion with your children about serving and missionaries. Tell about the missionaries that you have in the display. Recall ideas children have named about ways to help others. **Today we're going to think of ways we can help our missionaries.** Print children's ideas on the board.

Distribute final "puzzle" piece and art materials for children to decorate. If enough missionary material is available, let children use it on their puzzle pieces. Help children attach their last puzzle piece to the wall.

Option
Ask a member of the mission committee or the pastor to visit your class and talk about the missionaries during this section of the lesson. They can show photos or slides of the family and the mission work.

❷ Read the Bible Story

Materials
• *The Young Reader's Bible,* pages 424-429
• photocopies of the two-page Bible story (page 252)
• photocopies of page 255
• *The Young Reader's Bible Audio Cassette* or a cassette on which you have recorded unit stories
• cassette player(s), earphones optional
• a large sheet of paper
• metal chain link or handcuffs
• scissors
• crayons
• tape

"The Night the Prison Shook"
Gather children in the story center. Display a metal chain link or handcuff. Ask volunteers to try and pull the chain apart. **How could we pull this apart? Somebody in our Bible story needed to know! Listen to find out** *who* **and** *why.*

Listen
Read with suspense and animation "The Night the Prison Shook."
Who needed to know how to get out of prison chains? (Paul and Silas) **Why were they in chains?** (Some people didn't like them talking about Jesus.)
How did they get out of their chains? (God caused an earthquake.) **Who did Paul and Silas preach to in jail?** (jailer) **How did the jailer know Paul and Silas knew about Jesus?** (They prayed and sang in the jail.)

Participate
Give each child a copy of page 255, crayons, scissors and tape. Instruct children to color puppets on page 255. When they have finished coloring, they may

Option

A law enforcement officer who is a member of your congregation may be able to demonstrate leg irons or hand cuffs to introduce today's story.

Who Said This?

"Don't worry! We are all here!" (Paul)

"Beat them, put them in prison!" (judges)

"What must I do to be saved?" (prison guard)

"Believe in the Lord Jesus." (Paul and Silas)

Snacks

Serve foods from the missionaries' countries.

Materials

• Bibles
• cardboard strips
• cardboard circles
• tape
• photocopies of the bookmark (only) page 133
• stickers, or glitter, or bits of confetti
• pencils, markers
• clear adhesive plastic
• scissors

Verses for strips

"Serve the Lord with gladness."

"Go and make followers. . . . Teach them to obey."

"Jesus went everywhere doing good."

"For God so loved the world He gave His only Son."

References for circles

Acts 10:38; Matthew 28:19, 20; Psalm 100:2; John 3:16

Option

Use all ten of the unit key verses for this matching activity.

cut them out; then cut the slit near the bottom and tape them around two fingers to make finger puppets.

When everyone has completed their puppets, assign each child a character in the story. Seat the children in a circle, grouped according to character. Read the story again, pausing to let the different character groups "speak" their parts by nodding their puppets.

Next, play "Who said this?" Children should nod the appropriate puppet to answer each question.

Give each child a copy of the Bible story excerpt (page 252). **Find the sentence that ends with a question mark.** ("What must I do to be saved?") **Find one that ends with an exclamation mark.** (He was filled with joy!) Practice reading each sentence so it sounds like a question or exclamation.

Who can tell Psalm 100:2? (choose volunteer) **Who was serving the Lord in our story today?** (Paul, Silas)

Read

Using Bible-story excerpt (page 252), children can find, underline, and read the names that are on the puppets: *guard, Paul, Silas, family.* (*Judge* does not appear on the two-page excerpt.). They can put puppets on both hands and listen to the cassette story, using their puppets as the characters move and speak.

❸ Practice Using a Bible

Using My Bible

Before class, copy the verses from the narrow column on cardboard strips. Print the Bible references on cardboard circles.

Conduct a hands-on review of the parts of the Bible. **Find the Old Testament, New Testament, Genesis, Psalms, Revelation, Matthew, Mark, Luke, John. Name the four Gospel books.**

Attach verse strips to a classroom wall. Read each verse. Arrange reference circles in random order below strips, reading each reference as you put it up.

Finding Bible Verses

Explain that they must locate the Bible reference in the Bible to correctly match the verses and references on the wall. Work together to match each reference circle with the correct Bible verses. Congratulate class when the matches are correct.

Give each child a copy of the bookmark (page 133). Have the children choose their favorite Bible verse from the wall. They can copy the verse or the reference or both onto the back of the bookmark. Then they can color or add stickers or glitter to the bookmark. Check spelling before sealing the bookmark in plastic.

When the bookmarks are ready, place them on the clear adhesive plastic. Add another layer of plastic and seal the edges. Cut apart the bookmarks and give them to the children to take home in their Bibles.

❹ Share What We've Learned

Print four categories on a large sheet of paper: **Bible People; Bible Books; Bible Words; Bible Places**

Play "Find That Verse!" Divide class into two teams. Each team's player chooses from the categories on the board. When a player correctly answers a question from the chosen category, the player adds a felt church piece to the flannel board. The first team to complete the church wins. There are four questions in each category. When all questions from that category have been answered children must choose from other categories.

Questions for "Bible People":

1. One night at work I got all shook up! Who am I? (jailer)

2. Since I met Peter and John, I've started a new exercise program! Who am I? (lame man at temple gate)

3. Because I preached the very first sermon, people sometimes call me the first preacher. Who am I? (Peter)

4. First God changed my eyes and then He changed my name. Who am I? (Saul/Paul)

Questions for "Bible Books":

1. Name an Old Testament book.

2. Name a New Testament book.

3. Name the first Bible book.

4. Name the last Bible book.

Questions for "Bible Words":

1. This word named a Jewish holiday, but we call it the birthday of the church. (Pentecost)

2. This word names people who worship and follow Jesus. (Christians)

3. One way the church serves is by telling about whom? (Jesus the Son of God)

4. What do we call the group of people who help each other and tell about Jesus? (church)

Questions for "Bible Places":

1. Paul and Silas praised God in this kind of a building, but I am not a church. What am I? (jail)

2. It was in this city that Ananias helped Saul. (Damascus)

3. Peter gave a new message from God in what city? (Jerusalem)

4. Before I could walk, I sat near this building. What is it called? (temple)

"Find That Verse!" (Children must find and read.)

Psalm 100:2; Matthew 28:19, 20; Acts 10:38; Psalm 92:5

Have each child draw a happy face on a square of sandpaper. Children should color the face as heavily as possible. Give each child a paper sign lettered "Good News."

Have a helper fold an old towel and put a piece of cardboard on the towel. Place the sandpaper colored side down on a poster board "Good News" sign. Place the sign and sandpaper on the cardboard. (The cardboard will absorb excess crayon wax.) Press the sandpaper gently with a warm iron for about 30 seconds, then carefully remove the sandpaper.

Children can re-color the faces after each transfer, decorating the "Good News" sign. Use the signs to emphasize that the church tells good news about Jesus. Punch two holes at the top of the poster and tie with yarn to hang.

Ask children to tell about the puzzle piece they decorated at the beginning of class. Display the missions poster. Ask volunteers to pray for the missionaries.

Gather everyone in a circle to talk about what they have been doing and learning. Use the lesson and unit aims as an outline for the kinds of questions you ask.

They can offer sentence prayers, "Dear God, thank You for (*missionaries' names*). Please help them (*name a need*). In Jesus' name. Amen."

Children can take home their life-size "puzzles." Help children take puzzles from the wall.

Materials

- felt church-building pieces used in lesson 47
- flannel board
- Jeopardy-style game board
- missions display
- large sheet of paper
- paper signs lettered "Good News"
- scissors
- sandpaper cut in 4-inch squares
- crayons or glitter crayons
- towel
- cardboard
- iron
- paper punch
- yarn or ribbon

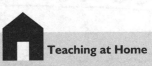

Teaching at Home

Plan to correspond with a mission family.

Reading tip

Volunteers can pantomime action words they find. When children correctly guess the action word, a volunteer can read the sentence in which the word is found.

God sent a man named Ananias
to the house where Saul was.

Ananias laid his hands on Saul.

"The Lord Jesus sent me
so you can see again
and be filled with the Holy Spirit."

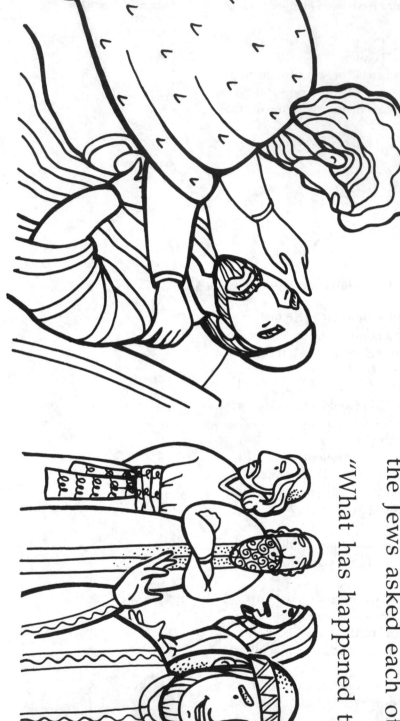

Later, Saul began to preach
to the Jews in Damascus.

"Jesus is truly God's Son,"
he told them.

"Isn't this the man
who arrests believers?"
the Jews asked each other.

"What has happened to him?"

Timothy Joins the Journey

Saul became known as Paul.

Paul traveled from place

to place, preaching about Jesus.

In each town,

the new believers met together

as a church.

Timothy was happy

to join the journey.

So Paul, Silas, and Timothy

traveled together

to cheer the churches

and tell others about Jesus.

Paul learned to love

young Timothy

like a son.

And the churches

grew stronger in faith,

with new believers

added every day.

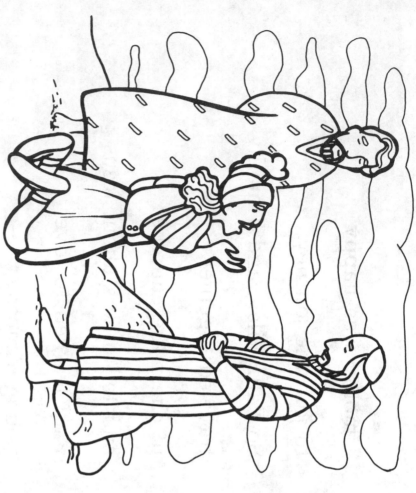

"What must I do to be saved?" asked the thankful guard.

"Believe in the Lord Jesus," said Paul and Silas. "He will save you and your whole family."

Paul told the guard and his family more about Jesus.

The guard washed Paul and Silas's wounds. Then he and his family were baptized. He was filled with joy!

Block a Story

Cut out these pictures. Put them in the correct order. Copy the letters from the bottom of each picture to write a Bible reference.

Write the Bible reference here:

_____

- -

_____

Letter to a Friend

Dear _____ ,

I want to tell you about my friend _____ .

I read in my _____ that He is the Son of

_____ .

Jesus is in _____ . Someday He will come

back for everyone who trusts Him.

Come to _____ _____ and learn about

my _____ .

Your friend,

_____

Word Bank

Jesus   Bible   God

Bible school   Heaven   Savior

Let Your Fingers Do the Talking

Color these puppets. Cut out and tape the tab to make finger puppets. Use your puppets to tell the story of Paul and Silas.

Paul

Silas

prison guard

guard's family

Paul and Silas

judge

52 New Testament Celebration

Remember New Testament stories.
Practice finding verses in the New Testament.
Recognize New Testament vocabulary words.

Materials
- streamers and tape
- twelve balloons
- construction paper
- photocopies of activity charts, page 319
- markers
- paper punch
- yarn, twine, or curling ribbon
- stickers (optional)

Option
Bible costumes for everyone to wear (sheets or towels with strips of cloth to hold them in place).

Get Ready to Celebrate

Before class, prepare twelve balloons by printing one letter on each: *N-E-W T-E-S-T-A-M-E-N-T*. Also, fold colored construction paper in half widthwise and staple along the sides. Print each child's name at the top. Glue an activity chart cut from a photocopy of page 319 to the folded construction paper. Punch holes near the top corners of each paper. Tie the ends of a 32-inch piece of yarn, twine, or curling ribbon to both holes.

Today's lesson celebrates the completion of a study of New Testament stories. To encourage a festive atmosphere, decorate the room. The fun setting can be maintained and the lesson aims will be accomplished using activity tables. You will need three tables or areas to offer three activities each. You will need at least one adult or teen helper to assist at each table. Children can choose the order in which they will do the table activities.

Divide into three groups. Follow this three step lesson plan, allowing twenty minutes for each step.

1 Children choose a table at which to begin (blue, red, yellow).
They complete their choice of three activities offered at that table.
The class gathers for Group Time 1.

2 Next, children complete their choice of activities at a different table.
The class gathers for Group Time 2.

3 Children complete their choice of activities at their last table.
The class gathers for Group Time 3.

Remember What We've Learned

Can you guess why we have balloons and streamers in our room today? (We're having a party.) **Who can read what the letters on the balloons spell?** (New Testament)

We learned that the Bible is divided into two parts, the Old Testament and the New Testament. We've been reading stories from the last part of the Bible, the New Testament, so we're having a party to celebrate.

Each of you will get to choose from nine fun activities. You can wear this small activity chart. When you complete an activity, we'll mark that box (or give you a sticker for it). Each time you complete the activities at a table, our class will gather as a group for some fun.

Snacks
Serve party cupcakes and ice cream or frosted muffins and frozen yogurt. See Group Time 2.

A–Make New Testament story televisions.

Before class, print these instructions on blue construction paper: *Glue the picture strips together. Color the pictures and trace over the words. Put the strip through the slits of your story television. Glue the other end of the story strip together. Pour enough beans into the sack to cover the bottom.*

Also, cut out the holes and make slits in the lunch sack. Cut apart the photocopied picture strips. Mark these measurements on a lunch sack: from one edge make two marks at 1 inch, at 1¾ inch, at 3½ inches and at 4½ inches. Draw four lines 2¾ inches long near the middle of the lunch sack. Add clear transparent tape along those lines to reinforce them before cutting. Cut along the lines with a single edge razor tool. (Putting cardboard inside the sack will prevent cutting through both layers of the sack.)

If the children need help in class, read the instructions aloud, show how to glue the strips together, how to trace over the dotted letters and insert the story strip through the slits.

B–Unscramble stories.

Before class, print these instructions on blue construction paper: *Sort the word strips by color. Put each color set together to make a sentence.*

Also, cut strips from colored paper and print a sentence part on each.
Green: An angel / told Mary, / "You will have / a baby, God's Son."
White: John the Baptist / baptized Jesus / in the / Jordan River.
Yellow: Zaccheus / climbed a tree / so he could / see Jesus.
Purple: When Jesus died / on the cross, / He was punished / for our sins.
Orange: When Jesus left, / angels said / Jesus would return / the same way.

If the children need help in class, let them sort the colors. Show how to put them together in order. Read the strips aloud.

C–Make story-telling party hats.

Before class, print these instructions on blue construction paper: *Color the pictures and glue them onto your hat. Ask someone to choose a picture on the hat. You tell the story.*

Also, cut apart the story pictures (one set per child).

To make party hats, cut half circles (10 inches along the straight edge) from colored poster board or shiny gift wrap. Form each half circle into a hat by bringing the straight edges together and sliding one side over the other to form the cone shape. Staple. Punch a hole on each side of the hat and tie an 18-inch piece of curling ribbon to each hole. Add glitter. Show how to glue pictures on the hat randomly.

D–Play jacks and find a verse.

Before class, print these instructions on red construction paper: *Spin or toss the jacks (or pennies) until they land on a book, chapter and verse. Find that reference in the Bible.* (See the sample on page 319.)

If the children need help in class, show how to spin a jack (or flip a penny). Recall how to find a verse.

E–Toss the dice and find a verse.

Before class, print these instructions on red construction paper: *Toss the dice. Look up that chapter and verse in the first book of the New Testament, Matthew. Say the reference.*

For example, "If you roll a two and a six, look up Matthew 2:6 or 6:2."

If the children need help in class, read the directions aloud, give the example, and show how to find Matthew and the chapter. Let the children find the verse.

Blue Table
Review New Testament stories. (A, B, C)

Materials
- blue construction paper
- photocopies of page 319
- paper lunch sacks
- transparent tape
- glue stick
- pens or pencils
- beans to hold the paper sack in place

Materials
- blue construction paper
- construction paper (green, white, yellow, purple, orange)

Materials
- blue construction paper
- photocopies of page 319
- crayons or markers
- glue sticks
- party hats
- curling ribbon
- glitter

Red Table
Locate New Testament verses. (D, E, F)

Materials
- red construction paper
- three jacks (or pennies)
- Bible
- game board grid

Materials
- red construction paper
- pair of dice
- Bible

Materials
- red construction paper
- dominoes (or index cards drawn to look like dominoes) in a bag
- Bible

Yellow Table
Read Bible vocabulary.
(G, H, I)

Materials
- yellow construction paper
- slips of white paper
- hat
- Scrabble game tiles, alphabet macaroni or cereal, or letters printed on small index cards cut in fourths

Materials
- yellow construction paper
- cassette player with earphones
- cassette tape on which you have recorded a message
- pencil and paper

Materials
- yellow construction paper
- small snack crackers
- a can of aerosol cheese
- paper plates
- pen
- list of New Testament vocabulary words (for teacher or helper use)

F–Play a domino dot search.

Before class, print these instructions on red construction paper: *Pull a domino out of the bag. Find the chapter and verse in the last book of the New Testament, Revelation. Say the reference.* Helpers can offer this example, "If your domino has five dots and three dots, you would look up Revelation 3:5 or 5:3."

If the children need help, read the directions aloud, give the example, and show how to find Revelation and the chapter. Let the child find the verse.

G–Play letter matching.

Before class, print these instructions on yellow construction paper: *Pull a word out of the hat. Find letters to make each word.* On each slip of white paper, print one New Testament vocabulary word (from the lists on the unit pages). Put the papers in a hat. In class, after the children make the word using the matching letters, guide the conversation about the meanings of the words.

H–Listen to a riddle.

Before class, prepare a cassette tape. (Making a backup would be wise.) Read these instructions onto the cassette:

"Here's a riddle for you. I'm a word that means ___ . *(Tell the meaning of a vocabulary word.)* What word am I? Print your guess. *(Pause.)* I'll give you a hint. *(Spell the word slowly.)* Please turn off the tape player now."

Repeat with enough vocabulary words so that each child in each group can listen for one definition.

Print these instructions on the yellow construction paper: *Listen to the riddle and print the word.* Copy the list of words on construction paper as well.

In class, each child will listen to one riddle. Help children put on earphones and turn on the tape. When they have printed a word, turn off the tape and praise them. If they can't print the word that was spelled, ask them what the word was and print it for them. Let them copy or trace the letters you wrote.

I–Feast on the Word.

Before class, print these instructions on the yellow construction paper: *Unscramble the crackers to find one of your Bible words.*

In class, print letters of a New Testament vocabulary word with aerosol cheese on individual crackers. Move the crackers out of order and let the children put them back in order. If they need help, tell them the word and let them try to put the crackers in order. If they can't figure out the order, print the word on the paper plate so they can match the crackers to the printed letters. Let them eat the crackers.

Group Time Celebrations

1 Picture Charades
Divide the class into three groups so that each has at least one story strip TV (made at the blue table). Have volunteers pantomime a story. Children try to put the matching story picture on their TV screens. Discuss the story or read it from *The Young Reader's Bible*.

2 Snack
Serve cupcakes and ice cream or muffins and frozen yogurt. Top each cupcake or muffin with a candy or frosting letter: N-E-W T-E-S-T-A-M-E-N-T.

3 Singing
Sing songs that children have especially enjoyed.

Note
See the unit pages for song ideas.

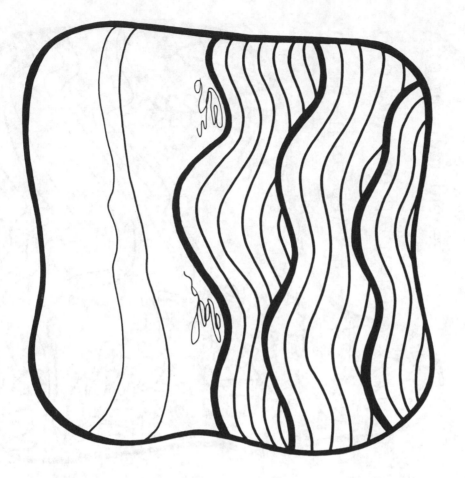

The Beginning

from Genesis 1 and 2

God is the beginning

of all things.

God made the heavens

and the earth.

The earth was empty and dark,

with water everywhere.

Then God said,

"Let there be light."

And there was!

There was evening and morning.

This was the first day

Next, God put a wide space

above the water.

God called the space *sky*.

This was the second day

On the third day,
God gathered the water
into its own places.
Now there were seas
and dry ground.
"Let plants grow in the ground,"
God said. And they did!

Then God said,
"Let there be lights in the sky
for day and for night."
God made the sun,
the moon, and the stars.
This was the fourth day.

On the fifth day,
God made fish for the seas.
He made birds for the sky.

260

On the sixth day, God made

living things for the land.

Then God said,

"Let us make human beings.

Let them rule

over the fish of the sea,

the birds of the air,

and the living things on land."

God made the first human being

from the dust.

The first man was called Adam.

God breathed into Adam

the breath of life.

God looked at all he had made.

It was very good!

On the seventh day, God rested.

He made that day a holy day.

Water, Water Everywhere

from Genesis 6 — 9

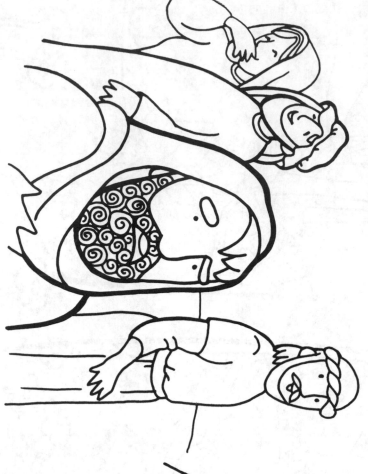

Soon many people lived on earth.
But everywhere God looked,
people were sinning.
Only Noah loved God.

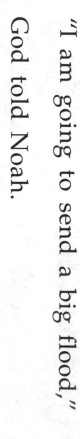

"I am going to send a big flood,"
God told Noah.
"Water will cover the whole earth.
Every living thing will die."
Noah listened carefully.
"I want you to build an ark,"
said God. Noah obeyed God.

262

Water covered the whole world.

Two of every kind of animal

came to Noah to live on the ark.

Then Noah and his family

went inside.

God closed the door,

and the rain began.

God sent rain for forty days.

263

Then Noah sent out a dove

to look for dry land.

And one day,

the dove did not come back.

"It is time to go out now!"

called Noah.

Noah and his family

thanked God

for keeping them safe.

God was pleased.

He put a beautiful rainbow

in the sky.

"This is a sign of my promise,"

said God. "I will never send

another flood like this one."

264

Ten Terrible Troubles

from Exodus 5 — 12

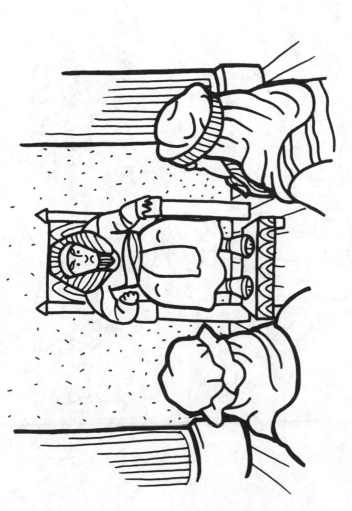

Moses and Aaron told Pharaoh,

"God says, Let my people

go into the desert to worship me."

"No!" said Pharaoh.

"Why should I obey your God?"

"Go back to Pharaoh," God said.

"Tell Aaron to throw down

his staff."

Aaron's staff became a snake.

"My magicians can do that, too,"

said Pharaoh.

Aaron's staff swallowed

the staffs of the magicians.

But Pharaoh still would not

let God's people go.

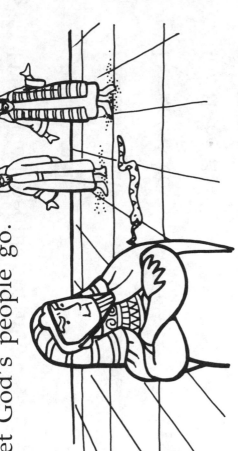

Then God sent troubles
on the Egyptians.

First the water turned to blood.

Then frogs covered the land.

Dust turned into biting gnats.

Flies swarmed everywhere.

All of Egypt's livestock died.

Egypt's people broke out in boils.

Hail killed people, plants,
and animals.

Hungry locusts ate the crops.

Darkness covered Egypt
for three days.

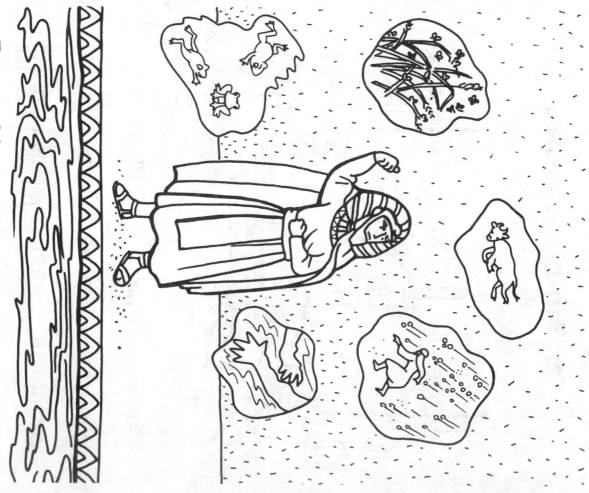

But stubborn Pharaoh still
would not let God's people go.

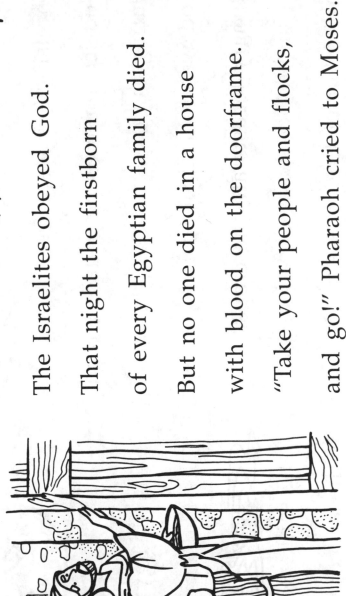

Then God told Moses,

"Every firstborn in Egypt will die.

Even Pharaoh's firstborn.

Tell my people to roast lamb

for their last meal in Egypt.

Tell them to smear the blood of

the lamb on their doorframes."

The Israelites obeyed God.

That night the firstborn

of every Egyptian family died.

But no one died in a house

with blood on the doorframe.

"Take your people and flocks,

and go!" Pharaoh cried to Moses.

Pharaoh's Biggest Mistake

from Exodus 12 — 15

The Israelites were free!

God led them along a desert road.

During the day,

God went ahead of them

in a pillar of cloud.

At night, God went ahead of them

in a pillar of fire.

But in Egypt, Pharaoh was sorry

he had let God's people go.

"Who will work for me now?"

he said. "We must bring

those people back!"

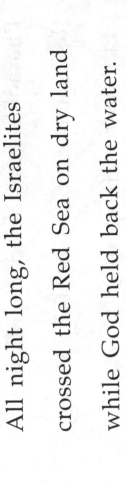

All night long, the Israelites

crossed the Red Sea on dry land

while God held back the water.

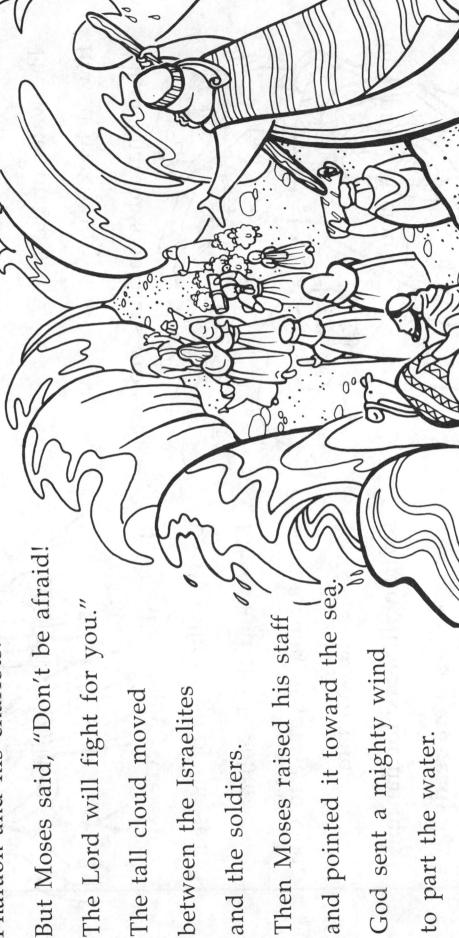

The Israelites were camped

beside the Red Sea.

They screamed when they saw

Pharaoh and his chariots.

But Moses said, "Don't be afraid!

The Lord will fight for you."

The tall cloud moved

between the Israelites

and the soldiers.

Then Moses raised his staff

and pointed it toward the sea.

God sent a mighty wind

to part the water.

Pharaoh's army tried to follow
the Israelites. But God told Moses,
"Lift your staff again."
Moses obeyed.
The water of the sea
flowed back into place.
All of Pharaoh's soldiers drowned.

But God's people were safe
on the other side of the sea.
Moses and the Israelites
sang a song of praise to God.
Moses' sister, Miriam,
led the women in a dance.
The Israelites were ready
to follow God anywhere.

Faith or Fear?

from Numbers 13 and 14

God told Moses

to send twelve men

to explore the land of Canaan.

"I will give this land

to my people," said God.

"See what the people are like,"

Moses told the twelve men.

"See what their towns are like."

After forty days,

the men came back.

"The land is flowing

with milk and honey," they said.

"Here is its fruit.

But the people are strong,

and their cities have walls."

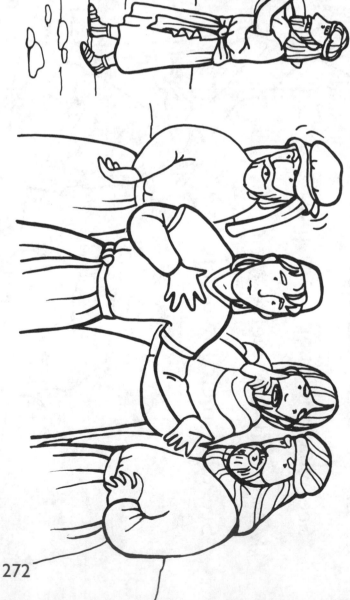

Caleb said,

"We should not be afraid.

We can take the land."

But other men said,

"The people are stronger

than we are.

We can't fight them and win."

God's people grumbled to Moses.

"It would be better

if we went back to Egypt,"

they said.

Then Caleb and Joshua

stood before the people.

"The Lord will lead us

into the land," Joshua said.

"He will give it to us."

But the people talked about

killing Joshua and Caleb.

God was angry

with his people.

"You will live and die

here in the desert," God said.

So it was forty years

before the people

went into the land of Canaan,

the land God had promised them.

Seven Times and a Shout

from Joshua 5 and 6

"What does God want to tell me?"
Joshua asked the angel.

"I have given you this city,"
was God's answer.

"Here is what you must do.

March your army
around the city.

Do it once a day for six days.

Carry the stone tablets
with the ten commandments
in their special box.

Have seven priests
blow trumpets as you march."

The gates of Jericho
were shut tight.

No one went out or in.

Then the angel of the Lord
came to Joshua.

God told Joshua

that the battle would be won

on the seventh day.

"March around the city

seven times on that day,"

said God. "On the seventh time,

shout,

and the walls will fall down."

Joshua obeyed God.

With the army and the priests,

he marched around the city

of Jericho.

275

Early the next morning,
Joshua and the army
and the priests marched again.

They did this for six days.

On the seventh day,
they marched seven times
around the city.

On the seventh time,
Joshua called out, "Shout!
For the Lord has given you
the city."

The priests gave a loud blast
on the trumpets.

The people shouted.

With a crash, the walls of Jericho
fell to the ground!

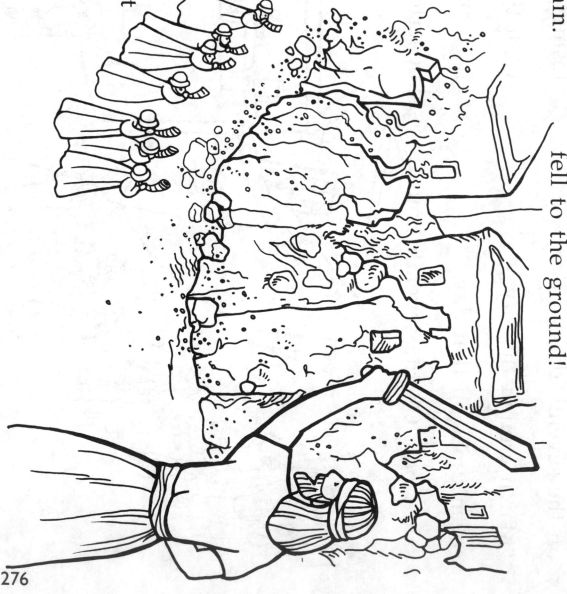

The Lord, He Is God!

from 1 Kings 18

For three years, there was no rain.

Crops did not grow.

Then God told Elijah,

"Go to King Ahab again.

Soon I will send rain on the land."

When Ahab saw Elijah, he said,

"You are a troublemaker."

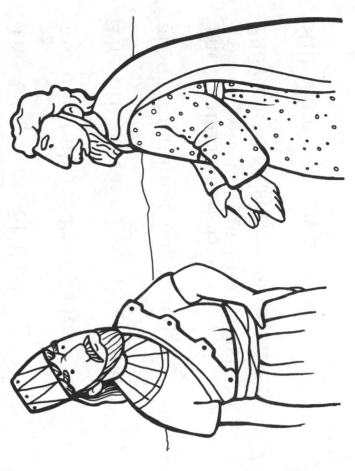

"Trouble came

because you did not obey God,"

Elijah said.

"Now call the people

to meet me on the mountain.

It is time to choose

between the Lord and Baal."

277

Elijah asked for two bulls.

"Call on the name of your god,"
Elijah told the people.

"I will call on the Lord.
The god who answers by fire,
he is God."

The 450 priests of Baal
put one bull on Baal's altar.

The priests called on their god
all day. Nothing happened.

They called louder.

They cut themselves with swords.

Still there was no answer.

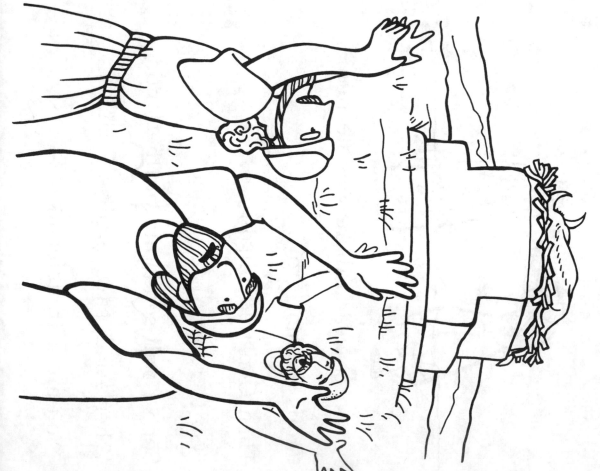

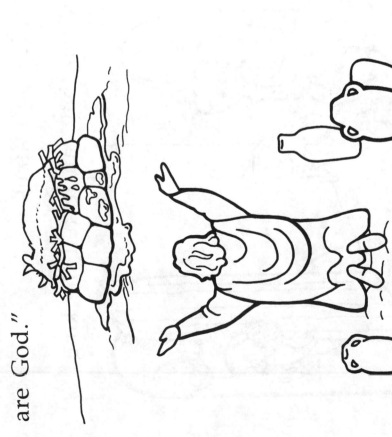

Then Elijah fixed God's altar.

He put the bull on the altar

and poured water all around.

"O Lord," prayed Elijah,

"let everyone know that *you*

are God."

The fire of the Lord burned up

the bull, the wood,

the stones, and the soil.

It licked up all the water.

The people fell down and cried,

"The Lord, he is God!"

Then the rain came.

Daniel for Dinner?

from Daniel 6

Daniel was the king's
favorite helper.

The king's other helpers
were jealous of Daniel.

They tricked King Darius
into making a new law.

Pray only to the king for thirty days,
or be thrown into the lions' den.

Daniel heard about the new law.

But Daniel loved God.

He kept praying to God,

three times every day.

The king's helpers

spied on Daniel.

Then they ran to tell the king.

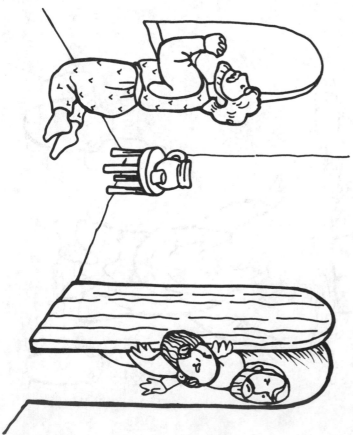

"Daniel broke the law!"

said the king's helpers.

King Darius was sad.

"Do what must be done," he said.

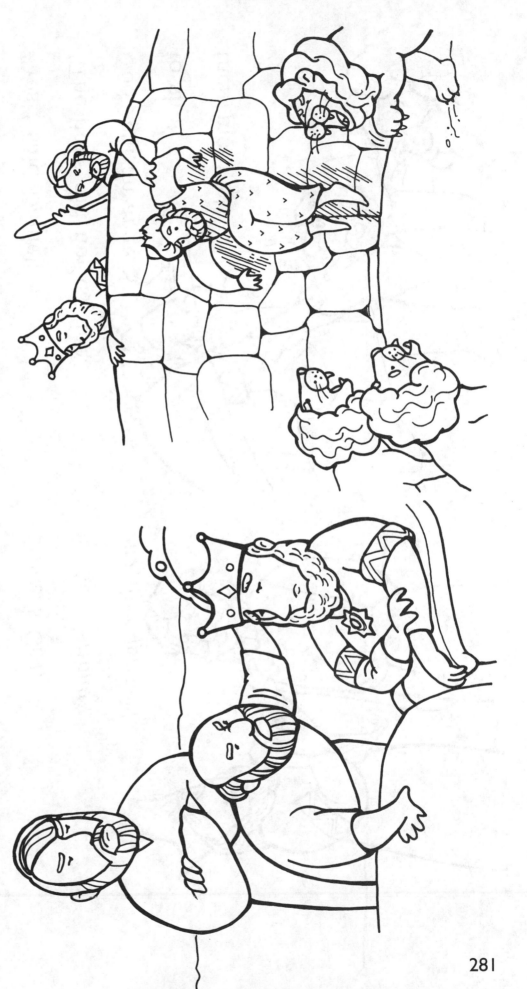

Daniel was tossed into a den

of hungry lions.

He could not escape.

And the king could not sleep.

In the morning,

the king hurried to the lions' den.

"Daniel!" he called.

"Has your God rescued you?"

"Yes!" said Daniel.

"The lions did not eat me.

God sent an angel

to shut

their mouths!"

The king set Daniel free.

Then he made

a brand-new law.

Everyone must worship

Daniel's God,

for he is strong

and lives forever!

282

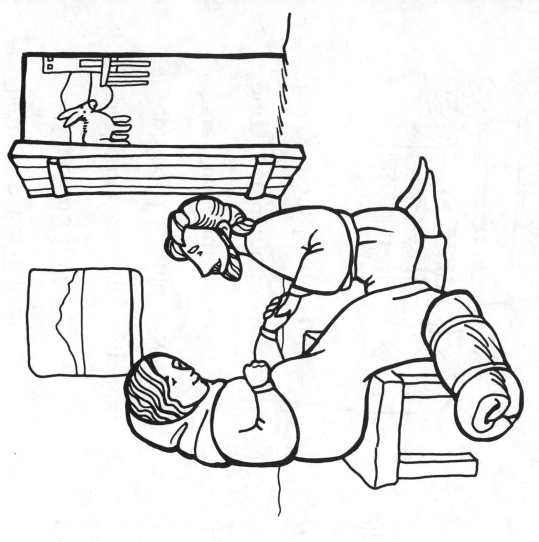

One Night in Bethlehem

from Luke 2

"The king wants to know

how many people

are in his kingdom,"

Joseph told Mary.

"We must go to my hometown

and be counted."

Mary patted her large middle.

"Bethlehem is far away, Joseph,"

she sighed.

"And the baby is due

any day now."

"Please don't worry,"

Joseph told Mary.

"God will watch over us."

The trip to Bethlehem
was long and dusty.
And Bethlehem was crowded.
Joseph tried to find a room
where they could stay.
"Sorry," said the innkeeper.
"Every room here is full."

284

But Mary and Joseph
found a warm, clean stable.
And there Mary's baby was born.
The baby was a boy, Jesus,
just as God's angel had said!

Mary wrapped her newborn baby
in cloths to keep him warm.
Tenderly she laid him
in his first bed —
a simple feeding box
under the stars,
one night in Bethlehem.

Good News of Great Joy

from Luke 2

On the hills near Bethlehem,
shepherds watched their sheep.
Suddenly the night was bright!
And standing near the shepherds
was an angel of the Lord.

The shepherds were afraid!
But the angel said,
"Calm down, for I have come
with good news of great joy!
Tonight in Bethlehem
a Savior has been born to you.
Christ the Lord, has come!"

286

Then there were angels all around,

praising God and saying,

"Glory to God in the highest!

And peace to his people

on earth!"

"You may go to see him,"
the angel told the shepherds.

"This will be a sign for you.

You will find the baby

wrapped in cloths

and lying in a feeding box."

When the angels were gone,
the shepherds said,
"Let's go to Bethlehem!"
They hurried into town
and found Mary and Joseph
and the baby, just as the angel
had said.

Then the shepherds went back
to their sheep,
praising God all the way.

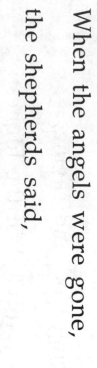

Inside and Out

from Matthew 9, Mark 2, and Luke 5

Jesus was teaching in a house.

A crowd of people

filled the house to hear him.

Then four friends came,

carrying a man

who could not move.

"This crowd is too big,"

the four men said.

So they took the man on his mat

up on the roof.

The four men made a hole
in the roof. They lowered their
friend down into the house,
right in front of Jesus.

Jesus saw that the four men
had great faith.
"Your sins are forgiven,"
Jesus told the man on the mat.

The teachers of the law
were saying to themselves,
Who does Jesus think he is?
Only God can forgive sins!

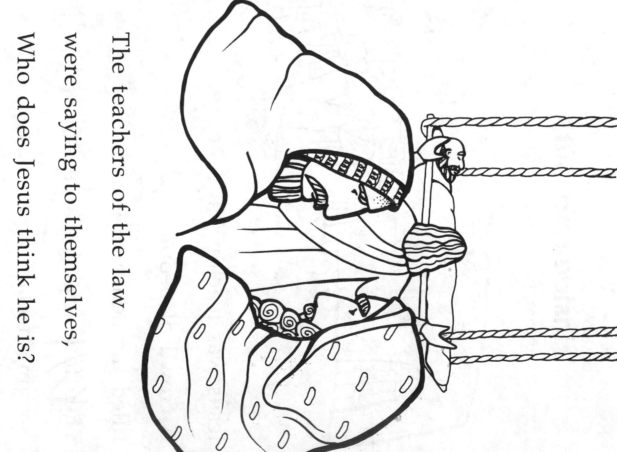

Jesus knew what the teachers

were thinking. He asked them,

"Is it easier to forgive sins

or to say rise and walk?"

Then Jesus told the man

on the mat, "Stand up.

Take your mat and go home."

The man jumped up.

He picked up his mat

and walked out of the house

praising God.

Everyone was amazed.

Jesus had healed the man

on the mat — inside *and* out!

Wild Winds and Waves Obey

from Matthew 8, Mark 4, and Luke 8

Jesus was tired.

All day long he had been teaching

from a boat on the lake.

When evening came,

Jesus said to his disciples,

"Let's go over to the other side

of the lake."

In the back of the boat,

Jesus went to sleep.

Then a wild storm began.

The wind howled, and waves

came over the sides of the boat.

"We are in danger!"

cried the disciples.

The disciples woke up Jesus.

"Teacher, Teacher, save us!"

they cried.

"Don't you care

that we are going to drown?"

293

Jesus got up.

He turned to the roaring waters.

"Quiet!" he said. "Be still!"

The wind went away.

The waves were still.

Jesus said to his disciples,

"Why are you so afraid?

Where is your faith?"

"What kind of man is this?"
the disciples asked each other.

"Even the wind
and the waves
obey him!"

The Right Thing to Do

from Matthew 3, Mark 1, and Luke 3

When John grew up,

he preached to God's people.

"Get ready!" he told them.

"Change how you live.

The kingdom of heaven

is coming soon."

At the Jordan River,

many people said,

"John, we are sorry

we have not obeyed God."

Then John baptized them

in the river.

Jesus came to John
to be baptized.
But John knew
that Jesus had never sinned.
"I need to be baptized
by *you*," John said.
"Why do you come to me?"

"It is important to baptize me,"
Jesus said.
"It is the right thing to do."
So John baptized Jesus.

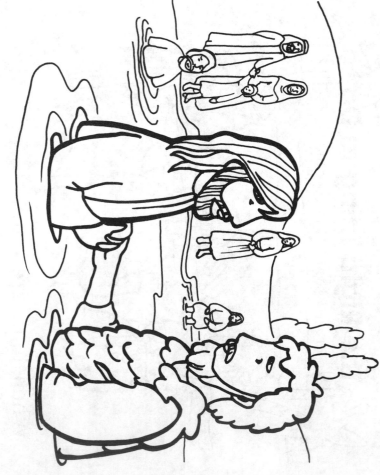

When Jesus came up

from the water,

heaven opened.

The Spirit of God

came down like a dove

and landed on Jesus.

Then a voice came

from heaven.

"You are my Son,"

said the voice.

"I love you,

and I am very pleased

with you."

Jesus the Teacher

from Matthew 5 — 7 and Luke 6

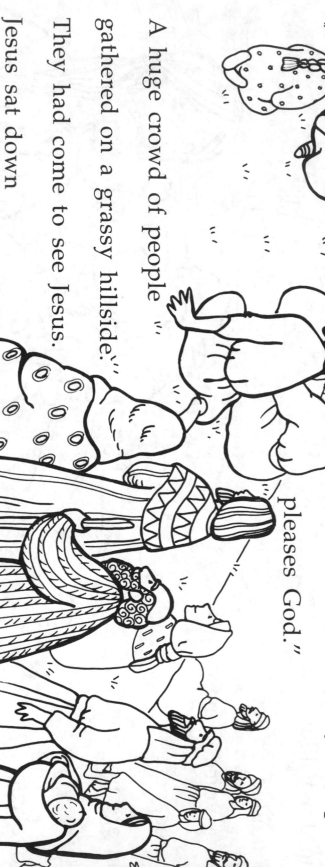

"Happy are the humble,"
Jesus said.
"Heaven belongs to them.
Whoever is sad will find comfort.
Whoever loves mercy and peace
pleases God."

A huge crowd of people
gathered on a grassy hillside."
They had come to see Jesus.
Jesus sat down
and began to teach them.

Jesus looked into the faces of the crowd.

"Love your enemies," he said.

"Forgive those who do wrong to you."

Jesus also taught about money.

"Don't worry about getting rich here on earth," Jesus said.

"Live to please God. Someday he will reward you in heaven.

Pray always," said Jesus.

"Seek and you will find."

Then Jesus told a story.

"Everyone who hears me today
and obeys me is like a wise man
who built his house on rock,"
he said.

"When the rain and wind came,
that house stood strong."

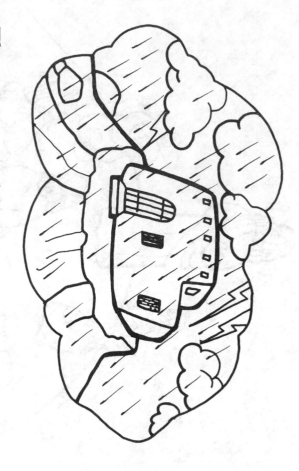

"But a foolish man built his house
on soft sand," said Jesus.

"When the rain and wind came,
his house fell down with a crash.
Anyone who doesn't listen to me
is like that foolish man."

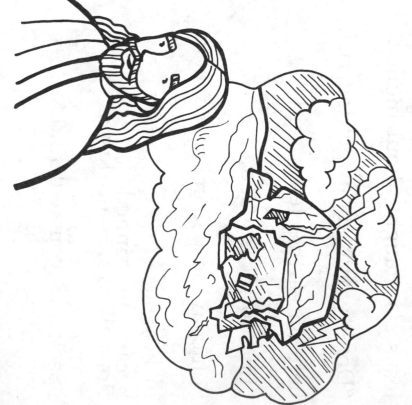

Now I See

from John 9

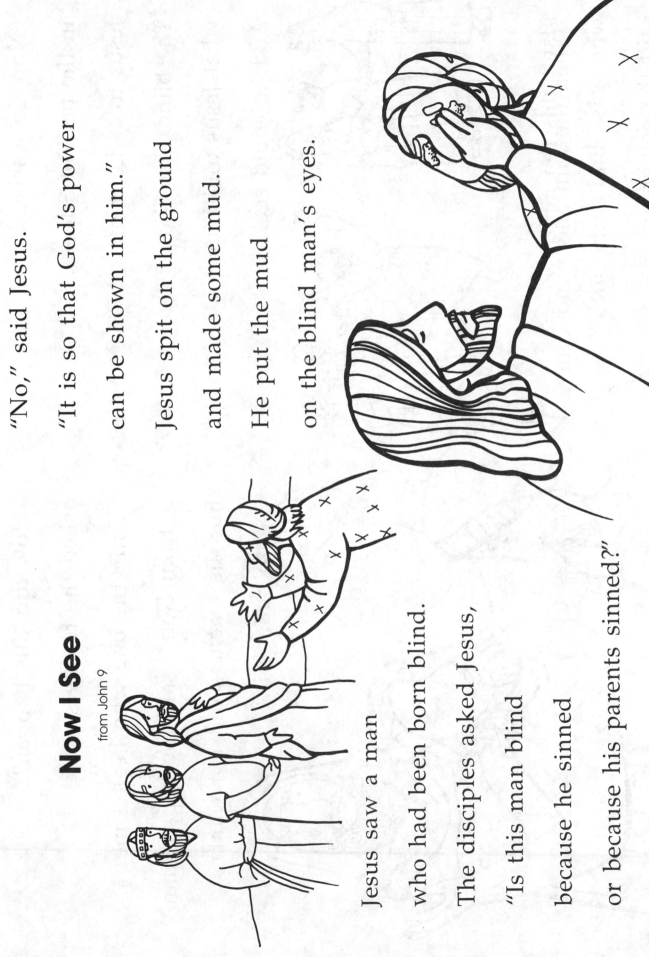

"No," said Jesus.

"It is so that God's power

can be shown in him."

Jesus spit on the ground

and made some mud.

He put the mud

on the blind man's eyes.

Jesus saw a man

who had been born blind.

The disciples asked Jesus,

"Is this man blind

because he sinned

or because his parents sinned?"

"Now go wash in the pool of Siloam," Jesus told the man.

The blind man did what Jesus told him. And he could see!

"How did this happen?" asked the teachers.

"Truly the one who healed me is from God," said the happy man.

But the teachers did not want to believe it.

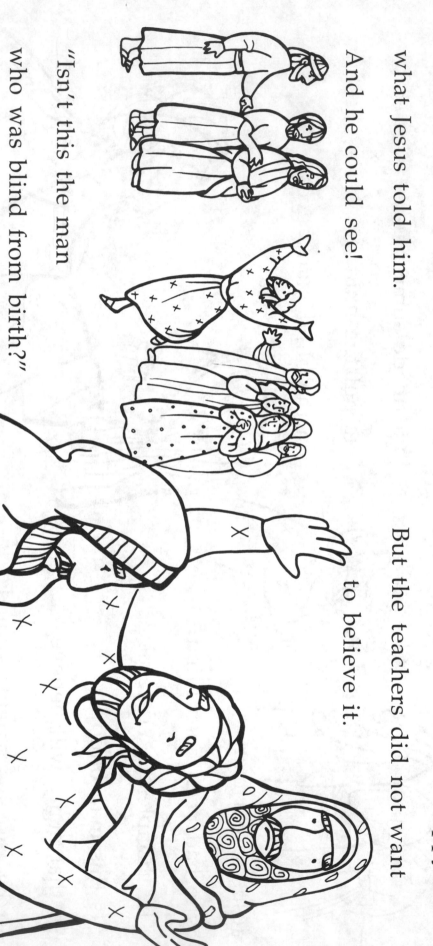

"Isn't this the man who was blind from birth?" said the neighbors.

302

Jesus found the man again.

"Do you believe
in the Son of Man?" asked Jesus.

"Who is he?" said the man.
Jesus smiled.

"You have seen him now,
and he is the one talking to you."

"Lord, I do believe in you!"
cried the happy man.

"I came into this world
so that many will believe,"
said Jesus.

One Thankful Man

from Luke 17

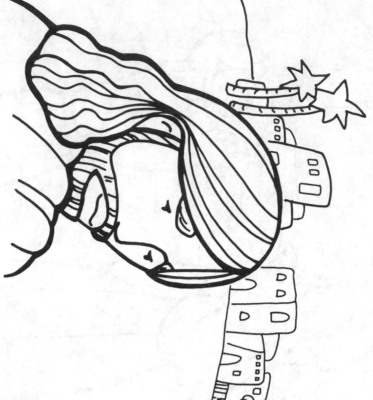

Jesus came near a village
between Samaria and Galilee.
There he heard a loud cry,
"Master, please help us!"

Jesus saw ten men
standing by themselves.
They had a terrible skin disease
called leprosy.
No one wanted them around.

But Jesus was not afraid
of the sick men.
He wanted to help them.
"Go show yourselves
to the village priests,"
Jesus told them.

The ten men obeyed Jesus.
And as they were walking
to find the priests,
suddenly their sores disappeared!

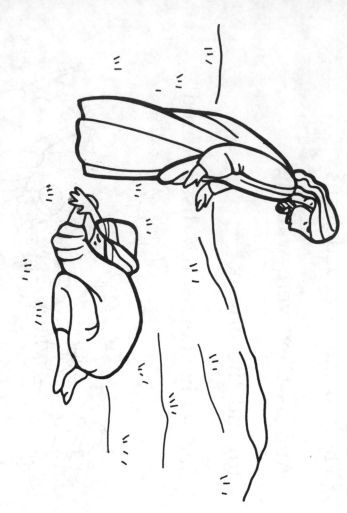

Jesus looked around.

"Where are the others?" he said.

"Did I not heal *ten* men?

Is this Samaritan the only one

who gives praise to God?"

Then Jesus smiled at the man

and said, "Get up and go now.

You were healed

because you believed."

One of the men ran back to Jesus.

He bowed down at Jesus' feet.

"Oh, thank you, Master!"

he cried.

And he was a Samaritan,

not a Jew like Jesus

and the disciples.

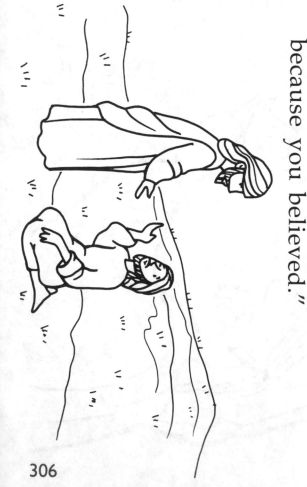

King of a Different Kingdom

from Matthew 27, Mark 15, Luke 23, and John 19

A judgment was made.

Jesus would have to die

on a cross!

Soldiers put a purple robe on him.

They put a crown of thorns

on his head.

Making fun of him, they said,

"Here is the king."

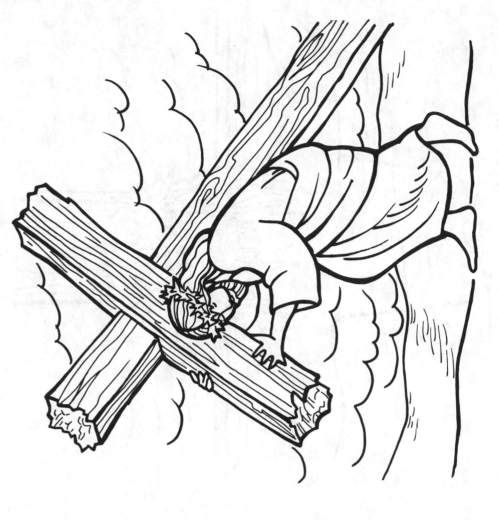

Then Jesus had to carry

a heavy wooden cross

to a hill called Calvary.

A crowd followed him.

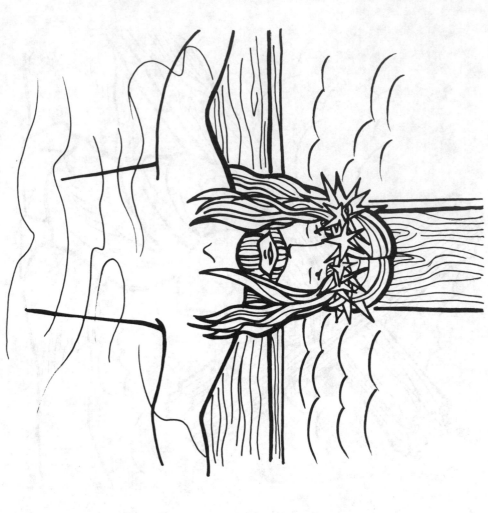

On the cross, Jesus said,

"Father, forgive them.

They do not know

what they are doing."

Two robbers hung on crosses
beside Jesus.

"Jesus, remember me
when you are king," said one.

"Today you will be with me
in my heavenly kingdom,"
Jesus told him.

Then darkness covered
the whole earth.

Jesus called out
in a loud voice,

"Father, I give myself to you!"
And Jesus died.

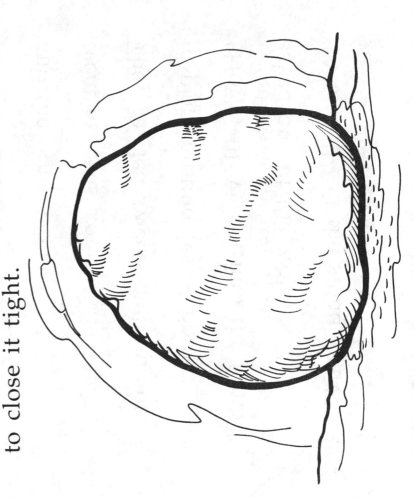

A rich man named Joseph
wrapped Jesus' body
in clean linen cloths.

He put the body into a new tomb.

Then a big, heavy stone
was rolled in front of the tomb
to close it tight.

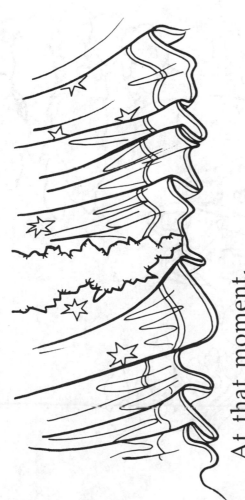

At that moment,

the temple curtain in Jerusalem

ripped in half.

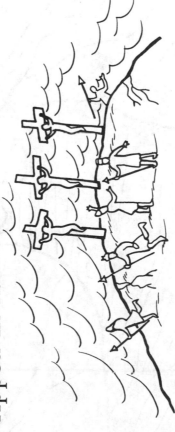

The earth shook and rocks split.

The soldiers at the cross said,

"Surely he was the Son of God!"

Could It Be True?

from Matthew 28, Mark 16, Luke 24, and John 20

It was the first day of the week.

The sun was coming up.

Mary Magdalene

and the other women

went to Jesus' tomb.

They carried sweet-smelling spices

to place around Jesus' body.

"How will we get into the tomb?"

asked one of the women.

"Who will roll the stone away?"

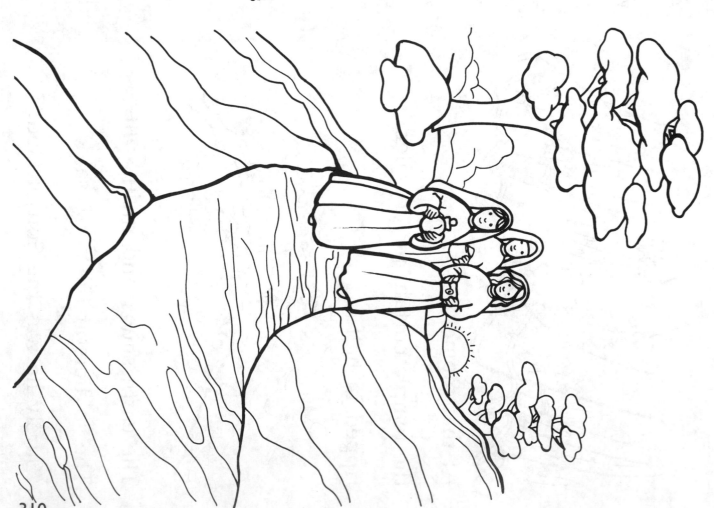

310

Mary ran to tell Peter and John.

But when the women got there,

the stone was rolled away already!

An angel from God had done it.

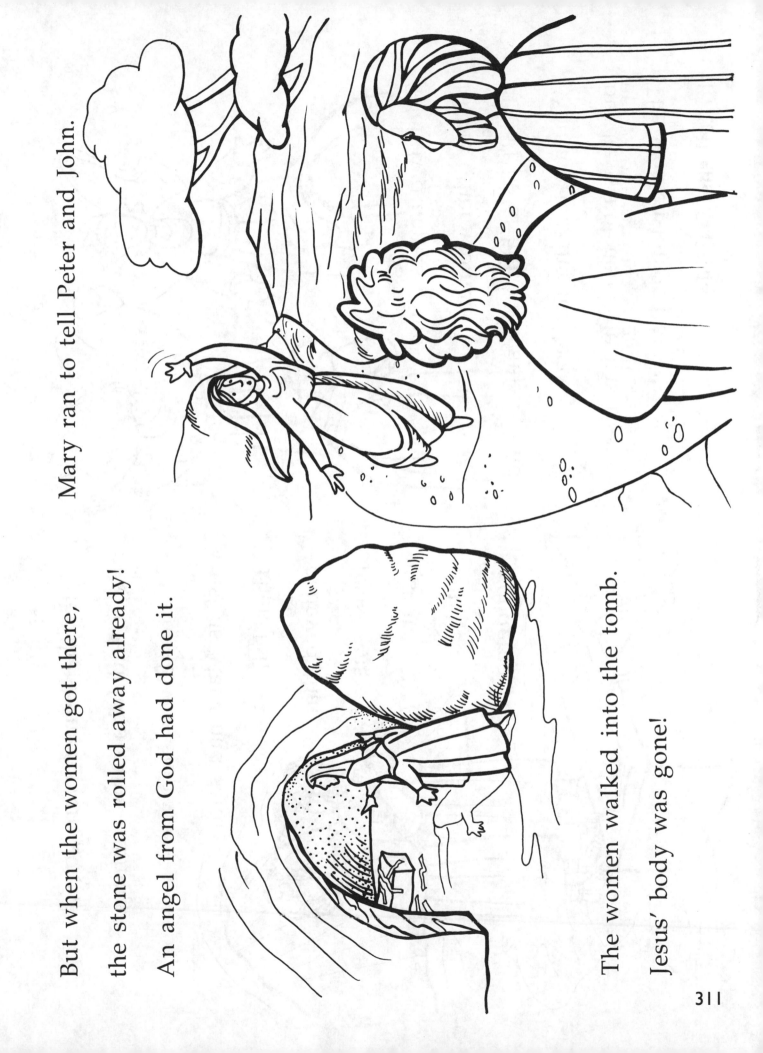

The women walked into the tomb.

Jesus' body was gone!

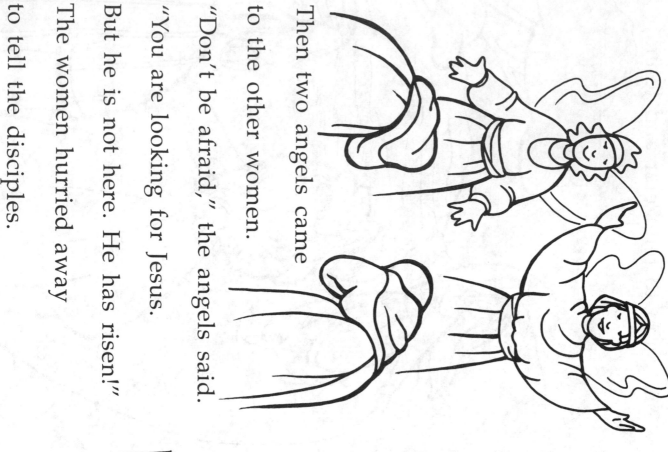

Then two angels came
to the other women.
"Don't be afraid," the angels said.
"You are looking for Jesus.
But he is not here. He has risen!"
The women hurried away
to tell the disciples.

After the women were gone,
Peter and John came running.
The tomb was empty,
just as Mary had said!
Then John
believed that
Jesus was alive
again.
But Peter
wondered.

The Very First Church

from Acts 2

On the Jewish holiday

called Pentecost,

the disciples met together

in a house in Jerusalem.

A sound like a strong wind

suddenly filled the house.

Then what looked like tongues

of fire rested on the disciples.

God's Holy Spirit

filled the disciples.

They began to speak

in other languages.

313

People heard the noise
and gathered around the house.
"What's going on?" they asked.
Everyone could hear
his own language being spoken,
even the people from other lands!

Peter said, "Listen!
What the prophet Joel
wrote about is happening today.
God says, I will pour out
my Spirit upon all people.
And everyone who trusts
in the Lord will be saved."

314

Three thousand people

believed in Jesus

and were baptized that day!

"Jesus was killed," said Peter.

"But God made him alive again.

We have seen him!

He is in heaven now.

Jesus is the Christ,

the one God promised to send."

The crowd gasped.

"What shall we do?" they asked.

"Repent," said Peter.

"Be baptized for the forgiveness

of your sins.

And you will receive

the gift of the Holy Spirit."

Jumping for Joy

from Acts 3

Peter and John

went to the temple to pray.

At the temple gate sat a man

who could not walk.

Every day, his friends carried him

to the gate to sit and beg.

The man asked Peter and John

for money.

"I have no money," said Peter.

"But I have something else.

In the name of Jesus,

rise and walk!"

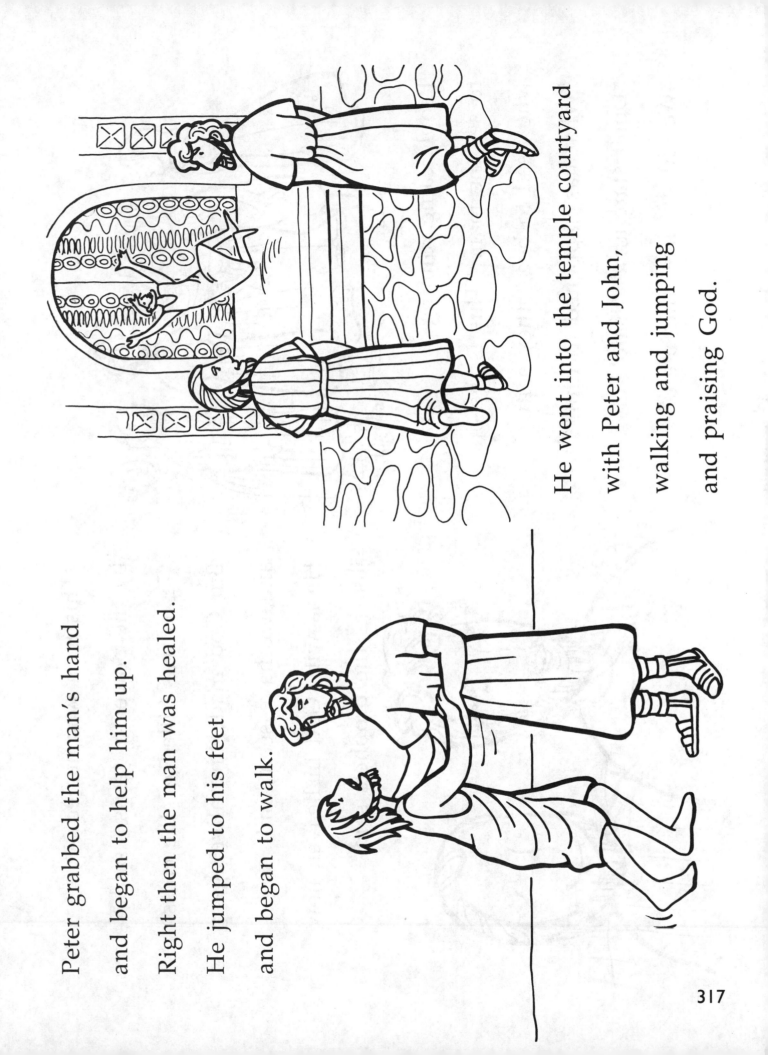

He went into the temple courtyard

with Peter and John,

walking and jumping

and praising God.

Peter grabbed the man's hand

and began to help him up.

Right then the man was healed.

He jumped to his feet

and began to walk.

"This man was healed
by the power of Jesus," said Peter.
"Jesus was killed on the cross.
But God made him alive again,
and we have seen him!
He is with God in heaven now,
just as the prophets said."

People came running
to see the man. "This is the one
who used to beg," they said.
"What has happened to him?"
"Don't stare at us," said Peter.
"We did not heal this man."

heal | rock | still | 5,000

water | see | come | Jesus

Photocopy one activity card for each child, cut out, outline with blue, red, and yellow markers, and glue to construction paper. Add a ribbon so the card will hang around the child's neck.

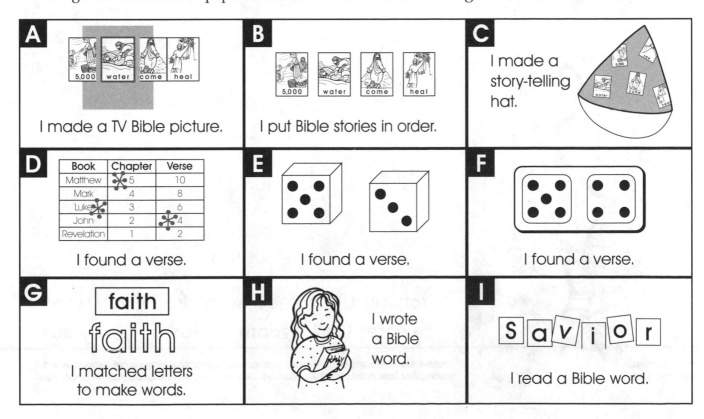

A I made a TV Bible picture.

B I put Bible stories in order.

C I made a story-telling hat.

D I found a verse.

Book	Chapter	Verse
Matthew	5	10
Mark	4	8
Luke	3	6
John	2	4
Revelation	1	2

E I found a verse.

F I found a verse.

G faith / faith — I matched letters to make words.

H I wrote a Bible word.

I Savior — I read a Bible word.

"You must become like children if you want to enter the kingdom of God."   —Jesus